DATE DUE

APR 3 0 2014	

BRODART, CO.   Cat. No. 23-221

The Death and Life of Main Street

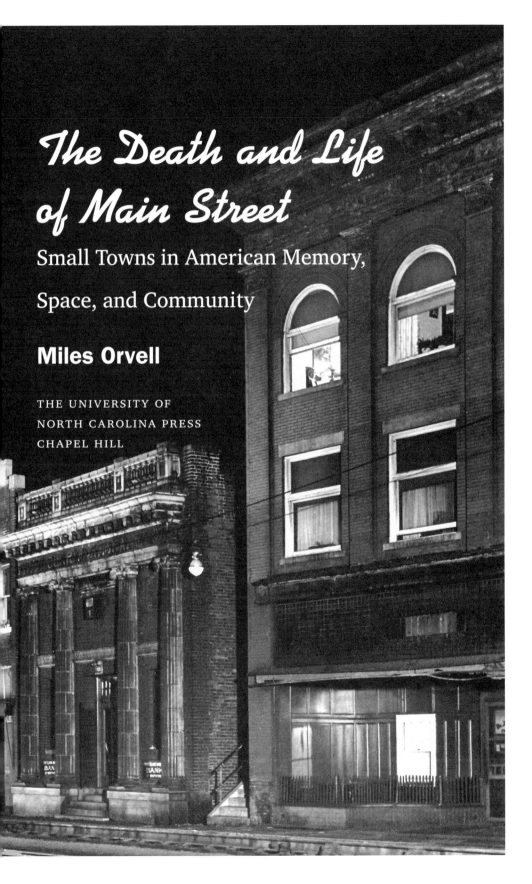

The Death and Life of Main Street

Small Towns in American Memory,

Space, and Community

Miles Orvell

THE UNIVERSITY OF
NORTH CAROLINA PRESS
CHAPEL HILL

© 2012 The University of North Carolina Press

Manufactured in the United States of America

Frontispiece: Photograph by O. Winston Link, *Main Line on Main Street* (1958), North Fork, West Virginia. Sharing space with the railroad on its main street, this narrow valley town was in its last phase when Link photographed it in a shocking image bordering on surrealism and suggesting the clash between the nostalgic image of Main Street and the forces of change. Courtesy of O. Winston Link Museum, with the permission of Conway Link.

Set in Charis, Franklin Gothic, and Koffee

The paper in this book meets the guidelines for permanence and durability of the Committee on Production Guidelines for Book Longevity of the Council on Library Resources.

The University of North Carolina Press has been a member of the Green Press Initiative since 2003.

Library of Congress Cataloging-in-Publication Data
Orvell, Miles.
The death and life of Main Street: small towns in
American memory, space, and community /
Miles Orvell.
    p. cm.
Includes bibliographical references and index.
ISBN 978-0-8078-3568-5 (cloth : alk. paper)
1. Small cities—Social aspects—United States. 2. City and
town life—United States. 3. Community life—United
States. 4. Community development—United States.
I. Title.
HT123.O78 2012
307.76'20973—dc23
                                        2012005086

16 15 14 13 12   5 4 3 2 1

To Gabriella, Ariana, and Dylan;
and to brother Barry and Bliss Street

It was not only the unsparing unapologetic ugliness and the rigid straightness which overwhelmed her. It was the planlessness, the flimsy temporariness of the buildings, their faded unpleasant colors. The street was cluttered with electric-light poles, telephone poles, gasoline pumps for motor cars, boxes of goods. Each man had built with the most valiant disregard of all the others. Between a large new "block" of two-story brick shops on one side, and the fire-brick Overland garage on the other side, was a one-story cottage turned into a millinery shop. The white temple of the Farmers' Bank was elbowed back by a grocery of glaring yellow brick. One store-building had a patchy galvanized iron cornice; the building beside it was crowned with battlements and pyramids of brick capped with blocks of red sandstone.
—Sinclair Lewis, *Main Street*

Denton had its hidden streets, its sense of languorous history, an old American stillness, wistful and unchanged, and these older traces too, older ideas and values scored in limestone and marble, in scroll ornaments atop a column or in the banknote details of a frieze. The Old Main, the county courthouse, the broad-fronted homes, the homes with deep shady porches, the trees, the streets named for trees—all this pleased her, made her think that happiness lived minute by minute in the things she saw and heard.
—Don De Lillo, *Libra*

Contents

A section of color illustrations appears after page 144.

Preface

Writing a book about Main Street requires some explanation. At first thought, nothing could be more familiar, banal even. Main Street is the essence of what is already known. And yet, during the years I have been working on this project, I have come to realize its immense and surprising complexity: "Main Street" in its material reality has been battered for decades in small towns across the United States, yet even today—especially today—the idea of the small town lies at the heart of the American ethos, with a strong and continuing appeal for Americans. This book attempts to capture some of this complexity in a series of chapters that explore the small town as constructed space in American culture and as a powerful ideology with both symbolic and material dimensions throughout the twentieth century and into our own time. And if Main Street is the most "American" of places, it is at the same time a place of paradox, a symbol of American democracy, yet a place of exclusion. It is the most mundane and dreary of places, and yet at the same time a place that has been fashioned—in its avatar as Disneyland's Main Street—into one of the most festive public spaces in the entire world.

My own route to this subject has followed several channels, so that in the end, for me, all roads led to Main Street. I had written many years ago on authenticity, and that led me to an interest in that most inauthentic of places, the Disneyland theme park. At some point I had also noticed, in working on the thirties photography of the Farm Security Administration, how pervasive was the representation of the small town in the archive of thirties government photography. In fact, as I looked some more into the culture of the 1930s, the small town—"our town"—seemed to be everywhere. Teaching a course called "Place in America," I became interested in the way the idea of community ran throughout the history of planned communities, of suburbia, and of the contemporary New Urbanist movement. In fact, it was the New Urbanism that I was most interested in understanding, especially in terms of its historical roots and its pervasive influence on contemporary place-making.

But these academic interests in the small town and in Main Street were preceded by my own experience growing up in America. This would be the point where you might expect me to acknowledge my small-town roots and to look back with nostalgia on my boyhood on Main Street. But actually, growing up as I did in an apartment house in Sunnyside, which is adjacent to Long Island City in the populous borough of Queens, and with the sounds of an elevated subway outside my bedroom window—a subway that could take me to Manhattan in just fifteen minutes—my own background is decidedly not small-town America. Whatever sense of community I did have came from the public schools I attended or from the neighborhood Cub Scout (and then Boy Scout) troop.

But on another level, the mythical level, I was acutely aware of what small-town America was like, at least in the television version; for my small town was the people and families I saw on American TV in the fifties, and who is to say they did not embed themselves deeply in my psyche? My own family and urban circumstances might have been closer to the Bronx apartments of *The Molly Goldberg Show*, but it was the charismatic midwestern banality of *Ozzie and Harriet* that most caught my imagination, or else the mild charm of the Hansens in *I Remember Mama*, who occupied a corner of immigrant San Francisco. Fortunately I had stopped watching television by the time *The Andy Griffith Show* came along in 1960, so I was spared the placid inanities of Andy Griffith and Don Knotts. But the fifties shows got to me, coming from a zone of popular desire, providing me with fictitious archetypes of the neighborhood and the small town, against which the realities of urban life would be measured.

My TV world was shared by millions, of course, influencing a whole generation of kids coming of age after World War II, but I also had the more distinctive experience of growing up in a place that really was a part of the history of the small town and community that I want to tell in this book, though I had no way of knowing it at the time: Sunnyside, Queens, was, after all, the site of a planned community of the 1920s whose historic importance I would understand only many years later, and urban Queens Boulevard was my Main Street. When I was about to go to high school, my family moved a little farther away from Manhattan, to Rego Park, which is adjacent to Forest Hills, itself another planned community from even earlier in the twentieth century. I now reside in Chestnut Hill, a late-nineteenth-century railroad suburb, now incorporated into Philadelphia, that comprises both a Main Street and elements of a planned town, and that is yet another point of inspiration, one that I discuss in a later chapter.

I knew vaguely, growing up, that Sunnyside and Forest Hills Gardens, so different from one another, were also quite different from the rest of the urban world, and that they were very special places. As to their history, how they got that way and why, it was all a blank to me, but one I got to fill in, in the process of writing this book.

That my own emphatically urban experience growing up in a borough of New York City could so inevitably, yet improbably, relate me to the small towns of America, both in myth and in reality, is part of the point of this study and part of the premise on which this inquiry stands—that there are, in the diversity and cacophony of American experience, these connecting chords. If Main Street is a microcosm of American life, and deeply tied up with the American's desire for the perfect community, then we need to understand its meanings and above all its contradictions, both historical and contemporary, if we are to understand its continuing power to influence the shape of American society and culture.

I WANT TO THANK my colleagues at Temple University for their support for this project in various forms over several years, including the award of a study leave and a College of Liberal Arts grant for research expenses. Particular thanks to the English Department and to my American studies colleagues. Treading as a relative newcomer in fields relating to urban studies, I have been fortunate to have the tolerant understanding, advice, and support of colleagues at Temple who have spent their lives in these areas, especially Carolyn Adams and Anne Shlay.

I have also been lucky to have in Mark Simpson-Vos, editorial director of the University of North Carolina Press, an editor of remarkable insight and efficiency, whose advice and assistance along the way to publication have been indispensable. And to the supporting staff at the press, especially Zachary Read and Paula Wald, more thanks for their always helpful encouragement and support. Many thanks to Howard Gillette, whose reading of the manuscript pointed me to many sources on the New Urbanism, and whose own book, *Civitas by Design* (2010), I encountered after writing my first draft, but still in time to add much to my understanding of planned communities. And I likewise owe a strong debt to Joy Kasson, another reader of the manuscript for the University of North Carolina Press, whose wise advice and astute comments helped immeasurably.

It is a pleasure to acknowledge the assistance of archivists, librarians, and others who have responded amiably to my calls for help, including especially Barbara Natanson at the Library of Congress; Liz Jarvis and Alex

Bartlett at the Chestnut Hill Historical Society; Brenda Galloway-Wright at Temple University's Urban Archives; Alix Reiskind, head of visual resources at the Harvard Graduate School of Design; Bob Singleton, executive director of the Greater Astoria Historical Society; Barbara Kellner and Jeannette Lichtenwalner at the Columbia (Maryland) Archives; Cathy Eiring, manager of the Forest Hills Gardens Corporation Office; Jan Pasek of the Philadelphia Housing Authority; and Kimberly Parker, director of the O. Winston Link Museum. Thanks also to these artists: photographer Sandy Sorlien for generously making available her extraordinary series of Main Street photos; Michael McCann, for kind permission to use his Celebration renderings; and photographer Scott McAuley for *Plasticville*. Without all of their help and the assistance of the efficient staff at the Library of Congress and the Smithsonian, my work in gathering illustrations would have been far more arduous.

To Lloyd Wells, about whom I write in one of my chapters, my special thanks for his warm and generous assistance in sharing his experiences and papers. Thanks also to historian David Contosta for sharing his insights on Chestnut Hill and Philadelphia with me. And to Don Hinkle-Brown, president of the Reinvestment Fund of Philadelphia, my gratitude for sharing his perspective on the city with me. My warm thanks also to Jane Lyle Diepeveen, Fair Lawn borough historian, for kindly sharing her knowledge of Radburn. I thank Robert Venturi and Denise Scott Brown for the inspiration of their work and for their generous insights.

To other colleagues and friends who have invited me to talk on this subject and greatly helped me think about it, I offer additional thanks, including Klaus Benesch, Peter Betjemann, Simon Bronner, John Haddad, Rob Kroes, Mark Meigs, David Nye, Sharon O'Brien, and Lauren Rabinovitz. And I must thank especially scholars whose work and friendship have long been an inspiration—Peter Bacon Hales, Udo Hebel, Carolyn Karcher, Jean Kempf, David Lubin, Jeffrey Meikle, Jan Radway, Thomas Riggio, Maren Stange, and Alan Trachtenberg. Among my former students, now colleagues, I want to thank especially Jaime Harker and Keith Gumery.

And to the many scholars in a range of fields whose work I have drawn on in this study, and whose work I have found indispensable to my own thinking, I offer particular gratitude. My notes reflect the range of my debt.

Those who tolerated my talking about this subject for so many years, even if they did so from the obligations of family or friendship, must also be thanked. I count myself lucky to have benefited from the insights and encouragement of Barry Orvell, Mark Rudd, and Paul Wachtel. Finally, my warmest gratitude to my family, who have endured years of "vacation" trips that often included excursions or detours to small towns and planned communities, even over their protests: thanks to my son, Dylan, whose creativity has inspired my own sedentary labors; thanks to my daughter, Ariana, whose study of cities has likewise inspired me, and for her many astute comments on the manuscript; and thanks to my wife, Gabriella Ibieta, for her generous editorial help and for her endless encouragement of a seemingly endless task.

The Death and Life of Main Street

Introduction

What is the best place to hide in America? Three films of the 1940s offer the same answer: small-town America. In Alfred Hitchcock's *Shadow of a Doubt* (1943), serial killer Charles Oakley hides out in a small California town, Santa Rosa, with his sister's family, though suspicion and the pursuit of the law eventually drive him to flee. In *The Stranger* (1946), Orson Welles uses a small town in Connecticut as the refuge of Nazi mastermind Franz Kindler, who has escaped from postwar Europe and assumes a new life as a professor at a small college before he is hunted down by a war-crime prosecutor. And in the 1947 film noir, *Out of the Past*, Jeff Bailey chooses to settle in Bridgeport, California, not much more than a few stores, where he runs a gas station as he tries to create a new identity for himself, following his traumatic years as a private investigator in New York. The small town has been, since the mid-nineteenth century, a part of the fictional imagination, and while it has served as a microcosm of America on many occasions, it has also served, as in these post–World War II films, as the epitome of the backwater, a place no one would dream of looking for much of anything: out of the mainstream, the small town is a place of refuge, a place of invisibility. Though it is far from the madness of the world, the town's tranquility is invaded in these films by strangers who bring that madness into the town. What could be more disturbing, more unsettling to the postwar imagination? In exploiting the image of the small town as a safe backwater, these films also point to one of the many paradoxes of Main Street, that it is vulnerable to outside forces that can blow through it and destroy it.

"Main Street" has pervaded the discourse of American culture for more than 150 years, molding both the physical and mental space we inhabit and serving as a global symbol of the United States. The most recent sign of this was an assumption that took hold in the media and the popular imagination late in the first decade of the twenty-first century, an assump-

1

tion that completely reverses the notion of the small town as backwater, far from the madding crowd, namely, the idea that we *all* live on Main Street: Main Street had become one element in a definitive national binary, the other being Wall Street. Wall Street, of course, has been a perennial symbol of the banking and financial services industries since the mid-nineteenth century at least, and when it imploded in 2008, bringing mortgage foreclosures, soaring unemployment, and a huge drop in the stock market, Main Street suddenly assumed a far broader constituency than it had ever possessed. In business parlance, "Main Street" had meant the small businessman, as opposed to the bankers; now it meant everyone in the United States who was *not* Wall Street. Unlike Wall Street, Main Street was what we all shared, it was symbolically where we all lived, it was the common space, the public space, as opposed to the private, as if all Americans lived in one immense small town, an image that emerged based on the function of any Main Street—which is to provide a place where people can come together for chance meetings, a place for shopping, for planned civic meetings, a place for parades and festivals.

For many years previous to the economic meltdown, Main Street's political valence had been Republican (as in the self-appointed congressional group, the Main Street Republicans): Main Street was associated with small-town culture and mores, with traditionalism, with conservative social values, as against the values of the city—diversity, multiculturalism, the arts, bohemianism.[1] But since the 2008 meltdown, Main Street has become a metaphor for a much broader political spectrum, encompassing the whole of the social structure (save the very top), whether Republican or Democrat, urban, suburban, or rural: suddenly the vast majority of Americans were pictured as victims of an extremely wealthy, narrow, blundering, and plundering predatory class—Wall Street. (The Occupy Movement, arising in 2011, with its distinction between the 99 percent and the 1 percent, was yet another manifestation of this idea.) I am not suggesting any realignment of class interests in the United States as a result of this metaphor, but there might have been the glimmer of a truly heterodox idea, even a proscribed idea: that many more of us than we had previously thought possible were in the same boat, and it was not a luxury yacht.

But Main Street has not always had this cachet: in fact, the trope of Main Street has taken many turns over the last 100 or more years, most dramatically in its move from being an image of the dullness of provincial life in the 1920s to being the bedrock of American democracy in the

1930s. In this book, I explore the small town as constructed space in American culture, from the nineteenth century to the present; I also explore Main Street as a powerful ideology, looking at its symbolic dimensions, throughout the twentieth century and into our own time. In short, I view Main Street as both a *place* and an *idea*.

But as a "place" it holds a peculiar status: there is not a single "Main Street"; there are countless versions. We have all been on some particular Main Street, but there are so many historical variations that it escapes a singular identity. At the same time, there is something generic about the place: Main Street is the principal thoroughfare of a given town and accordingly has a defined status within the hierarchy of a local geography that is consistent from one place to another. I am interested in the brick-and-mortar aspects of Main Street and in its generic attributes. But I am also interested in the larger emblematic meaning of Main Street—the place it occupies as cultural icon in our society. It is the dual reality of Main Street—as place and as idea—that gives it its centrality in American culture: we have all been there, in its local variations; and we all also have some broader set of associations with Main Street as a cultural ideal and an icon of American culture. And of course place and idea are interconnected, for it is Main Street's force as an idea that has powered its creation as place; and it is the place, Main Street, that has embodied and perpetuated the idea.

My aim is not simply to demonstrate the power and persistence of the idea of Main Street as a shaping force in American culture and as a global symbol; I am also aiming to problematize this major icon by asking how a model that connotes harmony and community functions in a society that has become increasingly diverse. How does the small-town ideal reveal the fault lines of the social compact? How does a symbol of dullness and banality become a symbol of excitement and entertainment? How does a place that stands for repression also stand for a core democratic process— the town meeting? In short, I am interested in Main Street as an icon and as an ideology that contains contradictions and tensions visible at each critical stage of its evolution through the twentieth century. As Robert Pinsky puts it, "The town is the imagined locale for American ambivalences about culture itself."[2]

Given the broad questions that motivate this study, I will be taking a multidisciplinary approach, dealing with the discourse of Main Street in political and social terms as well as in terms of representation and physical embodiment. Accordingly, my materials will be drawn from the historical archive, from literature and visual representation (including photography and film), as well as from architecture and urban planning. In doing so, I am taking my bearings from the work of scholars in many fields, and I might mention a few major points on the compass. Thus, the literary study of Main Street has a long tradition, beginning with Ima Honaker Herron's *The Small Town in American Literature* (1939) and including the still valuable study by Anthony Channell Hilfer, *The Revolt from the Village, 1915–1930* (1969). More recently, poet Robert Pinsky has written a short but penetrating memoir and meditation on the literature and culture of Main Street, *Thousands of Broadways: Dreams and Nightmares of the American Small Town* (2009). Richard Lingeman's *Small Town America: A Narrative History, 1620–the Present* (1980) is a landmark in historical studies, as is the more recent and more narrowly focused *Downtown America: A History of the Place and the People Who Made It* (2004), by Alison Isenberg. Richard V. Francaviglia's *Main Street Revisited: Time, Space, and Image Building in Small-Town America* (1996), by a cultural geographer, is likewise a major work in this area. And I have taken inspiration from the work of sociologists, from Robert and Helen Lynd to Robert Putnam.

I take my license to thus range across disciplines from the very nature of the problem and the kinds of questions I want to ask. In doing so, I am aware that I am transgressing methodological boundaries that have been as carefully cultivated as hedgerows, but I hope I can claim a temporary easement, and that the breadth of the subject provides some justification. (What F. O. Matthiessen observed in introducing *The American Renaissance* many years ago still holds true today, or ought to: "The true function of scholarship as of society is not to stake out claims on which others must not trespass, but to provide a community of knowledge in which others may share.")[3] I also hope that this study might, in bringing together so many different components, help to provide a broader picture of a central value in American culture that profoundly influences our way of thinking and building today and whose full measure we have not yet taken.

MY SUBJECT IS "Main Street," but I take that phrase not only on its own terms, denoting the commercial strip of a small town, but in the larger set of meanings that have accrued to it over the years. Main Street, the heart of the small town, is also a synecdoche for the small town itself (as in Sinclair Lewis's novel). More than that, Main Street encompasses the idea of community as well, and the term *community* is another of those words, like *Main Street*, that comprises both a physical space and an idea of association among people who live there. One classic study of the history of community defines the word in terms of place, often associated with the idealized image of the small town; but the author also rightly insists that community entails "an expectation of a special quality of human relationship," and that it is distinguished by "a network of social relations marked by mutuality and emotional bonds."[4] In short, community is most obviously the conjunction of place and people, of the land and human beings.

But we can also speak of communities that exist irrespective of place—religious communities, subscribers to newspapers and magazines, fans of radio or television programs, business communities, and so on. Thus, if we turn the angle of perspective, we can speak of individuals who belong to multiple communities, and a nuanced view of "community" requires this more layered sense. Nevertheless, the notion of community as place (and as a place of social connection) remains strong, even in the virtual realms of twenty-first-century American life, resting often on the most concrete and material sense of place, namely, where children play. Since the mid-twentieth century at least, where children play—whether they can be watched, whether they are safe from traffic and safe from strangers—has been a key factor in creating the sense of what a community is, and the sentiment of the small town is imbued with the sense that it is a place where children can grow up safely and can participate indispensably in such communal festivals as the Fourth of July, with its customary decorated bike parade, pie-eating contest, and three-legged race. Insofar as Main Street and the small town have embodied this idea of amicable public association, the term *community*—as a kind of shorthand—is a recurrent and central one in this narrative, and it figures largely in my account of the planned community (as place and as social experience), from the early twentieth century to the New Urbanism, which occupies the last three chapters of this book.[5]

In short, the three key terms for my discussion are *Main Street, small town*, and *community*. These terms are not synonymous, but they have in practice overlapped in the discourse of place in America, and I take the intersections of these terms and their cross-influences as a part of my subject. To complicate things further, each of these terms has both a denotative and a connotative meaning: thus, Main Street is the particular name of a place in many towns, but it also evokes an ethos, a culture, an ideology. The small town likewise can refer to a historical place or a larger political culture. And *community* too can mean not only the place but also the social composition of the place, as I suggested earlier. And while I am claiming in my narrative the interconnections among these terms, I am also assuming the reader will deduce from the context the more specific meaning intended.

But I am getting ahead of the story in raising these complexities. Let us begin, rather, with an understanding of Main Street in its seeming simplicity, for we usually do in practice assume a unitary conception of Main Street, and we oppose this putative unity to the radical complexity and diversity of the city. One way to put it, in starkly demographic terms, is to say that the small town is white and the city is nonwhite. These stereotypes are to some degree borne out by teens' stated preferences of where they would like to live: 35 percent of white teens (age thirteen to seventeen) would prefer a small town, as opposed to 29 percent who prefer a city; among nonwhites, only 19 percent prefer a small town, compared to 40 percent who would choose a city. For both groups, the suburbs gain the adherence of about 20 percent, and rural areas even less than that.[6] As I show in a later chapter, the small town has historically labored hard to keep its racial homogeneity intact, until about 1970 at least. But as I also hope to demonstrate in the pages that follow, the formulation of Main Street as a place of unity and homogeneity, even granting its relative racial consistency, is too simple to begin with and hard to find in fact.

If we can most obviously oppose the small town to the city, we can also, more abstractly perhaps, oppose it to the notion of the Borderland—a place of mixing, a margin of culture clash and reformation, a place where identity is defined against the mainstream. And it is the Borderland— especially the border culture between Latin America and North America, centered on the Chicano/a experience and the experience of hybridity— that has generated a rich culture of difference in contemporary America and that has understandably gained the attention of many scholars in American studies. On the face of it, Main Street and the Borderland are opposites: Main Street exists as a place of relative homogeneity and security, defined in opposition to the "world outside." Conversely, the Borderland, which exists by definition *between* two places and straddles the uncertainties of identity that result from that ambiguity, gains its vitality from the clash of cultures. Yet even as Main Street and the Borderland derive their power from their oppositional force, each contains, paradoxically, an element of the other, and these formulations—Main Street and Borderland— in fact have a certain codependency.[7] As Robert Bellah has suggested, the desire for "diversity" in the homogeneous American schoolhouse comes from a fear that sameness will create an inability to deal with the world as it in fact is; and the pervasive nostalgia for the small town and for community, a staple of our mass culture, conversely may come from "the fear that there may be no way at all to relate to those who are too different."[8] In fact we must allow for both Main Street *and* the Borderland if we are to have a complete picture of the tensions in American culture: on the one hand, the diversity of cultures that constantly merge and fuse within the mainstream and, on the other hand, the ideal of a shared community, represented by this notion of "small-town America."

But again, stereotype and reality are often in conflict: in asserting an interest in Main Street, I must from the outset resist the notion that the phrase will inevitably conjure up—that Main Street represents a unitary culture. Although I have opposed it, heuristically, to the Borderland, the cultural history of "Main Street" does not reveal a society that is monolithic. Rather, the story I want to tell is of Main Street as a place and an idea that has been subject to definition and redefinition, even contestation, for more than 100 years, and that the struggle to define its rule or its ideals has been part of its cultural meaning. The meaning has not been fixed but has been and continues to be in flux, and the debate over its meaning is precisely its cultural meaning. To assert an ideal of community—Main Street as utopia—is not necessarily to possess that ideal, and the story of Main Street is also, repeatedly, a story of the effort, and the failure, to define community. As Christopher Lasch observed, "Social solidarity does not rest on shared values or ideological consensus, let alone on an identity of interests; it rests on public conversation."[9] And it is precisely the conflict between Main Street as ideal and as sometimes harsh reality that we will see again and again.

My title, *The Death and Life of Main Street: Small Towns in American Memory, Space, and Community*, is meant to suggest both this book's specific focus—Main Street—and a larger sense of that term's place in American consciousness. Americans dream of Main Street, as an ideal place; they have also dreamed it into being, created it, and re-created it, as a physical place, the material embodiment of the dream. Moreover, my tacit assumption is that there is an equivalence of sorts between Main Street and America, that Main Street, in its broadest significance, *is* America. Given the extravagant heterogeneity of American society, not to mention its conflictual elements, there is undoubtedly something hyperbolic in this formulation. At the same time, I am asserting the right to speak about American culture in general terms.

That last point needs elaboration. The idea of any kind of national consensus or national consciousness came under attack in the 1960s and 1970s in response to some of the classic works of the "myth and symbol" writers in American studies (e.g., Henry Nash Smith, Leo Marx, R. W. B. Lewis), who seemed to be extrapolating something like a "national" consciousness from a few select literary texts. Though I agree with much of this critique, it has tended to simplify the methodology of these writers and set up a prohibition against synthetic narrative. Meanwhile, from the social sciences, there has been an equally strong skepticism about generalizations, in favor of explanations that are grounded only in individual cases. Although I am not assuming any unitary ethos or unified mentality among the many agents who comprise the society of the United States, I am assuming the existence of a popular culture, created out of American traditions and the mass media, in which a common knowledge of signs and symbols is shared. To the extent that we participate in a society dominated by mass media (one that began with the newspapers, magazines, and chromolithographs of the mid-nineteenth century and continues into the digital age), there are familiar and universal symbols that we all understand, even if we do not share the values they imply, such as "Santa Claus" or "cowboys" or "television." "Main Street" is one of these shared symbols, and to live in the United States and not know the meaning of "Main Street" is impossible. To that extent, there is a commonality of knowledge, though not necessarily a community of values. We may not subscribe to the Main Street ethos, but we know what it means. And we know also that it is a constant, a recurring meaning, a recurring symbol, a recurring icon in American culture. We see the small town in films, sitcoms, and fiction; we see it in our built environment, from the actual small town to the urbanized renditions of it that have been promulgated by the New Urbanism. It is in that sense that I am speaking about "Main Street America" as a metaphor for that shared knowledge of a common culture, despite the enormous heterogeneity and difference that also characterize American culture. For we often assume, in emphasizing difference, that there is nothing at all held in common To the extent that Americans share a place, we share an idiom, and that idiom includes the notion of "Main Street."

IN YET ONE MORE respect, my approach may need some explanation, in that this is primarily a study of an "American" idea and place, hardly venturing at all into transnational comparisons. Surely the transnational turn that American studies has taken in the last fifteen years has significantly changed the way we think about the United States: placing our understanding of America in the context of global cultural power as well as global economic and military power; observing the parallels, similarities, interactions, and differences between North and South America or between the United States and Canada; observing the flow of culture between the United States and other countries—in both directions—all of this has brought a new understanding of American culture in the twenty-first century. But my subject is more narrowly defined: and my interest here is in the evolution of Main Street as idea and place within the context of the United States. The study of national culture, I would argue, is not irrelevant to a contemporary understanding of American culture, and this does not at all argue for "American exceptionalism." To say that there may be characteristics of American culture that merit recognition and understanding is not to say that American culture is superior to other cultures or has a warrant to impose itself internationally. It is, however, to recognize that every culture, in addition to sharing features and interacting with other cultures, may also have its distinctive features.

This is not to say that there is no opportunity for transnational dimensions in the study of Main Street. Obviously we find towns wherever there are human habitations; and principal thoroughfares, whatever they are called, are an inevitable feature of town evolution and town design. The character of a High Street in England may be similar in many ways to the character of a Main Street in the United States. But the central arteries of small towns, especially in Europe, have often grown up over many centuries, and the accretion of history in places of settlements may go back to the Roman Empire and beyond. The small town in America, by contrast, has often been created overnight, relatively speaking, and the historic meaning of settlement in a country that otherwise has a history of wilderness and its perils is accordingly different. But the currents of influence run in both directions: the evolution of town design in the twentieth century draws considerably, as I show in a later chapter, on town planning ideas that were developed by an Englishman and on experimental garden cities that emerged in early-twentieth-century Britain; medieval German villages—to name just one more improbable foreign source—likewise contributed much to American twentieth-century thinking about town design. Today, the idea of Main Street reconstruction and preservation is itself a leading idea in China.[10] And who can as yet calculate the effect of Disney's replication of Main Street America in its worldwide theme parks? In fact, a transnational study of Main Street would be an excellent addition to the scholarly agenda. Admitting all of this, I would argue nevertheless that there is much to explore in a "national" study of Main Street and its cultural meanings, and given the inherent complexity of the subject as I have conceived it, the boundaries can be productively drawn in a way to emphasize the peculiarly "American" aspects of the Main Street idea.

Indeed, it is the self-consciousness about the idea of "Main Street"—from its inception as a nineteenth-century trope to its apotheosis in Disneyland to its productive embodiment in the New Urbanism—that marks it as an essential aspect of "American" culture. As early as 1849, a few years before writing *The Scarlet Letter*, Nathaniel Hawthorne wrote a historical sketch of New England, called "Main-Street," in which he lightly mocks the chauvinism of the Salem children who have grown up in town and regard it as the pinnacle of civilization.[11] The townsfolk proudly measure their own Main Street against the greatest thoroughfares of the world: their "Main-street" "is a street indeed, worthy to hold its way with the thronged and stately avenues of cities beyond the sea." Hearing of "Cheapside and Fleet-street and the Strand," Hawthorne writes, "the children listen, and still inquire if the streets of London are longer and broader than the one before their father's door; if the Tower is bigger than the jail in Prison Lane; if the old Abbey will hold a larger congregation than our meeting-house. Nothing impresses them, except their own experience."[12] Seventy years later, Sinclair Lewis, mocking the chauvinism of the townsfolk of Gopher Prairie, would call Main Street "the climax of civilization."[13] From Hawthorne to Sinclair Lewis to Walt Disney, nothing could be more American than the habit of regarding Main Street as an exceptional place, though only the first two would see that insistence as evidence of provinciality.

Part of the meaning of Main Street, adumbrated by Hawthorne in his tale, is that the town's main road, its central core, is a place of public spectacle. Hawthorne embodies that duality—Main Street as functional place and Main Street as theatrical spectacle—in the conception of his story, which features a showman who presents, on the Main Street of Salem, a painted panoramic representation of the very place itself, which he proceeds to unroll before an audience of townsfolk.[14] While doing so, the showman peoples the changing scenes with puppets from the various historical eras of New England, from the days of the Native Americans to the present, thus dramatizing the history of the town, with an emphasis—given Hawthorne's mentality—on the darkness and religious gloom of the inhabitants. And that notion—that Main Street is a space that doubles as a kind of public theater—explains something of Main Street's nature and also its necessity. The social order needs a town center where the drama of society can be enacted, where events can be witnessed, parades can be staged, and people can perform themselves as they go about their daily lives: Main Street as theater is part of its meaning as civic space; it is part of the reason we value it in a society that is otherwise placeless and suffering from atopia and anomie. Main Street stands for the rootedness of place and tradition in the historic small town, although ironically (as I discuss in the conclusion) it has been taken over by a consumer culture and re-made into a generic place, valued for its neutered associational qualities.[15]

This book is driven by a set of questions that have motivated my curiosity and that run throughout this book: How has Main Street maintained its hold on us, serving as the prison house of our culture and, at the same time, creating the map and model for urban development for well over 100 years? What is the collective fantasy, the myth of Main Street, as it has become embodied in our popular culture, and what are its material and political dimensions? What is Main Street's seemingly perennial and enduring appeal? What is the source of our deep nostalgia for the small town? And what, to turn the tables, are the pernicious effects of this seemingly benign myth, and the costs of keeping it alive?

My response to these questions takes the form of a series of chapters, beginning with "Main Street Mythologies," which examines the small town and Main Street as mythical constructions, removed from history and time, symbolic spaces that embody a perennial nostalgia. I then move to the historical plane of Main Street and the small town (chapter 2, "Fighting Extinction: The Reinvention of Main Street"), exploring the material existence of the traditional small town and its perennial struggle to survive in an industrial society and an economic order that have in many ways rendered it obsolete. In the chapters that follow, I go back to the 1920s and examine the history of the small town in roughly chronological order. Chapter 3, "Living on Main Street: Sinclair Lewis and the Great Cultural Divide," looks at the small town through the lens of the most celebrated book ever written about its claustrophobic culture, *Main Street*. I broaden the lens in the fourth chapter, "Main Street as Memory," and explore the reverse polarity of the small town in the 1930s, when it became the object of reverence, nostalgia, and all things good about America. In the fifth chapter, "Main Street: Belonging and Not Belonging," I examine the myth of small-town community, focusing especially on the Middletown studies. Chapter 6, "Utopian Dreams: From Forest Hills to Greenbelt," explores the tradition of town planning, modeled on the small town, that extends from the factory towns of the late nineteenth century to the Garden City tradition, up to World War II. In chapter 7, "Rethinking Suburbia: Levittown or the New Urbanism?" I look at the creation of new towns in the latter half of the twentieth century as part of the post–World War II response to the suburbs. Chapter 8, "Main Street in the City," explores the importation of New Urbanist thinking into the renewal of cities (especially affordable housing) that began in the late 1980s. And in the conclusion, "Consuming Main Street," I discuss the effort in the last twenty years to reinvent the downtowns of cities by going back to history, back to Main Street—via the New Urbanism—for the leading model.

This book traces, in effect, a circle, from the historical Main Street to the mythical, and from there to the extraordinary power of that myth to sustain a century of planning and development, from the suburbs to the inner cities. It is the power of this idea that has transformed place in America throughout the twentieth century and that now, in the twenty-first century, especially after the cataclysmic trauma of the attack on the World Trade Center, has created an eager society of consumers in search of community and of a world where 9/11 could never have happened.

Chapter One

Main Street Mythologies

Every town or settlement in the United States has a central artery running through it, and in most cases that road or avenue is called Main Street: it is the essence of the small town and synonymous with it. Yet for all its generic character, consider the range of referents embedded in this most familiar of icons: Do we mean the New England town with its traditional village green, with commercial streets bordering it, and featuring a steepled church that calls the community together into a symbolic whole, both political and religious? Or do we mean the southern town, with its courthouse square at the center, the streets coming into it, typically from four directions, forming a communal, commercial and legal center that gives precedence to secular culture? Or do we mean the linear Main Street of the Midwest, from one to six blocks long usually (depending on population), with commercial buildings fronting the street on one or, usually, two sides, providing a matrix for future growth that might expand laterally from the street itself as the town expands? The courthouse square or the village requires a deliberate act of town planning; but the linear Main Street, deriving from European models of row houses in villages and towns along main roads, can grow from nothing—a single building—and is driven by the commercial life of the surrounding population. Towns can also be constructed in one effort by giant companies for their workers— the so-called company towns of the late nineteenth century—or they can be built from a blueprint by land developers, as in the many New Urbanist towns of the late twentieth century. Their populations may range from 2,500 to 25,000 or more. (The U.S. Department of Housing and Urban Development limits their Main Street grants to cities with fewer than 50,000 inhabitants.) Multiply these general types by hundreds and thousands of individual places, of all sizes and populations, each with its individual character, and you get a picture of multiplicity almost too vast to be assimilated into a single phrase or concept, a point made evident by a web-

Main Street and common, Plymouth, New Hampshire, ca. 1908. Library of Congress, Detroit Publishing Co. Collection.

site initiated in 2010, *Mapping Main Street*, which documents the diversity of Main Streets in the United States through photographs and recorded interviews.[1]

Yet despite the wide range of particulars that are contained within the abstraction, there is an apparent consensus, a broad singularity of meaning that raises "Main Street" to an iconic and even mythical status that pervades our popular culture.

What is the myth of Main Street, and where does it begin? What are the constants of its imagining and iconography? As an idea, a Platonic form almost, Main Street exists on a plane apart from reality, and given its heterogeneity, in many ways Americans *have* ascribed a certain mythical character to "the small town," as if there were a single template, a type, out of which the myriad versions have emerged. Again and again we find the small town offered as a microcosm of America, yet an America in which conflicts are resolved, differences elided, a world that stands symbolically for order.

WRITING IN 1869, Susan Fenimore Cooper celebrated the virtues of the village in terms that spoke soothingly to a nation nearly torn asunder by the Civil War: "Probably much the largest number of the most pleasant and happiest homes in the land may be found to-day in our villages and

Main Street, Stroudsburg, Pennsylvania, ca. 1905. Library of Congress, Detroit Publishing Co. Collection.

rural towns—homes where truth, purity, the holiest affections, the highest charities and healthful culture are united with a simplicity of life scarcely possible on [*sic*] our extravagant cities." Although there was room for improvement (in fact, Cooper was promoting village improvement societies), she presents the village not as a benighted backwater but rather as a place that is as modern, as contemporary in its cultural resources, as New York or Philadelphia, with domestic use of gas for lighting, steam for heating, the morning paper, telegrams from Paris or London, new books, vegetables from Bermuda, and fruits from Cuba, not to mention lectures and concerts. She may have exaggerated a bit, but Cooper's engagement with the present and future of the rural village is positive and optimistic. She is creating a template for the small town that is an ideal to be pursued.[2]

One of the first intellectuals to articulate the broad cultural importance of the small town was the eminent and influential Randolph Bourne, who wrote in a 1913 essay for the *Atlantic Monthly*, "An American town, large enough to contain a fairly complete representation of the different classes and types of people and social organizations, and yet not so large that individualities are submerged in the general mass, or the lines between the classes blurred and made indistinct, is a real epitome of American life."[3] And Bourne went on to call for an anthropological analysis of social class and power in the town that would be answered, in 1929, by the first

Main Street and courthouse, Northampton, Mass., ca. 1907. Library of Congress, Detroit Publishing Co. Collection.

of the Middletown studies of Robert and Helen Lynd. The centrality of Main Street to American culture was likewise argued by the country's pre-eminent sociologist, Thorstein Veblen, in a 1923 essay that captured the mythic strength of the small town, when he wrote, "The country town is one of the great American institutions; perhaps the greatest, in the sense that it has had and continues to have a greater part than any other in shaping public sentiment and giving character to American culture." But of course to call it the "greatest" American institution is not necessarily to call it the most benign. Veblen also wrote of the small town that it is "the perfect flower of self-help and cupidity."[4]

Writing in the early twenties, Veblen assumed the immutability of the country town, failing to see that the vast rural lands of the Midwest would be drained of their populations, while cities correspondingly grew. On another level, however, Veblen was right: though the actual towns have in many cases been decimated, the institution of the small town, the institution of Main Street, remains of central importance, as he said, "in shaping public sentiment and giving character to American culture." Main Street's enduring power is as a symbol.

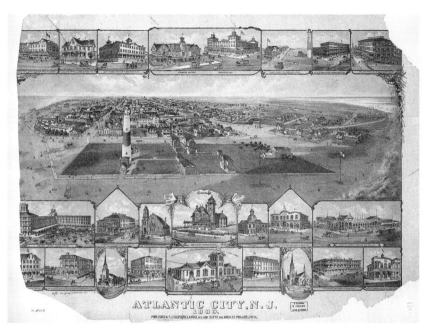

Perspective map by T. J. Shepherd Landis of Atlantic City, New Jersey, showing a plan of the city, with notable houses, churches, and hotels featured around the border, 1880. Library of Congress.

ONE OF THE MEANS by which the small towns were raised to another plane of meaning, even in the nineteenth century, was the chromolithographic map, which offered a visual representation of ordered space. Taking advantage of a printing process developed in the 1820s, itinerant artists would travel from town to town, making sketches of streets and buildings that could entice the townsfolk to become subscribers; given a critical mass, the artist would then invest the time in creating a map that would be lithographed and hung in the parlor. Such maps were decorative, but they were also of special use to land developers and town boosters, who could use the enhanced image of the town to attract workers and settlers, immigrants, industrialists, and builders. And during these years, town and city populations were growing exponentially: in 1840 8.5 percent of the population in the United States lived in urban places of 8,000 or more; by 1890, the figure had jumped to 30 percent (43 percent in the Northeast, around 15 percent in the Southeast).[5]

With towns ranging in size from the largest—New York, Boston, Chicago —to the smallest—Los Angeles (a mere sketch of a place in 1857), Reno, Bismarck—these views represent a wide range of particulars, yet the art-

Perspective map by T. M. Fowler of Wolfe City, Texas, showing a plan of the town, with railroads cutting across the map, and featuring border illustrations of hotels, banks, foundries, and oil mills, 1891. Library of Congress.

ist's treatment in most cases follows a convention that gave them all a certain common aspect. The convention, from the 1840s to the 1890s, the peak years of popularity for the chromolithograph maps, was to take a bird's-eye panoramic view of the town, showing the place as a distinct settlement positioned within a surrounding natural landscape of hills, mountains, rivers, or farms. Streets were labeled and buildings were drawn individually, so that the viewer, depending on the size of the town, would enjoy an almost three-dimensional effect. Tiny figures on horseback or in horse-drawn carts and carriages might also be seen in the busy parts of town. Meanwhile, around the border of the map, the artist would place a series of separate vignettes, featuring prominent buildings in the town, often commissioned by the buildings' owners. The name of the town was prominently printed on the bottom margin.[6]

By the early decades of the twentieth century, when the practice ended, artists had produced views of approximately 2,400 different places. Each was distinct, yet as part of a larger convention of town representation, they contributed to a collective sense of the cultural space of the United States, each image a snapshot or frozen moment in time, a record of the civilized space of human habitation in the nineteenth century. Or rather,

Frances Flora Palmer, Across the Continent: Westward the Course of Empire Takes Its Way *(1868), Currier & Ives lithograph. Library of Congress, Prints and Photographs Division.*

the civilized space of white habitation, for the Native American, who had occupied these spaces previously, was erased in all save a few images.

One popular print in particular, *Across the Continent: Westward the Course of Empire Takes Its Way* (1868) by Frances Flora Palmer, is worth special notice in this regard, though it pictures not the bird's-eye view of a settled town but rather the more general, and generic, process of founding a town. At a time when hundreds of towns were being founded across the Midwest and West, Palmer's popular Currier & Ives lithograph depicts a wilderness of plains, rivers, and mountains, with a railroad train bisecting the space diagonally. On the left side of the tracks, a log cabin village is springing into existence, thanks to the active energy of settlers who are cutting trees in the nearby forest; in the center of the foreground, children are playing outside a schoolhouse, the sign of settlement and civilization, with other houses scattered in the middle ground; townsfolk gather also at the siding where the train is stopped. Here is the process of civilization, in its rudimentary form—the beginning of the small town—and the railroad track, in a configuration that was not unusual, predicts the space that would in time become Main Street, running parallel to the track. Meanwhile, in an affirming but decidedly discourteous vision of Manifest Destiny, we see on the other side of the tracks, which lies undeveloped, two unfortunate Indians on horseback who are about to be engulfed by the smoke from the train's locomotive, which is blowing their way. Palmer's rendering of the founding myth of the small town—anticipating the history of Main Street—is a story of those who settle the place and those who are excluded or marginalized. We can see who the winners are and who the losers are in this process, but the rhetoric of the image and Palmer's sentiment are all for the winners.

At the height of the popularity of the chromolithograph views of towns and cities, Walt Whitman offered his own imagined community, in *Democratic Vistas* (1871), when he turned from his more typical celebration of the urban America that had birthed him poetically to imagine its polar opposite, the western town. In this powerful diatribe against the failures of democracy, Whitman draws the distinction repeatedly between the ideal structure of the polity and the corruption of politicians, between the magnificence of the material structures of the city and the depraved inhabitants. Yet he holds to his vision of an America of free individuals, of a superb democratic system, of invested homeowners. Against the present realities of American life, Whitman constructs an image of a utopian future that might even, he speculates, already exist in some places:

> I can conceive a community, to-day and here, in which, on a sufficient scale, the perfect personalities, without noise meet; say in some pleasant western settlement or town, where a couple of hundred best men and women, of ordinary worldly status, have by luck been drawn together, with nothing extra of genius or wealth, but virtuous, chaste, industrious, cheerful, resolute, friendly and devout. I can conceive such a community organized in running order, powers judiciously delegated—farming, building, trade, courts, mails, schools, elections, all attended to; and then the rest of life, the main thing, freely branching and blossoming in each individual, and bearing golden fruit. I can see there, in every young and old man, after his kind, and in every woman after hers, a true personality, develop'd, exercised proportionately in body, mind, and spirit. I can imagine this case as one not necessarily rare or difficult, but in buoyant accordance with the municipal and general requirements of our times. And I can realize in it the culmination

of something better than any stereotyped *éclat* of history or poems. Perhaps, unsung, undramatized, unput in essays or biographies—perhaps even some such community already exists, in Ohio, Illinois, Missouri, or somewhere, practically fulfilling itself, and thus outvying, in cheapest vulgar life, all that has been hitherto shown in best ideal pictures.[7]

There is much that is characteristic of Whitman here—the conflation of the "ordinary" and the "best" in describing the ideal townspeople, and the idealization of personality as a perfect synthesis of body, mind, and spirit. Opposing life and art, this imagined town is the "culmination of something better" than has been pictured previously by stereotyped literary representations or even in "best ideal pictures." What is less expected in the poet who had insisted we must unscrew the doors from their jambs is the picture of civic order Whitman projects, a community with trades, courts, schools, mail, all in perfect "running order." And most surprising is the place itself: not the city but the "pleasant western settlement or town," that is later given a locus in "Ohio, Illinois, Missouri, or somewhere."

Why did Whitman turn to "some pleasant western settlement or town" as the locus for this utopian vision? Given his excoriation of the contemporary state of democracy in the United States—he was thinking naturally of the eastern cities—Whitman seems to have imagined the western town as an escape into an idealized possibility of perfection, an order and simplicity that the poet had otherwise given up on. And in doing so, Whitman was going back to the "settlement"—to an earlier stage of civilization in the United States—in order to go forward to an idealized future, thus initiating the double movement of an act of recuperation that is at the same time an act of imagining, which would become exemplary in the American imagination.[8]

As it happens, such towns as Whitman imagined may already have been taking shape soon after he wrote *Democratic Vistas*. We have evidence from an 1888 *Harper's Monthly* article, at least, of a Montana town that comprises the kind of heterogeneous community the poet often invoked in his celebrations of American society: "Crowding the sidewalks are miners, picturesque in red shirts and top-boots; long-haired Missourians, waiting, like Micawber, for something to 'turn up'; ranchmen, standing beside their heavily loaded wagons; trappers; tourists; men of business. Chinamen and Indians, Germans and Hebrews, whites and blacks, the prosperous and the needy . . . all make Helena their home. No traditions, no old family influence, no past social eminence, hamper the restless spirit of the busy workers."[9] As here described, Helena comes close to exemplifying Frederick Jackson Turner's notion of the democratic openness of the frontier West, and it would be hard to find a comparable image of society east of the Mississippi. From our present perspective on the small town, it seems utterly fantastical, unless it represents some hypothetical first stage of civilization, the unformed mixing of a population without distinction, before the rigid lines of social difference and social exclusion set in.

Even while the towns of the Midwest and West were being settled, at a cost to the Native Americans that we can only grieve over, the older towns of the Northeast—many founded in the eighteenth century—were mutating into myth and memory. The "New England town" was deliberately created as a tourist destination, a nostalgic image, inspiring an attitude toward Main Street that would carry into and beyond the twentieth century. The recovery of the putative origins of New England village culture began as early as the 1850s, when Portsmouth, New Hampshire, sponsored a "hometown reunion" for townsfolk who had been dispersed to the far corners of the country. By the early 1900s, hometown week was a familiar ritual throughout New England, and Edith Wharton draws on the typical celebration for the background of her 1917 novel about social class and sexual awakening, *Summer*. Wharton sets her novel in the fictional town of North Dormer, of which Wharton observes carefully: "The incentive to the celebration had come rather from those who had left North Dormer than from those who had been obliged to stay there, and there was some difficulty in rousing the village to the proper state of enthusiasm."[10]

In addition to offering nostalgia for what was left behind as people moved to regions with greater economic opportunity, these hometown reunions also served as retreats to a past that was socially less conflicted. As the nineteenth century progressed, southern New England was becoming more and more "ethnic"—by 1890, 68 percent of Boston's population was made up of first- or second-generation immigrants—and the imagined purity of the old New Hampshire towns had even stronger appeal as a vacation spot for the urban elite.[11] In the last quarter of the nineteenth century, scores of New England small towns—Deerfield, Ipswich, Marblehead, Salem, as well as Nantucket Island—were undergoing transformation back to a colonial appearance that erased the accidents of history, positing an exaggerated homogeneity that satisfied the tourist in search of "heritage."[12]

TO THE EXTENT THAT Main Street has embedded itself indelibly as an archetype in the contemporary American mind, it is largely a function of *created memory*—not, we might say, firsthand memory, but a kind of secondhand, ersatz memory, a collective memory, given form in the many materializations of the small town—from Williamsburg to Disneyland—that have marked twentieth-century culture and continue powerfully into our own time. (See Plate 1.) As historian Max Page observes, "Memory is built into the physical landscape and individual encounters with buildings, natural sites, and whole regions."[13] Memories can also be built into fictitious spaces, where they produce a more comprehensive nostalgia for a generic small-town past that may have no personal connection to the individual. In effect, the mythologizing of the small town in these twentieth-century models has created a kind of vicarious memory. Such "memories" are constructed both physically and socially and can have, as psychologists have argued, positive psychological functions, generating feelings of social connectedness.[14]

I want to consider a few examples of such physical embodiments of the small town—real spaces constructed as imagined or fictitious places—from the miniature to the life-size replica, designed to recover an imagined memory of Main Street and serving as sites of vicarious remembrance and envisioned order.

One type of recuperation is the reproduction of the small town that is the common dream of model railroad enthusiasts. Like poetry, the miniature appeals to our desire for an alternate world, a cosmos that has a necessary coherence and order.[15] Perhaps the greatest model railroad setup, and the greatest miniature of Main Street, ever constructed is the work of an obsessive Pennsylvania craftsman, Laurence Gieringer. *Roadside America* first became a public exhibit in 1935 and occupied a succession of spaces, expanding in size, until it attained its present form and location in eastern Pennsylvania (Shartlesville) in 1953, where it occupies an indoor space larger than a basketball court. Though billed as "the World's Greatest Indoor Miniature Village," Gieringer's masterpiece of folk art is really more a miniature of the variegated industrial landscape of the entire United States. At its core is the small town.

Gieringer supposedly had the notion of building a miniature town at the age of ten, in 1905, when he climbed a mountain near his home and looked down below at the city of Reading—with what appeared to be its miniaturized houses. No doubt the youth experienced the usual intoxication of a godlike dream, but it was his astonishing perseverance over the

Laurence Gieringer's Roadside America, *a miniature railroad display, Shartlesville, Pennsylvania. Photograph by Christian Montane, 2009. Flickr.com.*

rest of his life (he died in 1963) that brought this vision to fruition, resulting in a dollhouse world (at a scale of three-eighths of an inch to the foot) that covers approximately 6,000 square feet. Gieringer's "America" comprises a variety of landscapes, from the frontier village to the small town, with shops, gas station, and movie theater; from ranches to anthracite mines, oil wells, and limestone quarries; from a wooden covered bridge to the San Francisco–Oakland Bay Bridge; from an Indian Village of teepees to a Pennsylvania Dutch farm; from a New England church to an alpine chapel with stained glass windows (perhaps an ancestral allusion). There is a railroad yard, an airport, a zoo, a circus, and a baseball field. Though Gieringer occasionally incorporated the specificities of history (e.g., the original Henry Ford shop in Dearborn), for the most part his constructions are generic types—"Joe's Barber Shop" or the "Yellow House Hotel."

For all its static quality as a miniature world, Gieringer's America is a world in motion. Many of the town settings show human figures and machines stopped in the midst of a typical moment: a car at a gas station, people going to the movies, foot traffic on Main Street. The town is shown here as the contact point between the individual and mass cul-

Laurence Gieringer's Roadside America, *a miniature railroad display, Shartlesville, Pennsylvania. Photograph by Christian Montane, 2009. Flickr.com.*

ture (movies, department stores, chain stores, and gasoline stations). But many other scenes—especially those featuring industry—are themselves subject to movement: the viewer can press a button that activates the repetitive motions of industrial production—the blacksmith hammering, the lumber mill sawing, the oil derrick drilling—while model trains, both freight and passenger, travel the landscape. For the most part, the temporal dimension of *Roadside America* is rooted in a sense of the everyday, the familiar, the typical—except here and there, where Gieringer has placed a sign to emphasize the aberration: "Note tree blown over by storm."

But as striking as what is present in this otherwise complete representation of American space is what is missing: the city and the suburbs. Given its terminal point in the 1950s, the absence of a suburban scene in *Roadside America* is not altogether surprising, but the years of its creation—1905 to 1950—correspond exactly to the great period of the construction of the modern city, which was expanding both vertically and horizontally; and this absence is the sign, we might say, of its ideology, a worldview that places the small town at the center of American civilization.[16] We can construct a cosmogony here that moves from the Native

Americans—posted at the corners of the exhibition space in life-size statues and occupying a miniature teepee village—to the typical farm, to the western frontier settlements, to the early-twentieth-century town; apart from their presence as the Original Owners of the land, sitting in the four corners of the model, the Native Americans are marginalized figures, displaced by the industry of the white man, whose toil and labor creates this representation of civilization. And in Gieringer's teleology, the town is the end point.

But all of this world is, in the end, presented to the viewer within an even broader frame of reference, supplied in a special display that is presented at least once an hour. When the lights dim, the stars (on the ceiling) come out, Kate Smith sings "God Bless America," and a couple of ancient slide projectors display photographs of the Statue of Liberty, the American flag, and a long-haired Jesus Christ. As Gieringer constructed his version of the American experience, through World War I, the Great Depression, and World War II, the preservation of order and sense must have become both the means and the end of *Roadside America*, a world where everything in the end made sense, open to the public for sampling. *Roadside America* has a Whitmanesque sweep to it, and like the poet in *Leaves of Grass*, Gieringer fills his space with endless details of American life, frozen in motion. But where Whitman was looking always to the future, Gieringer in his model looks always to the past.

WHILE GIERINGER WAS constructing his vision of small-town America, a miniature world that is, by its material construction, placed within a frame that allows only remote contact, others were breaking open the frame, re-creating the small town in historical versions that would likewise become symbols of order, yet ones that the visitor could physically enter. Yet in a way, these creations of the historical imagination—Greenfield Village, Colonial Williamsburg, Old Sturbridge, and a hundred more small-town re-creations—are themselves the fulfillment of dreams not unlike the humbler Gieringer's, only they were infinitely better funded, supported, and promoted. They are three-dimensional, life-size environments, not just models to look at from outside. And they have served, since the 1930s, as touchstones for the American imagination, shrines to the perfected memory of the village origins of the national life, ongoing representations of the living myth of small-town America that occupy a space somewhere between the work of art and actuality.

These "living museums" are spaces to walk into not only to view the past but also to interact with it through the presence of the employed guides, ersatz historical figures, personifications of "real" historical people or types of people. As such, they seem like literal illustrations of the reciprocal relationship between individual memory and group memory that Maurice Halbwachs posits. "Most of the time, when I remember," Halbwachs writes, "it is others who spur me on; their memory comes to the aid of mine and mine relies on theirs. . . . It is to the degree that our individual thought places itself in these frameworks and participates in this memory that it is capable of the act of recollection."[17] The mechanism of the re-created town museum, of "living history," is the embodiment of memory in the persona of the "villager," who is a paid repository for the forgotten culture of the past but who is employed to share it with the tourist through conversation and explanation.

There is no single formula for the freezing of place and time that these re-created towns represent, yet their evolution collectively demonstrates the popular form that "history"—fueled by nostalgia—has taken. And while these re-creations are inevitably collaborative acts, they are often inspired by the ambition and drive of an individual creator, and as such are acts of the historical imagination. Yet they are also part of the much larger movement of historic preservation that has taken place in the United States, beginning in the late nineteenth century and with roots in Europe, more precisely in the open-air museum of Skansen outside of Stockholm. Artur Hazelius, who created Skansen in 1891 as a collection of farms, churches, cottages, workshops, and manor houses taken from all over Sweden, is credited with founding the movement. He was motivated by a desire to preserve the folk traditions of the rural areas that, even in the late nineteenth century, were being visibly changed and challenged by modernity. He had begun collecting folk artifacts in 1872 and brought six lifelike tableaux, including costumed wax figures, to the 1876 Centennial in Philadelphia as part of the Swedish exhibition. The notion of separating space, isolating it from the everyday, is as old as the concept of "the sacred" itself, but sacred space is timeless; the idea of preserving space with a specifically historical meaning—whether as diorama, period room, house, town, or historical district—begins in the nineteenth century.

The American Centennial also featured a re-created "New England Farmer's Home," which was furnished with authentic heirlooms and costumed guides, who explained the setting.[18] Antiquarian George Francis Dow expanded this effort to replicate the past when he became director of the Essex Institute in Salem, Massachusetts, in 1898. In 1907 he installed three period rooms in the institute, and in 1912 he moved the 1685 John Ward House to its grounds, along with costumed guides. These were also the years that Wallace Nutting (1861–1941) was creating a series of popular photographs, hand-colored, that depicted an imagined colonial life, along with the bucolic landscape of the New England countryside, while he was catering as well to a growing taste for colonial furniture through an extensive series of carefully produced reproductions. Others in the late nineteenth and early twentieth centuries were also beginning to collect the preindustrial past, most notably the anthropologist Henry Mercer, who gathered his vast collection of artifacts in his own museum in Doylestown, Pennsylvania, where he also manufactured, in the arts and crafts style, a variety of decorative tiles.

BUT THE MOST RESOURCEFUL collector—with virtually unlimited re-sources—was Henry Ford, who used his network of automobile dealers to amass a huge collection of American artifacts. Ford's approach to resto-ration was personal and idiosyncratic: he had already been restoring his boyhood home when he visited Dow's Salem Essex Institute in 1923, and a few years later he completed the restoration of the Wayside Inn—"Built in the old Colonial day, / When men lived in a grander way," as Henry Wadsworth Longfellow wrote. And Mercer's collection of objects in his Doylestown museum was yet another inspiration.[19] Ford was the Janus of his age—looking ahead to the enormous changes wrought by the machine but also looking backward to, as Longfellow put it in introducing *Tales of the Wayside Inn*, a "region of repose":

> A place of slumber and of dreams,
> Remote among the wooded hills!
> For there no noisy railway speeds,
> Its torch-race scattering smoke and gleeds.

But just as the Model T was manufactured for the mass market, so were Ford's escapist fantasies to strike a responsive chord in the popular cul-ture of the early twentieth century, as his great project of preservation— the Henry Ford Museum and Greenfield Village, outside of Detroit—was to prove.

Most accounts of the Ford Museum and Greenfield Village discuss the complementarity of the two, with the museum housing the history of technology within a narrative of progress, while the village, with its historical buildings, evokes the past.[20] It is Greenfield Village that I am

*"Air View of Greenfield Village," Dearborn, Michigan, postcard showing the "green,"
as in early American communities, with public buildings surrounding it, ca. 1940.
Sapirstein Greeting Card Co. Author's collection.*

primarily interested in here, as a nostalgic representation of small-town
America that is at the same time a microcosm of America's material history, taking us from the early 1700s (in the Plympton Family House, imported from Sudbury, Massachusetts) to the late nineteenth century (with
several examples of dwellings). The village has several areas, distinctly
conceived yet spatially contiguous, that exemplify the social economy of
America before the twentieth century: there is an area of working farms
and related structures (e.g., a cider mill, a carriage barn); an area featuring craft production (e.g., pottery, weaving, glass, sawmills); an area
called "Main Street" that comprises shops and offices (e.g., a post office, a
tavern, the town hall, a general store, a jewelry store); and another area,
"Porches and Parlors," that primarily features homes from the eighteenth
and nineteenth centuries. In addition to this cross-section of American
buildings and functions, there are two more specialized areas—one devoted to Henry Ford himself and his early auto workshop and one devoted
to Thomas Edison and his early laboratories.

Ford's village is obviously eclectic and strives for a broad representation of material culture and the topicalities of place, but the whole of it
feels like a small town and is arranged with "Main Street" as its central
axis, with another leading avenue (Maple Lane) running off from Main

EARLY EQUIPAGE, GREENFIELD VILLAGE, DEARBORN, MICHIGAN

"Early Equipage," Greenfield Village, Dearborn, Michigan, postcard, ca. 1937. Artcraft Photo Co. Author's collection.

Street at right angles. Ford loved to stroll around the village for relaxation, enjoying an atmosphere that would be very far indeed from the industrial landscape he was building nearby during these same years: the River Rouge automobile plant, the epitome of advanced industrial production, begun in 1917 and expanded over the next decade.

If, in Greenfield, the small town is the cradle of American civilization, out of that cradle came the giants of American industry, invention, and practical knowledge whom Ford is chiefly celebrating in his village, beginning with Ford himself. Ford's factory and workshop are there, along with other buildings associated with his life; Ford's friend, Thomas Edison, does just as well, with several laboratories, shops, and offices from his early days. Noah Webster's substantial 1823 house is there, as is a house built in 1835 that Robert Frost lived in when he taught at the University of Michigan in Ann Arbor. So is the Wright brothers' family home, from 1875. But there are humbler buildings as well — William Holmes McGuffey's cabin, Charles Steinmetz's retreat, and Luther Burbank's garden office. A closer look reveals some anomalies, however: the Ford factory is one-quarter the original size; the workshop is largely a replica; Edison's labs are replicas; the cabin where George Washington Carver was born is modeled on Carver's memories of it. (Incidentally, Carver is the only acknowledgment, implicitly, that African Americans are a part of America's cultural history.) In addition to issues of authenticity, Greenfield Village raises questions about provenance: there is a Cotswold cottage from the 1600s, a Swiss chalet (built as a type with no original model), and a section of a London sweet shop (scaled down from five to two stories), all of whose connections with the American town are not immediately obvious.

In short, Greenfield Village is strikingly promiscuous, mixing the authentic object and the replica, in its representation of the great figures of the past. Though the website does inform the viewer when something is authentic and when it is reproduced, the casual stroller is much less aware, much less likely to read the fine print that supplies the information.

Does it even matter, one wonders? Everything has been moved to Greenfield Village from its original location anyway. One would surely notice the difference between an original factory and one reduced to one-quarter the original size (as with the Ford factory), but what is the difference, finally, between a real schoolhouse and a replica, between a real slave cabin and an imagined one? The difference may not be visible, but it goes to the essence of the "reality" being represented, for it is not the buildings per se we come to see, it is contact with "history." True, Ford had said, "History is bunk," but he revised that attitude significantly with the construction of Greenfield Village, coming to believe that history could best be learned through objects.

If it were authentic, we would feel, presumably, some sense of contact with greatness and with the past. If it were all fake, we might wonder if the point was somehow simply to remind us of some lost Platonic original. The sculpture collections of many art museums in the nineteenth century consisted of copies of famous statues, but the idea was to expose the viewer to an aesthetic experience, where the representation would at least appear to be the same as the original, and where the function of the work was to educate the eye. To the art market, of course, the difference between original and fake is ineffably important: a hundred fakes are worth nothing next to one original. But houses are not quite the same as works of art, especially houses that have little inherent aesthetic distinction as architecture but hold our attention as historical objects. And that is the heart of the issue: If the presumed interest of the object is historical, how can we accept the fake?

To Ford, evidently, the issue of authenticity had some importance, hence the effort to obtain the originals in the first place. But we experience an authentic object differently from a replica, and that is what makes

Greenfield Village a confusion of realms. As the creator of a culture of copies, Ford may have also felt that it was enough, in the end, to present a model of the original, just as the automobile purchaser was buying an authentic Ford that was at the same time one of a thousand or more. To the visitor who begins to ponder these issues, the metaphysical air of Greenfield Village is heavy with such questions, finally inducing a kind of intellectual vertigo.

COLONIAL WILLIAMSBURG, by contrast, is all sanity, all consistency, all perfection. It was conceived not as a collection of buildings associated with illustrious figures, but as a collection of buildings whose claim on our interest is precisely their authenticity. Moreover, Williamsburg is representing not some mythical place, but itself, the actual Virginia town that had formerly been the capital of Virginia and that, by 1900, had been largely eroded by the forces of change. The notion of restoring Williamsburg originated with the Reverend William Godwin, who had raised funds to preserve the Bruton Parish Church in 1907 and—following his return to Williamsburg after an assignment elsewhere—conceived the much grander idea of restoring the entire town. Henry Ford, whom he first approached, had no interest in Williamsburg and was already busy pursuing his own dreams. John D. Rockefeller Jr., however, was very interested: he had already financed the restoration of Versailles and Fontainebleau a few years earlier, thus helping to preserve the European storybook past; and the idea of Williamsburg appealed to him as a material and heuristic embodiment of American civic culture.

But Williamsburg was not simply a place; it was a moment—1790—chosen as the epitome of the symbolic tradition represented by the town itself. Certainly Williamsburg's national importance in the eighteenth century as Virginia's state capital encouraged the selection of 1790, but that date reflected the growing consensus among elite Americans that the high point of American history, the magical moment, was the War of Independence and its Federalist aftermath. The years of the long nineteenth century afterward saw the transformation of the United States from an essentially rural nation to an urban one, marked by factories, railroads and canals, giant turbines, and above all by the growth of cities and the importation of millions of immigrants. The immigrant laborers were building the wealth of modern America, but they were also the seedbed for socialistic and communist ideas—seen as anti-American—that were not especially welcome to the older stock; and World War I and its aftermath

The Raleigh Tavern, Williamsburg, Virginia, 1943. Library of Congress, Prints and Photographs Division, FSA-OWI Collection.

only fueled the xenophobia of the elite American, for whom the Bolshevik menace loomed improbably large. Colonial Williamsburg was obviously white history. Though Rockefeller's enthusiasm for Williamsburg makes sense in this context—and the restoration became his lifelong passion— it was also an expression of a cultural allegiance that in some ways ran counter to the more habitual inclinations of greatly wealthy Americans, many of whom were busy living a dream of European aristocracy, building castles on Fifth Avenue furnished with the finest handcrafted goods of Europe. (Madame Olenska's caustic observation in Wharton's 1920 novel, *Age of Innocence,* is on the Rockefeller money: "It seems stupid to have discovered America only to make it into a copy of another country.")[21]

Given the sacred moment of 1790, many hundreds of buildings had to be destroyed in Williamsburg to achieve the desired effect, while hundreds more had to be either restored or, in most cases, built anew on their original historical foundations. But it was the consistency and coherence of the effect, the homogeneity of the town in its desired state, that appealed to Rockefeller, who, as Mike Wallace has astutely observed, "was interested in totalities."[22] And although it was a colonial capital, the town's main street, Duke of Gloucester Street, with its restored shops, trees, and white

Barber and peruke maker's shop before restoration, Williamsburg, Virginia, 1943.
Library of Congress, Prints and Photographs Division, FSA-OWI Collection.

Barber and peruke maker's shop after restoration, Williamsburg, Virginia, 1943.
Library of Congress, Prints and Photographs Division, FSA-OWI Collection.

picket fences—would come to represent Main Street America. What Williamsburg represented was, above all, a complete environment, a sealed universe, an ordered dream town frozen in a moment in history. Also frozen in place were the various social strata that the town represented—from the largest structures of the ruling class to the humbler abodes of the artisans; all would have a place in Williamsburg, although it would be many years until the African American presence would be adequately acknowledged, and even then in a form that essentially cleansed the brutalities of slavery from the living record that Williamsburg was to be.

Williamsburg inspired scores of other restored and re-created towns (e.g., Old Sturbridge, Plimoth Plantation, the Farmer's Museum in Cooperstown, Winterthur) that were part of the larger movement to preserve the "American" heritage in a world that was rapidly changing, to create a "living history"—part authentic, part ersatz—that would in turn influence the future. Ironically, these memorial places—villages, living farms, and restored towns—were underwritten by those who had been best able to exploit the forces of change, accumulating fortunes in the new industrial America that would in turn permit acts of philanthropy powered by a nostalgia for a "free" society in which capital was yet a barely nascent force.

In the 1930s and 1940s, as thousands of small towns across the United States were struggling to survive, Main Street came to occupy a mythic plane in American culture. No better proof of this could be offered than the use of Main Street imagery by corporations during World War II, when the small town came to represent the heart of what the United States was fighting for, the American way of life. General Motors, Chrysler, Du Pont, General Electric, Republic Steel, McDonnell Aircraft, and others may have been doing everything possible to secure government contracts, eliminate regulations, harness labor, and moderate the unions, but in their World War II public relations programs, they associated their efforts strongly with Main Street. Through magazine advertising, factory town pageants, traveling revues, and radio programs, corporations like General Motors linked their own efforts to the "folks on Main Street," to the average worker and the small businessman.[23] One specific point of linkage, as Roland Marchand observes, was the corporation's praise of "American know-how," a legacy of the pioneer past "which had long been lodged in the technical ingenuity of small-town mechanics."[24] Where the corporation had identified itself at the 1939 New York World's Fair with futuristic visions of cities and transportation, now it was falling back on the virtues of the common folk and the preservation of small-town values.[25] "Free enterprise made small shops and factories into big ones—and then started more small ones," Republic Steel said, in one ad, to the folks gathered around the pot-bellied stove in the country store. Next to an illustration of a perfect small-town scene, at the center of which is the firehouse, the United States Rubber Company affirms, "It's hard to imagine the town without its fire trucks, without the trucks that haul farm products to market, and the rubber tired tractors that help the farmer grow those products."[26] Humanizing the corporation as it was gathering increasing power and authority in American life, the small-town imagery served to create the idea of a collective national effort founded on the most familiar of values—the small businessman and the public space of the commons. Though few would realize it at the time, the peculiar nature of Main Street was that it was a place for private enterprise that was also public space; the evolution of private corporations into giant containers of private space, whose costs would be passed on to the public in the form of "externalities," had already begun, of course, but we were looking the other way.

THE IDENTIFICATION OF CORPORATIONS with the Main Street mythos was a consolidating force that lasted through the war, but with the war's end the corporation began to assume a position of autonomy in American life, incorporating the bodies and souls of its workers in ways that were most effectively delineated in William Whyte's 1956 classic *The Organization Man*, which describes the slow but inexorable process by which the individual is merged with the corporation. In an episode from the first season of the great 1960s television series *The Twilight Zone*, Rod Serling captured the inner rebellion that might follow from this condition of spiritual captivity in an episode called "A Stop at Willoughby." Protagonist Gart Williams works in an advertising agency, the victim of an angry boss who keeps driving him to greater productivity, even while his shrewish wife wants nothing but the fruit of his labor to support her suburban, country-club lifestyle. Falling asleep on the commuter train to Westport, Connecticut (where Serling himself lived), Williams dreams of a town along the way—Willoughby—where it is the 1880s, and the kids are going fishing, a band is playing in the town center, people are riding by on penny-farthing bicycles, and the atmosphere is perfectly idyllic. At last, as the train stops at the imagined town of Willoughby, Williams decides to escape from his oppressive life and enter the "reality" of the small-town dream. But of course he has been dreaming, and as he steps from the moving train, he falls to his death. In a typical *Twilight Zone* touch, he is picked up by the Willoughby & Son Funeral Home.

SERLING'S WILLOUGHBY, in its 1880s embodiment, is the dreamed utopia, the archetypal response to the massive transformations in American life following World War II; and it follows by just five years the creation in 1955 of the apotheosis of the small-town myth, the "Main Street, U.S.A." section of Disneyland. One might say that Serling's Willoughby "explains" the necessity for Disney's creation and the reason for its continuing popularity into the twenty-first century.

Superlatives hardly seem equal to a description of Disneyland and its allure. The most powerful icon of American culture, Disneyland is America's utopia, the most desirable tourist destination in the world, the ultimate reward for work well done. "I'm going to Disney World"—the ad campaign begun in 1987 and featuring the greatest athletes of that time—became in the late twentieth century synonymous with victory of the rarest kind, whether Super Bowl or World Series. In effect, Disneyland is the reward for the highest achievement generally conceivable—the achievement of the professional superstar athlete. More than that, the place represents life itself: asked where he would go if released from the life sentence he was serving on a controversial murder conviction, the prisoner Jason Baldwin famously responded, "To Disneyland."[27]

Disneyland fused several elements not previously brought together in amusement parks: it was not just a single-theme park but an amalgamation of themes (fantasy, adventure, futurism); it was a fair with rides, but with an atmosphere friendly to families; and it exploited the Disney characters, moving them from the two dimensionality of the screen cartoon to the three-dimensionality of the street. Above all, it placed at the center of the Disney universe an image of small-town America that struck a deep chord with Americans after World War II, an affirmation of shared cultural values that symbolized the anchor for a ship of state that had recently survived a cataclysmic war and was now in the midst of an equally challenging Cold War. In 1947, when workers and artists at the Disney studios were being organized, breaking the founder's dream of a workforce that was a "family," Disney was called before the House Un-American Activities Committee as a friendly witness. Asked his personal opinion of the Communist Party, Disney answered,

Walt Disney pointing to Main Street on a display map of Disneyland, ca. 1955. Library of Congress, Prints and Photographs Division, Look Collection.

Well, I don't believe it is a political party. I believe it is an un-American thing. The thing that I resent the most is that they are able to get into these unions, take them over, and represent to the world that a group of people that are in my plant, that I know are good, 100 percent Americans, are trapped by this group, and they are represented to the world as supporting all of those ideologies, and it is not so, and I feel that they really ought to be smoked out and shown up for what they are, so that all of the good, free causes in this country, all the liberalisms that really are American, can go out without the taint of communism. That is my sincere feeling on it.[28]

Disneyland, still a glint in the founder's eye at this moment, would be everything that communism was not; it would be as authentically American as the House Un-American Activities Committee itself. Disney's Cold War defense of "American" values, the prelude to the creation of Disneyland's Main Street, would seem a perfect illustration of Miranda Joseph's point that in the second half of the twentieth century, "idealizations of community operate as conservative critiques of changes in the given social hierarchy."[29]

Disneyland occupies a unique metaphysical space.[30] Created in 1955, it quickly became a tourist magnet that united generations under the same big tent, until it was cloned in Florida in 1971 as Walt Disney World. (What California was to the West, Florida would be to the East.) Unlike the historical town—whether Sturbridge, Cooperstown, or Williamsburg—which is of interest because it is both unique and representative of its time and place, Disneyland is the essence of the inauthentic, the mother of all theme parks: it represents nothing but itself, its own factitious universe. Manufactured, it can be replicated, not only in Florida, but anywhere the population might support the requisite tourist activity—Japan, France, Hong Kong—for the mouse has a global notoriety.

Disneyland—in whatever version—is unique among theme parks not only because of the patented presence of Mickey and company, but on account of the peculiar Disney cosmogony, at the center of which is Main Street, U.S.A.[31] (See Plate 6.) There are differences from one park to another in the way Main Street has been imagined—Florida's version, for example, is more ornate than the earlier, simpler, California original, and other variations can be found in the versions outside the U.S. mainland—but the essence of Main Street is a constant.[32] It is the "center" of the theme park, the heart of it, the zone the visitor first enters, and it represents the core values of family, community, commerce, and entertainment that Disneyland embodies. (The shocking absence of Main Street from the planned Shanghai Disneyland may be the result of pressure from the Chinese government, which insisted on a park that would be "authentically Disney but distinctly Chinese," in the words of Disney's chief executive.)[33]

All of Disneyland offers the visitor amusement within a space that is meticulously designed and patrolled; the broad appeal of Disneyland is precisely the fact that it is safe "public" space, an increasingly rare commodity in contemporary society, and one most reliably found in property that is privately owned and patrolled by private security, as Disneyland is. But only the theme park's Main Street embodies the very concept of safe public space in its material form, by employing the architectural types that we associate with a nostalgic and idealized representation of small-town America. There are no amusements on Disney's Main Street comparable to the rides and shows in the other areas; instead, Main Street features the shops of a small town, reduced to seven-eighths scale to mark a smaller, more intimate environment for the shopper. Indeed, the shops *are* the entertainment, for there are no shoe stores, cleaners, hardware stores, or other practical establishments; instead, one finds a magic store, specialty food shops, and above all souvenir shops with Disney products. (There is also a standing-room-only movie theater showing Disney cartoons.) Yet

The Santa Fe & Disneyland passenger train chuffs into Main Street Station—one of the first sights visitors see at Disneyland.

Main Street, U.S.A.

Turn-of-the-century Town Square at Disneyland accurately recreates American town life of 50 years ago.

Disneyland's Main Street, U.S.A.: "Turn-of-the-century Town Square at Disneyland accurately recreates American town life of 50 years ago." From Disneyland, A Complete Guide *(1956). Author's collection.*

Main Street is teeming with activity—people walking, a tram passing by, a horse-drawn vehicle, Disney characters floating through the crowd, and, at regular intervals, a parade. Disney's Main Street is a perpetually active and exciting place, a place that implies a harmonious community and a democratic society. It is what Americans (and the rest of the world) want to think America stands for. It is the small town on a never-ending Saturday night, as remembered by Glenway Wescott: "As the sun hurried west . . . everywhere men and women and children were made eager by the thoughts of the night . . . for the night was Saturday night and they were going to town. . . . And in Middle America, in the numberless small towns that serve the people of the farms, there is no more magical time. It is the sweet reward of the long week's labor; it is their opera, drama, their trip to Zanzibar."[34]

Disney's imagined Main Street, a triumph of populist architecture, is a composite creation, modeled to some degree on Disney's memories of his hometown, Marceline, Missouri, as well as on designer Harper Goff's hometown, Fort Collins, Colorado.[35] The Victorian gingerbread of the shop fronts and the "public buildings" like the Railroad Station and the Town Hall have a dollhouse feeling and are as well maintained as a model railroad display—which indeed was one of Disney's inspirations for his Main Street. The town square provides a civic focal point, with its central fountain, while the general liveliness and good humor of the place conjures up a dream of the McKinley era at the turn of the century, when William McKinley could declare, with the economic depression and labor unrest of the 1890s over, "Now every avenue of production is crowded with activity, labor is well employed, and American products find good markets at home and abroad."[36] That feeling of confidence and comfort was doubtless augmented by the recent display of America's might in the Spanish-American War. However perilous that moment in fact was— anarchists lay in wait for McKinley, the Lower East Side was seething with socialists, events were progressing toward war in Europe—it was a time in which one could at least imagine a point of stasis.

In Disneyland, all roads lead to Main Street, and the other zones radiate from it geographically. These peripheral areas of the theme park also stand in a logical relation to Main Street that is the embodiment of the Disney cosmogony, which we can translate into a historical template: Frontierland is the American past, the encounter with the wilderness, the challenge of conquest and settlement; Adventureland represents the world outside the United States, a world that was once a place for exploration and the challenges of survival—the jungles of Tarzan, the desert island of the Swiss Family Robinson; Tomorrowland embodies the adventure of scientific discovery and the exploration of space beyond the planet. The trajectory thus progresses steadily, although Fantasyland steps outside the historical template in addressing the dreams of childhood, castles, fairies, and an escape from "reality" into the Disney version of classic fairy tales and cartoon creations. There are variations on this basic structure, accommodations to the specific cultural requirements of locale (e.g., Paris's celebration of Jules Verne) or to weather (e.g., Tokyo's indoor "World Bazaar"); but the basic structure, with Main Street at the center, is constant, a dream of America, a theatrical space at once deeply appealing to Americans and eminently exportable. Main Street is what makes it all possible: it is the bedrock of American dreams, imaginings, and values, the place we come back to and start out from, at least imaginatively.

DISNEY WAS SURELY one of the great mythmakers of American culture of the twentieth century; but he is equaled in some ways by the most popular illustrator of the century, born out of the same imaginative matrix: Norman Rockwell. If Disneyland's Main Street represents the material archetype of the American small town, Rockwell's illustrations, beginning with his first *Saturday Evening Post* cover in 1916 and continuing through the early 1960s, gave America a portrait of its inhabitants, creating an image that has endured into the twenty-first century as the archetype of small-town society. By 1929, editor George Horace Lorimer was well on his way to Americanizing his estimated 20 million readers through the *Post*, offering them a unifying "model against which they could shape their lives."[37] Rockwell's covers gave form to that model, incarnating a world of family doctors and family dinners, of drugstores and barbershops, of diners and train stations, of Christmas and Thanksgiving. In 1943, at the height of America's involvement in World War II, Rockwell developed a series of four paintings, *The Four Freedoms*, modeled on Franklin Delano Roosevelt's 1941 State of the Union speech, which featured images of freedom of speech, freedom of worship, freedom from want, and freedom from fear. Widely seen on the covers of the *Saturday Evening Post* and widely exhibited, Rockwell's images are rooted in these same small-town values—the family at the Thanksgiving table, religious worshippers, parents protecting their sleeping offspring in an attic bedroom, and a "common man," in a plaid shirt and worn jacket, speaking his mind at a town meeting where his words earn the solicitous attention of his neighbors in business suits.

Rockwell is the twentieth-century inheritor of the great genre tradition of such nineteenth-century painters as George Caleb Bingham, William Sidney Mount, Winslow Homer, and Eastman Johnson, who in turn had inherited the older Dutch tradition of portraying everyday life, focusing on common folk and on the dramatic incident. Rockwell inherited also the tradition of the hugely popular Victorian table-top sculptures by John Rogers, which depicted incidents from everyday life, as well as Civil War vignettes and theatrical scenes.[38] Rockwell took these popular traditions and gave them a twentieth-century form as magazine illustration, achieving mass celebrity by virtue of his uncanny ability to capture a recognizable psychological moment through the exact expression, the precise posture or gesture, that the moment requires: two kids at a party pull apart a noisemaker, waiting anxiously for the pop; an old man focuses intently on threading a needle; a young boy pours out medicine for his sick dog, who is wrapped in a blanket. In addition, Rockwell captured, through the perspectives of his cast of everyday characters, the quintessential moments of cultural change across the twentieth century: an old couple listening to a radio for the first time; the advent of the automobile; a man calling up to a worker placing a TV antenna on his roof, proclaiming excitedly the picture on his screen. And he reflected the most salient political events of the time—World War II and, in the sixties, the civil rights struggle, always touching on them through the perspective of his typical characters.

But it is Rockwell's depiction of Main Street that drove most deeply into American consciousness and that interests us here. More than any other artist of the twentieth century, Rockwell created the ethos of small-town America, even as a mass migration was taking place, from the towns to the cities, over the course of the twentieth century, a migration that would leave countless inhabitants of the metropolis feeling a sense of anomie, of dislocation. Rockwell might well seem alien to the urban sensibility that was fashioning itself around the *New Yorker* as opposed to the *Saturday Evening Post*;[39] but to many others, including city dwellers, he was the dramatist of the safely and humorously familiar, and his images carried the warm feeling of "home" in the sense that broadcast journalist Eric Sevareid meant it when he said, recalling his own childhood, that "the town was, simply *home*—and *all* of it home, not just the house but all the town. . . . Everything is home."[40] Rockwell's warmth is visible in the hundreds of vignettes he portrays for us—whether it is a couple applying for a marriage license, a schoolboy gazing out the window at a dog, a musical group playing in the back of a barbershop, or a doctor carefully examining a little girl's doll. All of Rockwell's imagery, capturing the particularities of everyday life, speak in unison of the order of the small-town universe. The whole is greater than the sum of its parts in Rockwell, and that whole harmonizes differences, placing the individual within a community that may be riven from time to time but that is basically benevolent.

Yet strangely, for one of the great creators of Main Street in the archive of American imagery, Rockwell provides us with very few concrete images of the small town itself. For the most part, the town setting is implicit, and we construct it, we fill in the background, however focused the scene is on the individuals. On a few rare occasions, Rockwell did portray the town itself, once notably for a *Saturday Evening Post* cover (*Crestwood Commuter Station*, November 16, 1946) when he pictured a railroad station filled with commuters dressed for the city: in the foreground, a dozen stragglers dash to catch the train, which is about to pull into the station; in the middle ground, the platform is crowded with men and women reading the newspaper patiently; while in the background, on the hill above the station, a handful of houses suggest a developing suburban community built beyond the older houses. It is a picture that prophesizes the postwar suburban future of the United States that was relegating the town to the status of bedroom community, breaking apart its traditional nurturing function.

Yet some towns were safely beyond the range of commuting, and they would remain (as they always had been) the center of Rockwell's imagination, backwaters of nostalgia that the commuters would retreat to and look to for inspiration. Rockwell did finally get around to portraying the archetype of Main Street itself in 1967, when he painted *Home for Christmas*, a summa of sorts, a panoramic view of Stockbridge, Massachusetts—Rockwell's adopted hometown—for *McCall's* magazine. (See Plate 5.) A horizontal composition, Rockwell's panorama could portray in detail the buildings lining one side of the street (from the library on the left, to the antique shop, general store, barber shop, town hall, bank, and, finally, the Red Lion Inn on the far right); and he could portray the parked cars, cars in motion, people carrying presents home, shoppers, and children playing in the snow, all set against the background of the Berkshire Mountains. With the shops glowing at twilight, decorated for the holidays, the scene provides as much Christmas sentiment as anyone could healthily tolerate.

Rockwell soared to popularity at the beginning of his career with the *Saturday Evening Post*, and he stayed there throughout his lifetime. Yet he has always presented a dilemma for the delineator of cultural levels, who faces the challenge of finding him lowbrow, middlebrow, or even highbrow. Rockwell is obvious, yes, but there is subtlety in his work that escapes first notice and keeps us looking. (Rockwell was deeply familiar with the history of art, from Rembrandt to Van Gogh, from Picasso to Pollock; and some of his paintings play with the conventions of illusion and framing in sophisticated ways.) The question took new currency when the High Museum in Atlanta originated a Rockwell exhibition in 1999 that traveled to the major museums of the United States in the following years, provoking tributes, uneasy confessions, and disclaimers.

Rockwell was extraordinarily versatile stylistically, but his genius as a popular artist was to go beyond realism to the point of comic exaggeration, into caricature.[41] We can see that process easily by comparing the photographs Rockwell used as the basis for his illustrations with the works themselves: normal people are turned into village grotesques, a back is arched to the point of a comic exaggeration; a nose is wrinkled and pointed more than any nose ever was; an expression of surprise or delight is forced to the point of idiocy; the cloying sweetness can be nearly intolerable, the coyness revolting.[42] As much as Rockwell peopled Main Street for the American imagination, he also turned it into a cartoon of sentiment (the progenitor of *The Andy Griffith Show* TV series), and his legacy is an ambiguous one. For better or worse, Rockwell has embedded himself as deeply into the American imagination as Disney, defining the image of Main Street powerfully, indelibly, and sentimentally.[43]

That same chord, blending high and popular art, has been struck more recently by Garrison Keillor, who writes for the *New Yorker* while also hosting one of the most popular radio shows in modern broadcasting. The core feature of Keillor's folksy *A Prairie Home Companion*, based in St. Paul, Minnesota, is the regular "news from Lake Wobegon," Keillor's fictitious hometown. Keillor's small-town stories are, in some ways, like Norman Rockwell come to life, though Keillor's town has a steady cast of characters, places, institutions, and customs. Lake Wobegone also has a marked ethnic tradition—Lutheran, Norwegian—that colors the town's emotional tone and lends it a homogeneity that makes all of its individual idiosyncrasies part of the same spectrum of white America. Keillor knows America has changed, of course, but he offers his characters as an exhibit from the past, inhabitants of a backwater of American society who have an endearing quaintness. What distinguishes Keillor above all, however, is the deliberate retrospective glow of nostalgia that the storyteller employs as a lens through which to see his town, and a storyteller's voice that narrates the foibles, absurdities, and limitations of the townsfolk with a carefully balanced blend of humor, love, and respect.

BEGINNING WITH THE FIRST visualizations of the town in nineteenth-century popular graphic art—Palmer's paradigmatic *Across the Continent, Westward the Course of Empire*—the idea of Main Street and the small-town community has acquired a mythical weight in American culture, a hyperreality that has been sustained in our popular culture through a variety of forms. Especially in the twentieth century and into our own day, from the model railroad village to Williamsburg and Greenfield Village, from Norman Rockwell's encyclopedic illustrations to Garrison Keillor's factitious reports on the mythical Lake Wobegone, and not forgetting that apotheosis of Main Street, Disneyland, the myth of Main Street has served to organize the feelings and perceptions of white America, but it has also provided, to a degree, a template for the broader population, including African Americans and Americans of ethnic descent who feel included in the American story, to think about culture, society, and space itself. The myth of Main Street, created as early as the nineteenth century, remains an essential element of American culture, a myth of order woven into its popular culture, its tourist culture and its visual culture, and providing the foundation for the common currency of shared values and symbols, especially in times of crisis, which is to say practically throughout the whole of American history from Whitman's day to ours. And yet, as the next chapter demonstrates, even as the small town has been enshrined in the national memory on a mythic plane, the actual small towns of America have struggled desperately to survive.

Chapter Two

Fighting Extinction
The Reinvention of Main Street

The small town has been dying for almost as long as it has been in existence. The product of geographic, social, and psychological forces that conduce to association and collective effort, the town is also a relatively fragile organism open to attack from a multiplicity of forces. From deserted ghost towns in the West, to Main Streets with boarded and vacant shops in the Midwest, to deserted towns in New England that stand like a memory of their former bustling selves, there are countless examples of failed and failing towns that have succumbed to a variety of elements. In this chapter I want to offer first a general picture of the larger historical processes that have worked against the small town in the twentieth century—competition from chain stores, mail-order catalogs, and malls. And second, I will consider how towns have survived, for many Main Streets have managed, despite the odds, to live on and thrive, and I want to explore that process as well, focusing on a significant case study—the town of Chestnut Hill, near Philadelphia—that offers a paradigm for Main Street's survival through self-reinvention.

From the very earliest founding of settlements in the colonies, villages have succumbed to an assortment of hostile conditions, including inadequate food supplies, disease and starvation, attacks from inhospitable Indians, and insufficient population. In these cases, the causes are relatively simple and straightforward. A more complex, and less violent, etiology occurs when a town has achieved a certain vitality and stability and then fades into a shadow of its former self, a "ghost town," as we say. And this process, beginning in the nineteenth century and continuing into our own time, might have a variety of causes, chiefly economic in nature. Some nineteenth-century towns in California and elsewhere in the West, for example, catered exclusively to a temporary population—such as miners —and when the local minerals were exhausted, many of the miners simply moved on. A more gradual decay faced towns that were based on a thin agricultural production and that lost their young people to manufacturing jobs, as happened in the industrial Northeast in the late nineteenth century. Similarly, towns that served the farms of the Midwest found their populations depleted as the farmers themselves lost ground—literally—to the eastern banks that increasingly took over mortgages in hard times; it was not long before giant agribusinesses devoured all available lands as they exploited the advantages of machines and the economies of scale. (This is the story John Steinbeck tells in *The Grapes of Wrath*.)

Even at the supposed peak of Main Street, the period of the 1890s, when so many iconic Main Street facades were constructed—facades that would provide the model for more than a century of nostalgic restorations and fabrications—the erosion of the small town was visible. Observing that growth and prosperity are identical, the author of an 1895 article, "The Doom of the Small Town," laments the "decay of villages." "One by one, family by family, their inhabitants slip away in search of other homes; a steady but hardly perceptible emigration takes away the young, the hopeful, the ambitious. There remain behind the superannuated, the feeble, the dull, the stagnant rich who will risk nothing, the ne'er-do-wells who have nothing to risk. Enough workers remain to till the soil, to manage the distribution of food and clothing, and to transact the common business of life; but the world's real work is done elsewhere."[1] The emotional effects of these losses on the remaining population were recorded sympathetically by many of the regional writers of this period, especially Hamlin Garland in his short-story collection *Main-Travelled Roads* (particularly the 1891 story, "Under the Lion's Paw"). More than one hundred years later, the small towns of the Great Plains and the upper Midwest are still trying to stop their young people from leaving and to attract new residents to Main Street, offering tax breaks, loans, and, in Plainville, Kansas, free land.[2]

Outside the sparsely populated Plains and Midwest, the problem was slightly different. In a 1900 *Atlantic Monthly* article, John Fiske, the Harvard philosopher and historian, celebrated his native town of Middletown, Connecticut, both for its history, calling it the birthplace of American democracy, and for its natural setting—"smiling meadows, such as Virgil and Dante might have chosen for their Elysian fields." Yet even in 1900, Fiske laments the loss of earlier homes and estates that have given way to the industrial revolution: "The complete destruction and disappearance of that noble landmark [the estate of Captain Hackstaff], to give place to a railway junction, is a typical instance of the kind of transformation wrought upon the face of things by the titanic and forceful age in which we are living." But on the whole, Fiske congratulates the town on maintaining, against "an age and country where material civilization has been achieving its grandest triumphs," some of the "old-time charm, something of the courtliness and quiet refinement" that marked the earlier days of Middletown.[3] Holding on to its past for dear life, Fiske's Middletown is feeling threatened by change, but in truth it has little idea what the twentieth century has in store.

For the fate of Middletown and thousands of other towns in New England and throughout the United States would be irrevocably altered by the advent of the mass-produced automobile, just moving into gear as Fiske was writing. When it arrived in mass production, however, it "was born into a roadless world," as General Motors declared in 1922, or rather, into a world of roads that were dirt hard, dusty, and bumpy in summer and wet, muddy, and rutted in winter. (Early cars could absorb far more road stress than our contemporary vehicles.) The need for roads was answered initially by the construction of local roads leading out of towns into the countryside and connecting one town with another.[4] While facilitating transportation between farm and town, the roads also allowed for escape from the small town, into larger regional towns and cities, all of which eroded the small town's centrality.

Roads that brought new customers into the town might also serve as conduits for regional traffic, thus clogging downtown Main Streets and destroying their function and character. And so the bypass was invented. But while some bypasses saved their towns—reducing local traffic to a tolerable level—others created a speedy way for travelers to avoid business centers, which were then left in the dust. The results were not always predictable. Following the creation of the interstate highway system, conceived in the 1930s and 1940s and built as a result of the Interstate Highway Act of 1956, the small town fell victim to yet another transformation in American culture as the growth of an automobile-dependent suburbia surrounding the major cities drained yet more people from the towns.

But the major and universal threat to the small town was the advent of a consumer economy that competed with downtown Main Street, a process that began in the nineteenth century with the creation of the mail-order businesses, made possible by a growing network of rail transportation. By the late nineteenth century, Sears Roebuck and Montgomery Ward were gaining a large share of small-town commerce, thus eliminating the town shopkeepers as middlemen. By the 1930s, the resulting economic and social forces threatened to tear apart the fabric of small-town life, a process acutely portrayed in the unjustly neglected 1936 novel by George Milburn, *Catalogue*.[5] *Catalogue* depicts the efforts by a group of merchants in Conchartee, Oklahoma, to compete with the Sears Roebuck and Montgomery Ward mail-order businesses that seem so attractive to their erstwhile customers. And they come up with a scheme—to buy up the town's supply of catalogues. At the end of Milburn's novel, the townspeople, having redeemed their catalogues for one dollar, and having seen them go up in flames, flood the post office with cards and letters requesting replacements from Sears and Montgomery Ward. The town's merchants cannot win, finally, against the force of consumer desire and the infinite variety of goods available from the major companies. What Milburn is depicting, in effect, is the struggle for the consumer soul that was taking place in the small towns of the American twentieth century: with chapters headed by excerpts from the Sears or Montgomery Ward catalogues, Milburn plays on the irony between the utterly commonplace, banal objects offered for sale and the intense dramas of desire that relate to them.

The end of the Depression and the end of World War II seemed to offer a whole new world of Main Street opportunities for the returning serviceman. The towns had been depleted of their young men and would need replacements for their elderly carpenters, mechanics, and plumbers. As the *Saturday Evening Post* declared, "Some of the best opportunities for returning war veterans will not be found in the cities or on the farms, but in the thousands of small towns in America."[6] So optimistic was this prospect that the United States Armed Forces Institute issued twenty books in 1945, offering instruction in a range of skills needed to work in, or start, a small business. For the 2 million returning servicemen, the choices, said the *Post*, "take in a whole block on Main Street—clothing stores, bakeries, groceries, drugstores, restaurants, electrical appliance and radio stores, beauty shops, filling stations, hardware stores, real estate and insurance offices, variety stores, shoe-repair shops, auto repairs, dry-cleaning establishments, laundries, metal-working shops, building and painting contracting, heating and plumbing, and sawmills."[7] The article was wise enough to warn of the risks attached to small businesses—every day in the United States, during "normal times," 1,000 small businesses fail—but in general the postwar social imagination could see nothing but blue skies over these small towns.

What it did not foresee was the enormous changes in store for the American postwar landscape, as the automobile came to figure ever larger in the social, geographic, and economic transformations of the United

States. The expanding roads in post–World War II America, and the expanding suburbs, would result in further major and continuing threats to the viability of Main Street—the outdoor shopping center, the regional mall, and its monstrous spawn, the big box mall and Walmart. But these postwar retail inventions continued a trend that had started earlier in the century and that I want briefly to delineate: the arrival of chain stores on Main Street.

As early as the 1910s, variety chain stores like Woolworth's, Kresge's, and Grant's were moving into Main Street. By 1935, Congressman Wright Patman of Texas was introducing a bill in the House of Representatives to impose a tax on chains and to mandate equal pricing, regardless of a store's size or efficiency. The bill died in committee, but the question would resonate throughout the thirties: "Does the Chain Store System Threaten the Nation's Welfare?" In a 1930 debate, arguing against chain stores, the National Wholesale Grocers' Association cited the numerous benefits to customers of a personalized retail service—catering to the community's needs, delivering goods, extending credit, and above all the qualities of "individual initiative, responsibility, self-reliance, citizenship and relations between the individual and his community" that are part of the small-business ethos that is "essential to America."[8] The small business was the heart of Main Street's economy and culture.

Taking the opposing position was the executive vice president of the National Chain Store Association, R. W. Lyons, who argued simply that the chains gave consumers what they want—lower prices and efficient delivery of goods. Lyons saw the chains as exemplifying "the science of merchandise turnover," which is associated with the science of mass production; both decrease waste and increase efficiency by standardizing procedures, records, and employee training. To the argument that the chains discourage individual initiative, Lyons replied that nine out of ten merchants fail anyway, and that nothing prevents the individual from joining his force and ambition to the chain store, which is itself in competition with other chain stores. Moreover, he argued, the chains do contribute to local economies, not only by employing locally and paying decent wages but by paying local taxes.[9] Of course these same arguments are heard today, with regard to the incursion of chains into small towns— whether it is the large drugstores or the Starbucks coffeehouses, the toy stores or the clothing chains—though today, given the perilous state of small towns, any business that commits itself to Main Street is going to win some gratitude there.

After World War II, the survival of the small town was threatened not so much by external forces moving into town in competition with locals as by competition based outside of town: the new malls that were by definition regional in nature and that therefore pulled consumers from a wide range of surrounding towns, all of which were affected. In some ways the malls emulated the logic of small towns, which often grew at the crossroads, accessible to the surrounding population; malls likewise were built near the intersections of roads—major highways and expressways—and could service a broader living area, which often grew to comprise suburban housing developments and industrial parks.[10]

But where towns developed organically, responding to the needs of an existing population, regional malls were deliberate acts of creation that sprang up fully grown. Malls were invented with the best of intentions, indeed utopian intentions, and as a response to postwar changes that were multiply determined: the creation of an interstate highway system that brought new mobility to the automobile, the flight from the inner city to the suburbs in search of a home, the gradual erosion of downtown retail centers, and the random creation of shopping strips along suburban roads. (From 1950 to 1992, the number of suburban shopping centers rose from 100 to 40,000.)[11] The regional mall would provide an ordered center for suburban retail commerce that would take advantage of the shift in population and the creation of new highway networks. It would provide a social and commercial center for that lynchpin of the new postwar economy, the consumer-housewife. And it would provide an environment that promoted itself as a simulation of Main Street, no matter how far from the type it might seem. The Mall of America, outside of Minneapolis, framed the paradox memorably in its 1992 brochure when it proclaimed, "This lushly landscaped, serpentine walk extends from the venerable Sears to the eagerly waited [sic] Nordstrom. With plant-covered balconies, wooden trellises, gazebos, bridges, and airy skylights, North Garden is Main Street, USA."[12] Main Street, U.S.A., rarely boasted such utopian trappings, but the malls were based on a new premise: what sells is the dream of Main Street. What sells is what is better than the real thing.

The individual most credited with the invention and proliferation of malls in America (and with their export to the rest of the world) is Victor Gruen, a Jewish refugee from Nazi Vienna who brought his architectural and theatrical talents to bear first on the redesign of downtown stores and then on selling the notion of the shopping center. The model driving his ideas was, ironically, an image of community drawn from the European town centers he knew from his youth: translated into the suburban mall, it was thus an imported urban image that threatened to destroy the small town—and the city—in America.

The idea of a planned retail zone was certainly in the currents of regional planning during the 1930s, as a way of combating the random commercial strips that were springing up along highways: the shopping center, it was argued, should "face toward green open spaces and turn its back to the road."[13] Gruen had entered this discourse with a project described in the pages of *Architectural Forum* in 1943, which gained him some notoriety, along with many commissions. In 1950 he gained the confidence of a Detroit department store, which invested in the construction of a huge suburban shopping center, Northland, designed with pedestrian malls oriented around a core department store. Gruen expanded his ideas in Southdale, outside of Minneapolis, designing the first enclosed American mall, where the mall was endowed with sufficient attractors—fountains, sculpture, benches, trees—to make it a new thing: both a commercial magnet and a cultural center, where people would come for entertainment and amusement, for civic events, holidays, and celebrations. A safe refuge from the city and from reality, it became, in effect, an idealized version of Main Street, moved inside and weatherproofed. Even better, it was safe from the intrusions of civic disorder—protests, demonstrations, and other expressions of eccentricity and free speech—thanks to its legal status as private space, a characteristic that maintained the sanctity and order of malls for decades in the United States.[14]

Gruen's ideal consumer, bedazzled and mesmerized by the multiplicity of stimuli, would helplessly and impulsively buy things: we call this eponymously the "Gruen Effect" or "Gruen Transfer." Paradoxically, the indoor mall, this most "American" of inventions—a machine for selling, as it has been called—had been inspired by the civilities of the public sphere in Vienna and the nineteenth-century European arcades, the first glass-covered shopping malls. (J. C. Nichols, who built the highly successful outdoor Country Club Plaza in suburban Kansas City in 1922, a Mediterranean-styled blend of residential and commercial structures, with fountains, sculptures, and pleasant public places to sit, had also been inspired by his early trips to Europe, where he saw the plazas and squares that America generally lacked.)

But Gruen's conceptions went beyond the suburban mall. Seeing the demise of the downtown city shopping districts, partly as a result of the suburbanization of America and the regional malls, Gruen then tried to

Central Court of Southdale Center, the first modern mall, designed by Victor Gruen, Edina (suburb of Minneapolis), Minnesota, 1957. Main Street as mall, a fabricated modernistic space designed to enhance the shopping experience. United Press photograph. Library of Congress, Victor Gruen Collection.

save downtown with the same theories of place-making that he had applied to regional malls. Interestingly, his plans for Fort Worth, Texas, which were never realized, elicited the praise of Jane Jacobs, who was otherwise strongly opposed to then current urban renewal projects ("They banish the street"). Jacobs said that Gruen's plan, which included "sidewalk arcades, poster columns, flags, vending kiosks, display stands, outdoor cafés, bandstands, flower beds, and special lighting effects," would create a rich downtown experience.[15]

His achievement in Rochester, New York—Midtown Plaza—was a giant indoor space that transformed a dying center city into a vibrant festival of commerce and entertainment. Gruen's practice was national in scope, for at its foundation was a sense of the universality of the civilized shopping experience and the fungibility of the material space itself. He nailed it at the beginning of his American career when he said, with a salesman's panache and a breathtaking contempt for the local, "If you know one American Main Street, you know them all."[16]

While some of Gruen's malls remain, in the twenty-first century, vital

Drawing by Victor Gruen and Associates of pedestrian downtown Fort Worth, Texas, "giving shoppers view of windows on both sides of street. Pedestrian bridge connects parking structure with hotel." From "A Greater Ft. Worth Tomorrow," Western Architect and Engineer *(January 1957).*

commercial centers, others—and many hundreds of malls that had emulated Gruen's model—have become dead space. The monotony of the same stores everywhere; the monotony of the same engineering in shopper control; the monotony of the music, the benches, the fountains, the trees; the dead air, always at the same temperature—all these things that had seemed so winning in the fifties and sixties had come to seem lifeless, ersatz space by the nineties, and the many undistinguished malls—pale imitators of Gruen's—that had failed to sustain their customers' excitement and interest began to close. From our present perspective, Gruen's utopian thinking had left out an important ingredient: the spontaneous vitality of public space, the randomness and unexpectedness of real life. What he had so admired in the Vienna of his youth—the cafés, the lively urban spaces, the open squares and public spaces, the statues, the density of population—were missing from indoor spaces controlled by the central authority of the mall operator, whether suburban or urban. Gruen had of-

Midtown Plaza, designed by Victor Gruen, with the Clock of Nations (evoking the traditional European village clock) in the background, Rochester, New York, 1963. Library of Congress, Victor Gruen Collection.

fered America a safe shopping environment with some great attractions, but it was a factitious environment, a fiction whose charm lasted for a generation but eventually expired. Even Gruen's famous and much loved mall in downtown Rochester—originally designed to draw people back to the city—was slated for demolition in the first decade of the twenty-first century.

As Main Street was struggling against the regional malls, it was also competing with a previously unknown and unimagined foe, the big box store, and chiefly its most successful avatar, Walmart (branded as Wal-Mart before 2008), which was draining the life out of not only the small town but the regional mall as well.[17] Growing from a single variety store in 1950 to a chain of eleven by 1960, Walmart was by the end of the twentieth century a global phenomenon, the largest retailer in the world, with enormous consequences for towns, cities, and regions. Enough has been written by now about "The Walmart Effect"—on manufacturing and markets, on retailing, on competing stores, on shoppers, on landscape and community—to make further discussion largely otiose, except to observe, in the present context, that Walmart has enjoyed the luxury of present-

Sam Walton's first 5-10 store on Main Street in Bentonville, Arkansas. Flickr.com.

ing its goods to shoppers at the most basic level of consumer satisfaction. With the slack service, no-frills displays, and monotonous building design (blue, gray, and red), Walmart is not a place one goes to willingly. In recent years, "listening to our customers," as the company proudly put it, some stores have undergone remodeling—including the creation of quasi– "Main Street" facades on the otherwise massive nondescript buildings— but there is no effort (and no need) to attract customers by providing the kind of entertainment experience that the malls have offered: festival markets, flowers, benches, cute sculptures, carousels, fountains, and so on. The shoppers' motivation is singular (low prices), and their satisfaction is accordingly achieved through bargains and a basic environment.

During the first decade of the new century, Walmart continued to ride the wave of retail success, with some moderation of profits as the world economy worsened, but at regional malls, meanwhile, sales declined far more dramatically (by 50 percent between 1995 and 2003).[18] During the past twenty years—because of the overbuilding of competing malls and because of competition from Walmart and the other big box stores—hundreds of malls have failed annually, becoming vacant and abandoned. Some of these newly created "brownfields" have lain fallow for years; others, ironically, have been created anew as New Urbanist communities, with mixed housing and town centers that include retail stores and restaurants serving the residents and surrounding populations. Still other malls have been reborn as "Townscape Malls," to use Michael Southworth's term, or what the industry calls "lifestyle centers," places that offer multiple attractions, from libraries to theaters to restaurants and of course shopping. In fact, many of these places incorporate the name "Main Street" and the associated generic signs and symbols of the place: street lamps, clocks, village greens, and so on.[19]

I WILL COME BACK to the dissemination of Main Street symbolism—the new commercial idiom of the twenty-first century—in my final chapter. But let me return now to the small town itself and its effort to survive the huge forces outside the town that have impinged on it for so many years. The attractive power of city stores, capable of pulling the willing shopper out of the small town, was noticed as early as 1929, as the automobile, now reaching a mass market, was making travel possible over distances previously thought impossible for a mere shopping expedition. Marketing specialist William Reilly called it the "Law of Retail Gravitation," whereby the housewife (long identified as the archetypal consumer) would travel long distances to retail centers in search of goods that had been promoted through the new mass media of radio, newspapers, movies, and magazines.[20] As Alison Isenberg points out, however, the small town could still, according to Reilly, survive nicely, if it accepted its niche in the national "distribution system," in short, by serving local and immediate needs.[21] What the town could also do, to keep itself attractive and competitive during the thirties, was modernize its storefronts, clean up the streets, and get rid of the clutter, all of which was done most easily in the postcard images of the small towns—airbrushed to perfection—that promoted an image of clean modernity.[22] The meaning of modernization during the thirties, as Gabrielle Esperdy has argued, was social (as a sign of coming prosperity), political (New Deal legislation guaranteed loans to small businesses), and economic (a lot of people were employed in these modernizations).[23] Ironically, these "modernizations" seem, from a twenty-first-century perspective, more like disfigurement than improvement, as they transformed what we have come to appreciate as the charm of the Victorian Main Street into an incongruous medley of original storefronts and the thirties version of modernity—streamlined design.

Main Street modernization continued as a strategy into the forties and beyond, leaving in its wake a stylistic jumble of incompatible storefronts, which, as they aged and grew frayed along the edges, looked graceless, incongruous, and desperate. All of which set the stage for the late-twentieth-century counterreformation, if you will, the preservation movement, the effort to restore Main Street to what it was, or what it was imagined to have been. Small towns sought to mark themselves in some distinctive way, as opposed to the generic "modernization" of the earlier twentieth century. The Main Street Project of the National Trust for Historic Preservation, begun in the 1970s, has undertaken this labor of preservation on a national scale, and I will return to it in a moment. But I want first to discuss in more detail one of the earliest such efforts, begun even before the preservation movement had a name, which took place in a small town that has technically been a part of the city of Philadelphia since the 1854 Act of Incorporation, though it has always seemed a somewhat distinct entity, outside of the downtown area and outside the industrial belt that encircled the city in the late nineteenth and early twentieth centuries.[24] I want to use Chestnut Hill as an illustration of the triumph, and the perils, of restoration.

Chestnut Hill, which reinvented itself in the fifties as a charming colonial Main Street, happens to be the place where I live and is partly the inspiration for this book. And the fact that the town was named one of America's "Dozen Distinctive Destinations" in 2010 by the National Trust for Historic Preservation certainly supports a view of the community's historic and aesthetic distinction. It is a place that, to some degree, also inspired New Urbanists like Elizabeth Plater-Zyberk.[25] It is the subject of a serious historical study by David R. Contosta; it plays a key role in sociologist Elijah Anderson's *Code of the Street*; and it has been celebrated by architectural historian Witold Rybczynski in a recent book on the New Urbanism.[26] At the risk of turning Chestnut Hill into an idyllic place of comfort, an idealized *locus amoenus*, the happy Bedford Falls of our time (as in Frank Capra's *It's a Wonderful Life*), I want to add my own view of the place, though from a somewhat different angle from that of my predecessors.

Rybczynski uses Chestnut Hill as a touchstone for community design, an example of a place that has been planned (by George Houston, in the late nineteenth century, and by his successors) and that has evolved over the years, evincing the kind of inspired charm that has an implicit authenticity, in contrast to the well-meaning efforts of the New Urbanists, who are struggling anew to create community. "Chestnut Hill, where we live," Rybczynski declares, "is as bucolic as its name." He describes the "arboreal tunnels of massive oaks and sycamores," the variously bounded properties, some with wooden fences, some with wrought iron, some stone, some open. He describes the architectural styles that have accumulated over the years: "There are mansions as big as small hotels, and little Hansel-and-Gretel cottages[,] . . . charming Queen Annes with picturesque bay windows and ornamental curlicues; rather serious half-timbered Tudors; elegant Georgian Revivals that make me think of Jazz Age financiers in wing collars and spats; and straightforward center-hall Colonials, as friendly and uncomplicated as the big golden Labs that play in their front yards."[27]

In his ekphrastic, and at times ecstatic, description, Rybczynski does justice, perhaps more than justice, to the neighborhood. He does not discuss the distinction between the houses on the east side of the main street and the west (the east is more modest, the west more affluent). More to the point, he does not discuss the main street at all—Germantown Avenue. But it is the avenue, a commercial strip that is the main artery through the neighborhood, which gives Chestnut Hill its distinctive character as a viable community.

Germantown Avenue is urban ethnographer Elijah Anderson's focus in his 1999 book, *Code of the Street: Decency, Violence and the Moral Life of the Inner City*, which offers a nuanced view of the gradations of neighborhoods—and the corresponding changes in street codes and behavior—that are visible along the length of the avenue, commencing in Chestnut Hill and moving through racially mixed neighborhoods to areas of deep poverty, a continuum that reveals the changing "role of violence in the social organization of the communities through which the avenue passes and . . . how violence is revealed in the interactions of people up and down the street." We move, in Anderson's narrative, from a "code of civility at one end" (Chestnut Hill) to a "code of conduct regulated by the threat of violence—the code of the street—at the other."[28]

Yet even in the relatively civil Chestnut Hill, Anderson perceives a degree of racial tension. Anderson was a Chestnut Hill resident at the time he wrote *Code of the Street*, and he portrays a neighborhood that is, at least on its main street, Germantown Avenue, uniformly middle-class. There is a small minority of black residents in Chestnut Hill, but a somewhat larger representation of black middle-class shoppers there, who come from surrounding neighborhoods to the upscale shops of Chestnut Hill and are joined there by white residents. With all this mix, "a pleasant ambiance prevails—an air of civility."[29] And yet, as Anderson observes, black males walking into stores, "especially a jewelry store," are "almost always given extra scrutiny," even when they are middle class, thus perceiving a failure on the part of whites to make distinctions between social classes that can be irksome to middle-class blacks.[30] Anderson adroitly reveals the tensions that can exist along Chestnut Hill's main street, and his depiction of Germantown Avenue anticipates the issue of a community's self-definition—by acts of inclusion and exclusion—that I will take up more generally in chapter 5.

What has not been discussed by Rybczynski or Anderson, and what interests me, especially in the present context, is Chestnut Hill's main street, Germantown Avenue, as a self-conscious invention of the 1950s that began to define itself not in terms of "modernization"—the prevailing strategy of the 1930s and 1940s—but in terms of history and nostalgia. Chestnut Hill is, to all present appearances, a charming colonial town, with a mix of Victorian buildings and more recent structures that have followed the vaguely colonial pattern book. Chestnut Hill, however, is a study not only in historic preservation but in self-invention as well, and it is a story that anticipates the movement to maintain the viability of the small town that would become more broadly national in the later twentieth century. And although Chestnut Hill can serve in some ways as an archetype of the American small town and its main street over the last 150 years, it is the latter part of the story—the post–World War II period—that I am especially interested in, and that bears detailed observation.

Chestnut Hill is representative of small towns with successful commercial centers everywhere that have managed to hold their own against the malls and big box stores, by defining a unique character that makes them attractive as shopping places and that also fulfills the basic local needs of the community. In order to survive, the small town must attract people from outside the surrounding residential area, and in Chestnut Hill's case its attractive power results from a mix of restaurants and specialty shops (antiques, crafts, exotic gifts, art and print galleries, boutique clothing stores), all with smart window displays. In addition, the avenue is decorated with "Main Street" style street furniture (hanging flowers, lights, benches, lampposts, etc.). Street festivals—arts and crafts in the fall, gardens in the spring—also bring people in from outside, with the streets thronging with music, food, children, and dogs. Meanwhile, the local community's daily needs are served by a hardware store that doubles as a kind of small-town general store, by numerous cleaners, a grocery, a flower shop, a cat hospital, and a chain drugstore. But the Chestnut Hill of the twenty-first century is not the same town it was in 1950.[31]

As early as the 1950s, Chestnut Hill was feeling the drain on Germantown Avenue business as a result of the new shopping centers in nearby suburbia. With roots in the colonial period, Chestnut Hill had grown from a nineteenth-century farming village to a Victorian railroad suburb of Philadelphia, maintaining a slow growth through the first half of the twentieth century, when it presented a mix of shops serving a local population— pharmacies, butcher shops, bakeries, cafés, garages, hardware stores, gas stations, auto dealers, a movie theater, and so on. Some shops featured large painted signs, others neon signs, the usual disarray and disorder of a declining main street. By 1950, the automobile was expanding the range of travel, making it possible for residents to go off to the new suburban shopping centers and leaving Germantown Avenue with many vacant stores. In fact, the blight had already affected the part of Germantown Avenue closer to the city (the Germantown section of Philadelphia), and with it came a general decline in housing values. Chestnut Hill could have reasonably feared such a fate, despite the affluence of the community.

Few small towns that have been positioned at this junction have survived and prospered, until the Main Street Project of the late twentieth century made outside intervention and assistance a matter of coherent strategies and methods. That Chestnut Hill did indeed change its fortunes, beginning in the 1950s, was likewise the result of an outside intervening force, but in this case it was an individual who had—until his marriage—no connection whatsoever to the town, Lloyd P. Wells. In claiming a singular importance for Wells, I should also say that the character of Chestnut Hill had, even before Wells, been molded by the strong influence of a series of enterprising individuals, from Henry Houston in the late nineteenth century to George Woodward in the early twentieth, and their succeeding families, who built hundreds of houses, often imitating European and English models, that gave a coherent architectural character to the neighborhood. More than that, they controlled who lived in those houses, for with a few exceptions, these properties—for the middle

Germantown Avenue, Chestnut Hill, Pennsylvania, showing a commercial street with billboards and heavy traffic before colonialization, ca. 1940. Urban Archives, Paley Library, Temple University.

and upper middle class—were rented to screened, white Anglo-Saxon, and preferably Episcopalian, tenants, who commuted to Center City Philadelphia on the commuter railroad. (There were always the more modest row houses, close to the avenue, for the working classes who labored in the area.) Since the Second World War, many of these formerly rented properties have been sold, and the previously "exclusive" character of the town—the intended result of a deliberate social policy—has given way to a somewhat more diverse population. Despite its elitism, Chestnut Hill as a physical place did benefit from the creation of public spaces (such as parks and community and recreational centers) as well as from the creation of private community spaces (including a church and a cricket and tennis club), all on land donated by the owners for their ideal community.

Wells entered this patrician world in the late 1940s, marrying into a prominent Philadelphia legal family. With a career as an airplane pilot behind him, Wells opened a hardware company on Germantown Avenue;

but he soon realized that his customers lacked parking, a problem that would obviously threaten a business where sometimes heavy items must be carried away. But Wells also saw the problem in a much larger context: with a vacancy rate of 30 percent, the town was already blighted, losing its competition with surrounding shopping areas where customers could drive and park.[32] Unless the town could revive Germantown Avenue, it would fall victim to the process that had already been occurring on the avenue closer to Philadelphia, where the deterioration of commercial areas had led to the decline of residential neighborhoods.

Seeing how attracted people were to the first shopping centers with parking lots, Wells came up with the simple but brilliant idea of creating a common parking lot in the back of his store, shared by the adjoining shops, though he had first to convince the other storeowners on the block to give up their backyards for this purpose. (Wells himself was fortuitously able to purchase adjoining property, which made things a little easier.) He then sought to convince the whole of Germantown Avenue to do the same, having conceived a second inspired notion: that each merchant had more to gain from cooperating and creating a consistent shopping experience than from going it alone. The idea, in short, was to create a "horizontal department store" along the town's main street, one that could compete with the suburban shopping centers.[33] By this one simple change—creating accessible, pleasantly landscaped parking lots out of the backyard spaces behind the stores—Wells changed the character of Germantown Avenue, transforming it into a walking town, so that even if you drove there, you could easily leave your car and free yourself to walk. You had the convenience of the shopping center and the variety of the town center, and it was his idea, only partially realized, to increase the commercial presence on the side streets leading into the main street, thus creating a "quadrangle" area of shopping.[34] (Then, as now, NIMBYism was strong, and Wells had to fight the avenue's closest neighbors, who resisted the increased parking, commerce, and traffic.)

Along with the logistical plan to make Germantown Avenue accessible, Wells had an equally important aesthetic strategy: to turn Chestnut Hill into a colonial town by creating a unified architectural style, planting trees on the street, eliminating neon signs in store windows, and installing wooden signs. The sources of this strategy were multiple: Wells had spent some of his earlier years vacationing with his family in Palm Beach and had been impressed by the architectural consistency that had evolved in southern Florida under the influence of Addison Mizner's

"46th store to be colonialized," showing Chestnut Hill, Pennsylvania's, conscious effort to re-invent itself, 1961. Chestnut Hill Historical Society.

Spanish colonial revival style. Unlike Mizner's Florida towns, Chestnut Hill had actually been a colonial village, with buildings dating back to the eighteenth century, so there was an authentic material base to build on; moreover, the "romantic fantasy" of colonial America was strong at the time, symbolizing old American values that were politically appealing in the postwar era.[35] Philadelphia was an especially likely place for a colonial revival, with historic Germantown restoring its Market Square area and, most notably, the area around Independence Hall becoming the object of a massive restoration effort, inspired in part by the success and appeal of Colonial Williamsburg.[36] Acting with the advice of the town's local architecture committee, Wells persuaded the merchants to convert their storefronts to the general theme of a colonial town, figuring moreover that the clean lines would be perennially tasteful. These changes would require the cooperation of the landlords, of course, and many were persuaded by Wells (assisted by free architectural advice, where needed) to historicize their properties, creating a look that was far from uniform but that worked as a coherent aesthetic.

In turning to history for inspiration, Wells was anticipating the larger cultural turn to the past that would make the idea of preservation a leading ethos of the late twentieth century. This turn, as Alison Isenberg has observed, represents a complete reversal of the "modernization" strategy that had dominated thinking about the revitalization of Main Street during the 1930s and 1940s.[37] Of course, in the case of Wells, the "colonial" theme was imposed on a main street that was at least in part authentically colonial; but other buildings, in various Victorian styles, were also on the avenue, and while some were stripped of their Victorian identities and turned into ersatz colonial facades, others were left more or less intact and allowed to blend in with the character of the town.[38] The result was a main street that, through its aesthetic and practical strategies, became a commercial success—with few store vacancies, increasing numbers of shoppers, and increasing sales. Within a decade, Chestnut Hill was competing successfully with commercial centers around the region.

GIVEN THE HUMAN RESISTANCE to change, one must credit Wells with a number of skills: patience, political strategizing, the labor of persuasion, the gift of cajolery, the ability to inspire, and a willingness to come back to the fight, even after he had resigned in disgust. Whatever natural endowments he had (including his determination to overcome dyslexia, which prevented him from earning a college degree) were nurtured, no doubt, by his upbringing in St. Louis, Missouri. There, after his father died, Wells was close to his grandfather, who had served as mayor of the city for two terms, including during the 1904 St. Louis World's Fair—*Meet Me in St. Louis*, that most iconic of small-town films, took place at that time—and was later a figure in national Democratic politics and in the banking and railroad industries. Along with Mizner's Florida, Wells credited as his inspiration several New England towns he had known well in his younger years—including Vineyard Haven (Martha's Vineyard) and the town of Nantucket. Interestingly, these are places that were sufficiently isolated to be relatively protected from the shopping center, towns that had a traditional regional architectural character that was relatively impervious to fashion and change. And like these places, Chestnut Hill was greatly developed in the late nineteenth century as a vacation retreat from the city, and so the idea of a festive "theming" of the place seemed to fit.

But Wells's vision was also one of a community governing itself through associations and committees, quasi-governmental bodies that would function—alongside Philadelphia's city government—as immediate agents of

The Eagle Hotel on Germantown Avenue in Chestnut Hill, Pennsylvania, literally a colonial building, ca. 1900. Chestnut Hill Historical Society.

The Eagle Hotel on Germantown Avenue in Chestnut Hill, Pennsylvania, attractively stylized during the 1950s as a "colonial" building, housing a flower shop. Photograph by Nancy Hubby, 1985. Chestnut Hill Historical Society.

change in the community. It was also a part of his vision that Chestnut Hill should be an integrated community, in housing and commerce.[39] (From 1970 to 2000, the African American population of Chestnut Hill increased from 1 percent to 15 percent.)[40] Wells had the support of a good many people in Chestnut Hill for many years, but in the process he had also been opposed by those who wanted to take the community in another direction on some issues, and after serving as head of the local community association for two terms, Wells was narrowly defeated in 1976. Feeling that his efforts of more than twenty-five years were now hitting a wall, he left Chestnut Hill for northern Maine.

If I have been speaking of Chestnut Hill so far as if it is a homogeneous and consistent whole, I must now complicate that picture in an effort to illustrate on a smaller scale the kinds of struggles small towns have endured, in dealing with both internal and external forces. For my description thus far largely belies the divisions and conflicts within the space of the town, omitting, for example, the fact that the community's main street is not entirely uniform throughout Chestnut Hill but instead is tacitly divided between an "upper" Germantown Avenue and a "lower" Germantown Avenue. In the upper part, there is a greater aesthetic consistency to the shops and storefronts, in line with the stone colonial buildings that have become the hallmark of the place. The lower section of Germantown Avenue, by contrast, is a mix of commercial space, some of it resembling that on the upper part, and some of it including newer brick buildings with large plate glass windows and small parking lots (from eight to twenty cars) in front of the store, including two mini strip malls, with anterior parking, as opposed to the rear lots of the upper avenue. In short, the space on the lower part of Germantown Avenue is not the "typical" Main Street scene, with sidewalks and shops directly on the street. It is a hybrid space of parking lots and shops. Parking in a lot in front of a store is quite different, psychologically, from parking on a street or parking in a rear lot and walking to the shops on the street. In the storefront lot, you feel anchored to that store, you tend not to walk to the next block, your car is a part of you that you "cannot" leave behind.

The community has not accepted this different character of lower Germantown Avenue, permitted by zoning, without challenge. Chestnut Hill's watchdog aesthetic committee (with no real legal authority) managed to get at least some cooperation from the store owners, so that the newer buildings—none stridently modern—do not look entirely incongruous. So, for example, when McDonald's came to town—itself the cause of community protest, to no avail—the franchise agreed to scale back its street front advertising, omit the giant golden arches, and modify the materials and design of the building to make it blend in more with the brick facades of the upper part of the street. When a large CVS drugstore arrived (with parking in front), it agreed to style the building with bricks, thus providing a kind of harmony with the businesses on the upper part of the hill. The drugstore even displayed large photographs of historic Chestnut Hill (from the Historical Society), thus connecting the place symbolically with its history; these disappeared after a year or two, though, leaving the windows blank and featureless. Perhaps it goes without saying that the coming of CVS meant the closing of three smaller drugstores that had served the community for years. Meanwhile, the recessions of the twenty-first century have not been kind to lower Chestnut Hill, where the vacancy rate has been high, including the demise of the local video rental store, one of countless Netflix casualties. For that matter, the local chain bookstore at the top of the hill (which had previously driven out independent booksellers in the neighborhood), was itself killed off by Amazon.[41] We are in the midst of a global transformation of commercial space as a result of e-commerce—visible on a local level in such changes as these in small towns—that we have not fully absorbed intellectually or in our urban planning and development.

The accidents of history can be fully determining of the fate of places, and every small town's history is accordingly unique. But the example of Chestnut Hill does allow us to draw several conclusions about the small town's survival into the twenty-first century. First, Main Street is vulnerable to external forces that can both create it (as, for example, a needed center of commerce in the nineteenth century) or destroy it (as an obsolete shopping area in the age of the automobile and the super mall). But second, communities can resist these outside forces and benefit greatly from leadership and cooperation, often the result of a single individual who can build cooperation. Third, history can be a source of renewal, through the appeal of historic properties that are tastefully preserved. Fourth, towns can market their images as a whole, competing with shopping centers. And fifth, towns can work to restructure their economic resources, recruiting new businesses and strengthening existing ones.

These are, in fact, the guiding doctrines of the National Trust Main Street Center, which has been the main agent for saving small towns in the United States for the past several decades, since the late 1970s. The Main Street Center has functioned by providing the kind of leadership that Chestnut Hill was able, by accident of history, to generate on its own in the fifties; and the center has helped towns merge private investment with government support (federal, state, and local).[42] The results are visible in hundreds of saved towns, which have seen dramatically increased sales tax revenues, renovated facades and preserved buildings, new downtown organizations, and low-interest loan pools. Some, on the initiative of local townsfolk and volunteer labor, have turned themselves into art communities; others have restored local movie theaters on Main Street to serve as entertainment and community centers; others have capitalized on their eccentricities and assets, whatever these might be.[43] And not a few towns—especially those surrounding New York City, in nearby northeast Pennsylvania and in the Hudson Valley region—have been reinventing themselves as Latino communities, as their demography has shifted. Where small towns had previously been written off entirely as victims of deindustrialization and the malls, many have been able to build on New Urbanist principles and have won government support and private investment, enabling them to sustain themselves economically and saving them from the slow death that might otherwise await them.[44] And with the American Dream Downpayment Act of 2003, HOPE VI funds were made available to support affordable housing in downtown Main Streets (a town's population must be under 50,000 to qualify), where the housing projects were in connection with Main Street revitalization programs and specifically targeted the conversion of outmoded commercial properties into affordable housing.[45]

Has Main Street been saved? It would be naive to think that even the most successful projects touted by the Main Street Project have created blooming festival marketplaces out of previously arid and moribund spaces.[46] Still, they are holding on, and they are beginning to attract people who even want to live on Main Street, in apartments above the stores that had been vacant in some cases for decades. Under the New Urbanist influence, retail stores are emphasized rather than law offices and banks. And here is the key point, at least for my own purposes: Even while the thousands of small towns across America struggle to survive, with varying degrees of success, the idealized vision of Main Street is enduring and powerful, a platonic image, an icon, a myth, that has inspired the American imagination for a century and one that has, for the past twenty-five years especially, been inspiring the revival of small towns and the renewal of both suburbs and cities. I will have more to say about the impact of the Main Street myth on the ongoing development of our cities in the last chapters, but I want first to explore the historical progression of that icon as a model for thinking about space and cultural values throughout the twentieth century. Understanding the power of Main Street as a force that has been organizing the construction of space in the United States for a century means first understanding the pivotal shift in meaning that Main Street underwent during the early twentieth century, from a culture that was held up to ridicule, an icon of convention and oppression, to a culture that was seen as nurturing in its healing powers, a culture that would, beginning decisively in the thirties, generate a passionate nostalgia well into our own time.

Chapter Three

Living on Main Street

Sinclair Lewis and the Great Cultural Divide

There is a perfect irony in the fact that the model for Sinclair Lewis's Gopher Prairie—Sauk Centre, Minnesota—now celebrates the author of *Main Street* as its favorite son. Lewis had excoriated the town in his 1920 novel, which would famously shatter the complacency of small-town America; and his satire was transparent enough for Sauk Centre to acknowledge, in a town website nearly a century later, that *Main Street* had indeed irritated the townspeople, who were not incapable of seeing that some of their leading citizens were models for the novel's characters. But Lewis would have appreciated the energy with which Sauk Centre has in the years since capitalized on its original embarrassment and turned dross into gold. This would not be the first time a prodigal son has morphed into a favored native son, and Sauk Centre (population 20,000 in the early twenty-first century) has been painstakingly thorough: the novelist's boyhood home, open to visitors, is located on what is now known as Sinclair Lewis Avenue; and the Sinclair Lewis Interpretive Center, opened in 1975, houses the author's writing desk and collected works. The high points of the summer season in Sauk Centre, where Lewis had been anything but happy in his boyhood, are the Sinclair Lewis Days, featuring parades, treasure hunts, a horseshoe tournament, fireworks, a street dance, and a royal pageant, all held in the Sinclair Lewis Campground. While Sauk Centre's website boasts of the town's "picturesque Main Street," the town water tower enthusiastically proclaims Sauk Centre as "The Original Main Street." Doubtless Lewis would admire the pluck and practicality that could make a virtue out of the notoriety his novel had brought the place.

Lewis's own visits to Sauk Centre (where his father and brother continued to live) after the publication of *Main Street* were often the occasion for renewing old ties and receiving accolades from those who knew him "back then" and whom he frequently did not remember. After receiving the Nobel Prize for Literature in 1930, Lewis became a prophet almost too honored in his own country, but the price of his celebrity may have been too dear, for the co-optation of *Main Street* by Main Street risks erasing our cultural memory of this once explosive book, muting not only its profound and divisive impact when it appeared in 1920 but also its enduring value as a work that has defined more clearly than anything before or since the split in American culture that became conclusive after World War I and that has remained a defining characteristic of our society, crystallized in more recent years as "the culture wars," the split between Main Street and Bohemia.

Lewis knew that *Main Street* would be a big book, and he was more correct in that estimate than he could have guessed. It was as shocking and iconoclastic in its way as *The Jungle* (1905) by Upton Sinclair (with whom he was occasionally confused), making Lewis the most widely read author of his time, with *Main Street* consistently the best-selling novel from 1920 to 1925. It was also, for Lewis, a break with his earlier writing, which had been deeply entrenched in the culture of the *Saturday Evening Post*, which had already begun in 1916 to publish Norman Rockwell covers, and which favored sentimental stories and conventional treatments that celebrated small-town virtues. Lewis's work was often satirical of commercial culture, but he knew that *Main Street* was a more serious work, and he was quite deliberate in making this break with the *Post*, refusing to serialize his big novel and keeping it virtually a secret from George Lorimer, his hitherto always supportive editor.[1] In fact, he was risking the publication of his new novel with a young publisher just about to open his own house, Alfred Harcourt, even investing his own money in Harcourt's new venture. In writing *Main Street*, Lewis felt he was jumping the divide in American culture, from convention to iconoclasm, from entertainment to a major declaration.

At a time when half the population of the United States lived in towns smaller than 2,500, *Main Street* defined the war between mainstream America and Bohemia, between the Village (as in Village Smithy) and Greenwich Village. In thus delineating the fault lines of American culture, Lewis provided a map of American society that is still viable, yet it is a far more complex map of the topography of Middle America than we have usually taken it to be, and understanding the place of Main Street in the literary culture of the United States compels us to comprehend Lewis's *Main Street* and the culture that produced it.

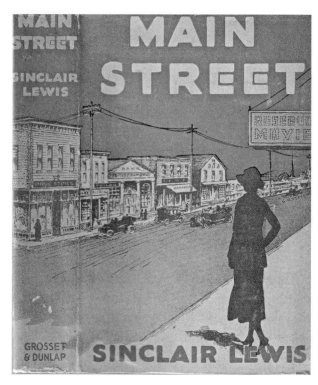

Cover by C. K.
Stevens of Sinclair
Lewis's Main Street.
In 1922, two years
after the original
Harcourt edition,
Grosset and Dunlap,
the major reprint
publisher of the
early twentieth
century, brought
out a mass-market
edition, "Illustrated
with Scenes from the
Photoplay, a Warner
Bro's Screen Classic."
Author's collection.

WHERE DOES LEWIS'S PORTRAIT of America come from? Carol Kennicott, his main character, herself distinguishes "two traditions of the
American small town," one in the popular magazines, the other on the
vaudeville stage and in newspapers. In the magazine tradition, says Carol,
"the American village remains the one sure abode of friendship, honesty,
and clean sweet marriageable girls," and the errant adventurer who might
leave his village returns in time to the joy of his childhood sweetheart. We
might call this the pastoral tradition, and in opposition to it is the vaudeville tradition, in which the small town is occupied by quaint Victorian
bric-a-brac and "whiskered rusticity," "shrewd comic old men who are
known as 'hicks.'" In fact, the pastoral tradition of the village that Carol
first invokes has a long history, going back to the eighteenth century and
Philip Freneau's "The American Village," which celebrates the ongoing vitality of the village tradition in the New World, as against English poet Ol-
iver Goldsmith's lament for the Old World's "Deserted Village."[2] And the
village or small town remains throughout the nineteenth century a place
that is fondly evoked by writers like Harriet Beecher Stowe, Mary Wilkins
Freeman, and Sarah Orne Jewett, a tradition carried into the twentieth

century in the more sentimental treatments of Booth Tarkington and Zona Gale. Lewis draws on both the pastoral and the vaudeville traditions in constructing his cast of small-town characters, a blend of quirky eccentrics and classic types who are placed at times within a fondly conventional comedy of manners. But more notably Lewis brings a third quality to his depiction of Gopher Prairie, a piercing satire that paints a bleak and miserable picture of small-town life on the prairie.

In this bleaker picture, Lewis was inspired by a rich lineage of gloomy and ominous realism, the "antivillage" tradition. There are several strands to this convention, beginning with the moral satires of Nathaniel Hawthorne, who established the archetype of the town that conceals beneath its seemingly placid surface the torments of suspicion, dread, and evil spite. Thus, Hawthorne's Young Goodman Brown returns from the woods to find the townsmen he had previously respected to be now uncannily evocative of the devil's crew he had met in the woods. And following Hawthorne, Mark Twain would give the Manichean trope his own twist in "The Man That Corrupted Hadleyburg," a dark moral fable in which a town that had prided itself on its virtue is exposed by a skeptical malcontent for what it is—a place of backbiting, chicanery, hypocrisy, and turpitude. In *Main Street*, Lewis draws on the antivillage tradition in characters like the villainous Mrs. Bogard (who willfully ruins innocent Fern Mullins). For Lewis as for many other authors, the isolation of the small town has made it a perfect laboratory for exploring the whole spectrum of human evil, and it has been used in this way throughout the twentieth century by writers as diverse as Grace Metalious, who anatomized the hypocrisies of the New England town in *Peyton Place* (1956), and playwright Lanford Wilson, whose *Book of Days* (1999) exposes the greed and corruption of a Missouri small town.

The trope that all of these antivillage works share is, we might say, the town as a rotten onion: we peel back the seemingly healthy outside layers to reveal the underlying moral decay and dishonesty, a structure as old as Sophocles yet still serviceable to the satirist. Precisely because the small town is treated as a microcosm of the larger world, the writer is less interested in portraying the etiology of evil as a function of small-town existence than in showing the town to be an instance of the larger human condition, a place where events unfold in ways that reveal the essential geometries of the moral and sexual life. Lewis's Gopher Prairie is a microcosm of human life generally and has been acclaimed as a universal fiction by multitudes of foreign readers who see their own town's pathologies in Lewis's American characters; yet Lewis is also more narrowly sociological in his biography of Gopher Prairie, and his understanding of the pathology of place encompasses the dense particulars of small-town life. By anchoring his social analysis in the specificity of a particular place and time, Lewis was anticipating our contemporary understanding of the way place affects our psychological and social being, associating our deepest emotions with the bounded memories, anxieties, and strictures of place.

Yet another strong literary impulse fed into Lewis's *Main Street*, one that was shared by a number of writers in the late nineteenth and early twentieth centuries and that was given a name by Lewis's friend, Carl Van Doren, in the title of a review he wrote for *The Nation* in 1921: "The Revolt from the Village."[3] In some ways the most powerful force acting on Lewis, this strain focuses on the individual's struggle against the oppressive constraints of the small town and includes works by Hamlin Garland (early Garland, that is—*Main-Travelled Roads* [1891], with its scathing portrayal of farming and rural village life), Edith Wharton, Willa Cather, Theodore Dreiser, Edgar Lee Masters, and the critics Van Wyck Brooks and H. L. Mencken.[4] For this group, emerging in the early years of the twentieth century, often from the Midwest, small-town life was a melting pot in which the character of individuality was dissolved under the pressure of conformity into the common run of the community. In the hands of these writers, the pastoral simplicity and egalitarian ideals of small-town life thus mutate into a cauldron of gossip, backbiting, malevolence, and thwarted sexual desire, a vision of America that can be taken as part of the general reaction against puritanism and its repressive heritage by a younger generation of writers. In this environment, the only healthy response to the town's repressive order is the path of rebellion—to leave the narrow confines of the local village for the tolerant cosmopolitanism of Greenwich Village, to light out for the big city, where tolerance of sexual difference and aesthetic ambition is presumably to be found.[5]

In the years leading up to *Main Street*, Lewis himself was living on the fringes of the radical Bohemian culture of Greenwich Village, and especially among the leftist activists, artists, and writers who gravitated around the journal *The Masses*. Lewis had come to New York in 1910 and was working for an advertising agency, but he numbered among his friends at the time Floyd Dell, John Reed and Louise Bryant, Mary Heaton Vorse, Art Young, and Randolph Bourne, among others.[6] (Bourne had written in 1913: "If a modern writer wishes to win an imperishable name as a historian, he has only to write an exhaustive monograph" on the life of the American small town.)[7] This is the world that Carol Kennicott dreams of, Lewis tells us, having contracted the disease of independent thought through her excessive reading of the likes of Theodore Dreiser, H. L. Mencken, Sherwood Anderson, and Edgar Lee Masters; in fact, their work, along with that of Cather and Wharton, provided Lewis himself with at least some of the inspiration for *Main Street.*

Cather's 1905 story, "The Sculptor's Funeral," for example, is an early and crystalline formulation of the problem: The artist Harvey Merrick, who has achieved national renown, is brought back for burial to his hometown by his friend Henry Steavens, who gradually realizes the depth of alienation the artist had suffered growing up amid the banality of Rogers group sculptures and green Brussels carpets, not to mention the meanness of the hard-headed townsfolk who mock him, even in death, for his dreamy impracticality. The clash of cultures—between the civilization of Boston, where Merrick thrived, and the ruffian frontier town he came from—could not be clearer, and it is summed up by the town lawyer, a man defeated in his own ambitions to rise above the dead weight of the town, who excoriates the mocking mourners as a "lot of sick, side-tracked, burnt-dog, land-poor sharks." Cather's postmortem on small-town culture foreshadows Lewis's own attack fifteen years later, though with the latter's Erik Valborg as the "artist," the treatment is lighter. By that point, in order to indict Main Street, it was not necessary to have an authentic alienated artist; it was enough to have someone with artistic inclinations and ambitions.[8]

Yet another catalyst for Lewis was likewise written in a far more somber mode than *Main Street,* indeed a tragic mode: Edgar Lee Masters's poem cycle *Spoon River Anthology* (1915). Masters had exploded the myth of small-town America just as it was settling into its genteel complacency in this collection of life stories that sang the song of a dysfunctional America, where every tombstone on the hill, with its conventional inscription, belied the tales of violence, arson, murder, and disappointment of those buried beneath:

One passed in a fever,
One was burned in a mine,
One was killed in a brawl,
One died in a jail,
One fell from a bridge toiling for children and wife—
All, all are sleeping, sleeping, sleeping on the hill.

. . . .
One died in shameful child-birth,
One of a thwarted love,
One at the hands of a brute in a brothel,
One of a broken pride, in the search for heart's desire,
One after life in far-away London and Paris
Was brought to her little space by Ella and Kate and Mag—
All, all are sleeping, sleeping, sleeping on the hill.

Masters's extreme vision of small-town America—a morgue of discontent, buried happiness, lasting grudges, and suppressed violence—is the obverse of Lewis's Gopher Prairie, where almost nothing happens except in the frustrated consciousness of Carol Kennicott. Melodrama at this extreme a pitch was not to Lewis's purpose, though his sense of the tension between the placid surface of Main Street and the dissatisfactions of characters like Carol and Erik echoes Masters.

CAROL'S ESSENTIAL DISCONTENT in Gopher Prairie likewise echoes a book published the year before *Main Street,* Sherwood Anderson's *Winesburg, Ohio,* which exposes a community of grotesques, of frustrated individuals who have repressed their life's impulses and free spirits in order to survive. Anderson portrays the town through chapter-vignettes that focus usually on a single character and that character's interaction with young George Willard, the book's hero. Only Willard will escape the fate suffered by the other townsfolk, it would seem, by leaving the small town at the end of *Winesburg* for the city, thus freeing himself from the consequences of repressed sexuality that otherwise characterize the town. (Freud was on many a bookshelf in those days.) Willard, the youth about to liberate himself from the suffocating nest, is thus left at the beginning of an imagined trajectory toward freedom and fulfillment. Lewis's Carol Kennicott, arriving in Gopher Prairie from the big city, is on a reverse trajectory and is being asked to accept conditions of limitation that go along with her life choice of marriage and that she will have to work hard to escape.

Carol is, in Lewis's hands, at once an exception to the rule of Main Street and a representative of a growing strain of discontent in American culture, "emerging in the minds of women in ten thousand Gopher Prairies," as Lewis writes.[9] In Carol's case, it is a disquietude based on her reading an "astonishing number of books from the public library"—works by "young American sociologists, young English realists, Russian horrorists; Anatole France, Rolland, Nexo, Wells, Shaw, Key, Edgar Lee Masters, Theodore Dreiser, Sherwood Anderson, Henry Mencken, and all the other subversive philosophers and artists whom women were consulting everywhere, in batik-curtained studios in New York, in Kansas farmhouses, San Francisco drawing-rooms, Alabama schools for negroes." But Lewis ends this passage on a note of irony, allowing the reader to feel sufficiently superior to Carol's otherwise expanded consciousness: "From them she got the same confused desire which the million other women felt; the same determination to be class-conscious without discovering the class of which she was to be conscious" (263). Carol was to be a heroine of discontent, but her confusions were the sign of Lewis's commitment to a realism that played one object of satire against another, keeping the reader off balance.

In Carl Van Doren's 1921 review mentioned earlier, the critic declared the lineage of Midwest writers, from Masters to Anderson to Lewis (and including the more ambivalent Zona Gale and Floyd Dell), to be the "newest style in American literature," overturning half a century of literary celebration of the village. Van Doren muted the antecedents of these writers, and he amalgamates them a little too easily, but his emphasis on a break from the past, symbolized by their collectivity, anticipates an enduring view of that revolutionary moment. The "American voice," as Van Doren hears it in Lewis's *Main Street*, "speaks of American conditions. The villages of the Middle West, it asseverates, have been conquered and converted by the legions of mediocrity, and now, grown rich and vain, are setting out to carry the dingy banner, led by the booster's calliope and the evangelist's bass drum, farther than it has ever gone before to make provincialism imperialistic; so that all the native and instinctive virtues, freedoms, powers must rally in their own defense."[10] Van Doren's delineation of the culture of the Midwest would remain a steady characterization of the region, if not a caricature, through the twentieth century, resonant with political overtones. Yet it is a culture whose peculiar synthesis of qualities is the result of native influences ranging from puritanism to the Chautauqua. As one of Carol's Washington friends puts it, toward the end of *Main Street*, "Your Middlewest is double-Puritan—prairie Puritan on top of New England Puritan; bluff frontiersman on the surface, but in its heart it still has the ideal of Plymouth Rock in a sleet-storm" (441).

TO UNDERSTAND THIS CULTURE, and especially to understand Lewis's understanding of it, we must go to H. L. Mencken, one of the writers on

Carol's preferred list. Mencken's view of America was caustic and bracing, and his essay, "Puritanism as a Literary Force" (published in *A Book of Prefaces* in 1917), which crystallized the revolutionary spirit of the post–World War I moment, was a diagram of American culture that was also a diatribe against the repressive and moralistic spirit that had culminated in what to Mencken was the triumph of Comstockery, Prohibition.[11] Following the lead of Leon Kellner's *American Literature* (1915), which had just been translated from the German into English, Mencken located the problem in the legacy of puritanism, which resulted in the hypertrophy of moral habits and a "delusion of moral infallibility."[12] Mencken's acerbic gaiety found its perfect nemesis in puritanism, and his opposition is comprehensive and absolute: "That deep-seated and uncorrupted puritanism, that conviction of the pervasiveness of sin, of the supreme importance of moral correctness, of the need of savage and inquisitorial laws, has been a dominating force in American life since the very beginning. There has never been any question before the nation, whether political or economic, religious or military, diplomatic or sociological, which did not resolve itself, soon or late, into a purely moral question."[13] (Given the persistent influence of evangelical Christianity in American politics into the twenty-first century, it is not hard to make a case for the continuing relevance of Mencken.)

Another source for Lewis was Van Wyck Brooks. Brooks is not mentioned as one of Carol Kennicott's favored authors, but he was surely one of Lewis's, and the latter might have imbibed a similar critique of American culture from Brooks's earlier *The Wine of the Puritans* (1908), which was followed by *America's Coming-of-Age* (1915). In these two books, especially in the latter, Brooks developed the distinction between what he saw as the two cultures of the United States, which were growing increasingly oppositional: the highbrow (which was spiritual and intellectual) and the lowbrow (which was practical and worldly). As Brooks outlined it in *America's Coming-of-Age*, these two traditions could be traced back to the legacy of puritanism and were peculiarly American, marking the extremes of American culture, which are "not expected to have anything in common."[14] For Brooks, the gulf was wide: "Incompatibility, mutual contempt between theory and practice, is in the very nature of the case."[15] And Brooks stood apart from the mass of Americans and from commercial society in asserting that what was needed was a sense of purpose beyond materialism, in short "an object in living."[16] But Brooks's theory of American culture was not a simple dualism: for lowbrow America needed the spiritual side of the highbrow as much as highbrow America needed the practicality of the lowbrow. Brooks was positing an ideal somewhere in the middle, and the same was true for American personality: from Abraham Lincoln and Ralph Waldo Emerson to John Rockefeller and Woodrow Wilson, Brooks saw "permutations and combinations of these two grand progenitors of the American mind."[17]

Unlike Mencken, Brooks did not see puritanism as the devil's work, exactly, but he did see it as the root of America's peculiar cultural configuration, and this view had a wide following among the young intellectuals of the teens and twenties. From Brooks's theory of the separation of the original whole wine of puritanism into the sediment (the business culture of America) and the aroma (the aesthetic culture), Lewis had taken the underlying framework of cultural analysis in *Main Street,* the division of American culture into highbrow and lowbrow. As Juanita, president of the Jolly Seventeen Club, declares, "Maybe we aren't as highbrow as the Cities, but we do have the daisiest times and—oh, we go swimming in summer, and dances and—oh, lots of good times. If folks will just take us as we are, I think we're a pretty good bunch!" (266). Carol notes early on in the book the opprobrium that attaches to the word *highbrow* when it is uttered by the townsfolk: "Except for half a dozen in each town the citizens are proud of that achievement of ignorance which it is so easy to come by. To be 'intellectual' or 'artistic' or, in their own word, to be 'highbrow,' is to be priggish and of dubious virtue" (122).

The Brooks/Mencken critique of America that Lewis translated into the powerful formulation of *Main Street* first enthralled the East but soon spread to the Midwest, where it reverberated through the small towns and cities that such champions of Middle America as Meredith Nicholson were simultaneously celebrating as the bedrock of American values. Nicholson, a best-selling Indiana writer and journalist, had published *The Valley of Democracy* in 1918, two years before Lewis's *Main Street,* in which he extolled the "spirit of the West" (he meant the Midwest, with Chicago at its core). But he was also respectful of the new writers—Edgar Lee Masters, Vachel Lindsay, Carl Sandburg—along with Willa Cather and Frank Norris, all of whose efforts at realism he applauded: "The West has proved that it is not afraid of its own shadow."[18] Nicholson's progressive outlook is visible wherever he turned his eye: "In every town of the great Valley there are groups of people earnestly engaged in determined efforts to solve governmental problems."[19] Yet Nicholson made no great claims for "culture," at least in the Arnoldian sense, with its emphasis on "things true, things elevated, things just, things pure." On the contrary, he admitted that the "combat with provincialism and the creation of a broad and informed American spirit" was yet to be won in the Midwest.[20]

One might expect that Nicholson would appreciate Lewis's *Main Street* for its realism, and indeed he does, finding that the characters and speech "bite into the consciousness." Yet he is also defensive of the small town and resists Lewis's claim to universal satire. "Nine-tenths of the American towns are so alike that it is the completest boredom to wander from one to another," Lewis had written, giving voice to Carol's confirmed perspective.

> Always, west of Pittsburg [*sic*], and often, east of it, there is the
> same lumber yard, the same railroad station, the same Ford garage,
> the same creamery, the same box-like houses and two-story shops.
> . . . The shops show the same standardized, nationally advertised
> wares; the newspapers of sections three thousand miles apart have
> the same "syndicated features"; the boy in Arkansas displays just
> such a flamboyant ready-made suit as is found on just such a boy
> in Delaware, both of them iterate the same slang phrases from the
> same sporting-pages, and if one of them is in college and the other
> is a barber, no one may surmise which is which. (268)

Nicholson, in contrast, argues that "there are very marked differences between Gopher Prairie and towns of approximately the same size"; Nicholson's diverse small towns possess a "sturdy optimism and unshakable ambition to excel other Main Streets."[21] Moreover, he sees Carol Kennicott as a failure, "a bore, and an unmitigated nuisance."[22] Presuming himself to speak on behalf of the Main Streets of America, Nicholson demands that we leave them alone, do not condescend to them, do not try to uplift or reform them, let them prize their sanitary conditions, regardless of whether they have read Walter Pater.[23]

But if Nicholson urges us to see Gopher Prairie as an aberration from the excellent small towns he is celebrating here, Lewis's satire would have it just the other way around: Gopher Prairie is among the better towns of the Midwest. Carol arrives in her new town with relief, glad that she and her new husband are not getting off the train at any of the barer specimens of midwestern settlement they have passed through; and she learns—during her sojourn in Washington, D.C., at the end of the novel—that her hometown is, relative to some other places, "a model of daring color, clever planning, and frenzied intellectuality. From her teacher-housemate she had a sardonic description of a Middlewestern railroad-division town, of the same size as Gopher Prairie but devoid of lawns and trees, a town where the tracks sprawled along the cinder-scabbed Main Street, and the railroad shops, dripping soot from eaves and doorway, rolled out smoke in greasy coils" (429).[24] Still, small-town pride dies hard, and Carol finds even in Washington the disappointingly familiar types she had also found in her California visit. "Carol recognized in Washington as she had in California a transplanted and guarded Main Street" (426). The émigrés are everywhere Carol goes, in churches, in boardinghouses, in motor processions, theater parties, and state dinners.

Without settling the question of how universal Lewis's portrait of the midwestern small town is, and admitting a wide variety in the species, we might still consider Gopher Prairie an accurate composite portrait, exact enough in its details that readers immediately recognize it as representative of the type. As a composite portrait, it offers us the basis for understanding a culture whose belief system is summed up by Uncle Whittier and Aunt Bessie, who experience, in the person of their niece-in-law, Carol Kennicott, a profound shock to their core convictions:

> They were staggered to learn that a real tangible person, living in Minnesota, and married to their own flesh-and-blood relation, could apparently believe that divorce may not always be immoral; that illegitimate children do not bear any special and guaranteed form of curse; that there are ethical authorities outside of the Hebrew Bible; that men have drunk wine yet not died in the gutter; that the capitalistic system of distribution and the Baptist wedding-ceremony were not known in the Garden of Eden; that mushrooms are as edible as corn-beef hash; that the word "dude" is no longer frequently used; that there are Ministers of the Gospel who accept evolution; that some persons of apparent intelligence and business ability do not always vote the Republican ticket straight; that it is not a universal custom to wear scratchy flannels next the skin in winter; that a violin is not inherently more immoral than a chapel organ; that some poets do not have long hair; and that Jews are not always pedlers or pants-makers. (244–45)

If we seek the source of these beliefs, we would find them in the tyranny of the institutions that shape small-town culture, which Lewis sums up at one point as "Polite Society, the Family, the Church, Sound Business, the Party, the Country, the Superior White Race" (430).

The hegemony of Main Street values that Lewis describes was shaped and reinforced through a multitude of cultural vehicles in small-town America, and we might step back from Gopher Prairie for a moment to survey them briefly. One was the ubiquitous and revered McGuffey Reader, which rivaled the Bible and Webster's dictionary in sales and was the prime vehicle for reading instruction and, consequently, the prime vehicle for moral instruction. As Henry H. Vail's *A History of the McGuffey Readers* (1911) puts it: "The school readers are the proper and indispensable texts for teaching true patriotism, integrity, honesty, industry, temperance, courage, politeness, and all other moral and intellectual virtues. In these books every lesson should have a distinct purpose in view, and the final aim should be to establish in the pupils high moral principles which are at the foundation of character."[25] Bible stories, historical tales, the maxims of sages, the wisdom of folklore, political rhetoric, essays, religious writings, poems and tales of sentiment—all were grist for the educational mill and helped lay the foundation for a body of belief that formed the common narcotic of the American mind going into the twentieth century. William Holmes McGuffey, who had a long and distinguished career as an educator in addition to his role as the creator of the readers, achieved his ultimate canonization when Henry Ford, one of his great admirers, re-created the McGuffey birthplace at Greenfield Village, as part of his tribute to American genius.[26]

Lewis Atherton's *Main Street on the Middle Border* offers a cogent summary of "the McGuffey code," as he calls it: that village and rural life was superior to life in the city; that all things fell within God's "master plan," and accordingly that all things, including evil, happen for the best. The code, promulgated through the McGuffey readings, was reinforced by the two major institutions of small-town life—the church and the school, which combined to celebrate the virtues of self-control; obedience to parents, elders, and teachers; and persistence through difficulties. Meanwhile, throughout, the McGuffey texts stressed the importance of family, at the center of which was the gentle force of Mother.[27]

Yet another force creating the ethos of Main Street was the Chautauqua, a strong presence in midwestern small-town culture circa 1920, and one to which Lewis devotes a chapter in his novel. The Chautauqua movement originated in the 1870s in the eponymous upstate New York summer vacation community that fused Protestant religious inspiration with education and entertainment; later in the century, taking advantage of expanded rail transportation, traveling camp meetings (called Chautauquas) brought the good news of Christian culture to the hinterlands and small towns. (To the extent that the goal of the Chautauquas was self-improvement, they were anticipated by the mid-nineteenth-century lyceum movement, which brought a more secular and commercial education to the small towns and cities of the Northeast and Midwest, in the form of lectures.)[28] The Chautauquas incorporated scientific learning and travel, but the essential dimension of the movement was more religious than secular. And though it eventually developed a somewhat pluralistic conception of American society, accepting Jews and Catholics by 1900, true citizenship was defined largely as a Christian, white, middle-class privilege.[29] How broad the Chautauqua culture was, how liberal, modern, and expansive it became in the twentieth century, are matters of debate.[30] But by the 1920s it had come to seem—to liberal, progressive, urban America—a backwater of conservatism.

And so it seemed to Lewis. Carol greets the arrival of the traveling cultural entertainment, which she imagines to be a kind of university on wheels, with great expectations, but the air slowly goes out of her tires. After attending virtually all the Chautauqua presentations, she realizes her disappointment: "It did not seem to be a tabloid university; it did not seem to be any kind of a university; it seemed to be a combination of vaudeville performance, Y.M.C.A. lecture, and the graduation exercises of an elocution class" (237). Yet there is one bright spot in the Chautauqua, when one of the lecturers, rather than indulge in the customary flattery of the typical circuit speaker, instead offers a critique of land use in Gopher Prairie that voices Carol's own sentiments: "the little man suggested that the architecture of Gopher Prairie was haphazard, and that it was sottish to let the lakefront be monopolized by the cinder-heaped wall of the railroad embankment." The speaker is dismissed by the audience as possibly right but merely a pessimist in the end (238).

In all of this, we might say, Main Street was aspiring toward mediocrity or what would first, in the mid-twenties, become known as middlebrow culture. Yet to examine Carol herself in relation to the culture of Main Street is to realize that Lewis has given us a careful portrait of her dissatisfactions and frustrations, one that affirms her aspirations toward highbrow culture but also shows us how far short she falls of the real Bohemian thing, for by the end of the book she is not uncomfortable with the middling mix of Gopher Prairie. This portrait of Carol begins in Chicago, where she had spent a year studying library science before marrying Will Kennicott, and where she "reveled in the Art Institute, in symphonies and violin recitals and chamber music, in the theater and classic dancing." In addition to this exposure to the institutions of certifiably high culture, Carol dabbles in Chicago Bohemian life—a "Studio Party, with beer, cigarettes, bobbed hair, and a Russian Jewess who sang the Internationale." She hears the conversation about "Freud, Romain Rolland, syndicalism," and so on, yet Lewis makes sure we understand his heroine's limitations: "It cannot be reported that Carol had anything significant to say to the Bohemians." Indeed, she was "shocked by the free manners which she had for years desired" (9–10). Yet "Bohemia," as a concept, the antitype of the small town, haunts Carol in Gopher Prairie, providing a place, partly mythical, that represents all that Main Street is not. At the height of Will's exasperation, as Carol threatens to run off from Gopher Prairie, he casts his wife into this model of Bohemia, reminding her of her obligations to him and to their marriage: "Never thought of that complication, did you, in this 'off to Bohemia, and express yourself, and free love, and live your own life' stuff!" (422).

WHETHER CAROL'S CONSCIOUSNESS is indeed identical to Sinclair Lewis's has been much debated over the years, but the matter is best settled by saying that although Carol's acerbic views surely do originate in Lewis's similar vision of small-town life, Carol is not Lewis, and he clearly stands outside of her, viewing her with an eye that is at times empathetic, at times satiric. We also know that Carol was to some degree modeled on Lewis's first wife, with whom he visited Sauk Centre in 1916 and through whose eyes he saw the place more freshly and more objectively than he could on his own. Perhaps that parallax view of his hometown's Main Street accounts for one of the telling early scenes in the book, when Lewis deliberately plays on the dissonance between two views of Gopher Prairie—one Carol's and the other Bea Sorenson's. Carol and Bea have both arrived on the same train, and as they stroll down Main Street, Lewis offers first Carol's caustic view of its banality and "touching fumble at beauty" (Ye Art Shoppe boasts vases "starting out to imitate tree-trunks but running off into blobs of gilt" [36]), while Bea sees nothing but splendor and luxury, large buildings, a department store, a hotel, and, in the "Art Shoppy," "the dandiest vase made so it looked just like a tree trunk!" (40). To Carol, there is "not one building save the Ionic bank which gave pleasure" (37) to her eyes; to Bea, the excitement is overwhelming—movies, electric lights, motorcars, and amusements to anticipate. Lewis's point is not to satirize the naiveté of Bea Sorenson, who comes from a town with sixty-seven inhabitants; rather, in suddenly taking us away from Carol's view, he offers us a perspective on Main Street that assures us that the author is operating from a lofty perspective, able to see the town for "what it is," but suggesting that what it is depends on who is seeing it.[31]

Where did Carol's perspective come from? Lewis portrays the process by which a spirited girl becomes a social reformer in the first pages of *Main Street*, rooting her transformation in her college experience, where she comes under the influence of an outsider to midwestern culture, her sociology teacher, who had lived "among poets and socialists and Jews and millionaire uplifters at the University Settlement in New York" (3–4). His field trips to the prisons and charities of Minneapolis and St. Paul open Carol's eyes to how the other half lived, and she conceives the desire to read George Bernard Shaw (one of Lewis's own favorite authors). More to the point, she reads a book on "village improvement—tree-planting, town pageants, girls' clubs. It had pictures of greens and garden-walls in France, New England, Pennsylvania. . . . Why should they have all the garden suburbs on Long Island? Nobody has done anything with the ugly towns here in the Northwest except hold revivals and build libraries to contain the Elsie books. I'll make 'em put in a village green, and darling cottages, and a quaint Main Street!" (5). Lured by Will Kennicott's photographs of Gopher Prairie and by her reading on town planning, Carol finds her vocation even before she finds Gopher Prairie.

Lewis's evocation of the progressive culture of "village improvement" affirms a central aspect of the cultural matrix in which Carol's ambitions were formed. For nearly a century before Carol came to Main Street, the villages of New England were being celebrated as models of community and beauty, an ideal that was based on such towns as Concord, Massachusetts, and Litchfield, Connecticut, and that was woven into the essays of Ralph Waldo Emerson and Henry David Thoreau and into the Romantic fiction of Catherine Maria Sedgwick (*A New England Tale*, 1822), Catherine Beecher Stowe (*Poganuc People*, 1878), and Henry Ward Beecher (*Norwood; or Village Life in New England*, 1868). In this collective image, the New England village was constructed as the center of commerce, law, church, society, and culture, a synthesis of town and country, rural virtue and urban amenities. This image of the "center village," powerfully influential as an icon of American place, was not, as Joseph Wood has argued, a feature of the geography of New England in the colonial period, when farms and houses were more dispersed across the landscape, but was rather a fabrication of the nineteenth century, made possible by increas-

Main Street, Sauk Centre, Minnesota, showing the beginnings of the town with wooden buildings, ca. 1880. Minnesota Historical Society.

Main Street, Sauk Centre, Minnesota, with structures now of brick and mixing residential and commercial buildings, ca. 1900–1910. Minnesota Historical Society.

Main Street, Sauk Centre, Minnesota, now more densely commercial, with awnings, automobiles, and electric lights, ca. 1915–25. Minnesota Historical Society.

Main Street, Sauk Centre, Minnesota, featuring a parade and spectators down the dense commercial street, July 4, 1915. Minnesota Historical Society.

ing population density, manufacture, and trade.[32] The ideal was translated into material form through the village improvement movement of the later nineteenth century, which carried over into the twentieth century (and into our own day), and which so strongly impresses Lewis's heroine.[33] Street beautification was a key part of the program, along with the planting of trees, and thus a practice that was urged as early as the writings of landscape architect Andrew Jackson Downing was carried forward into the many local societies that planted the elm tree as the sign and symbol of civility and pastoral urbanism in the New England town.[34] The model moved west, of course, and when Carol passes through Wilmette and Evanston on her way through Illinois, she is newly inspired by her college ambitions: she "discovered new forms of suburban architecture, and remembered her desire to recreate villages. She decided that she would give up library work and, by a miracle whose nature was not very clearly revealed to her, turn a prairie town into Georgian houses and Japanese bungalows" (10). But these ambitions are dormant as Carol pursues her brief career as a librarian, only to be awakened fully when she moves to Gopher Prairie.

Carol's desire for change remains strong, but never quite progresses beyond the chrysalis stage. Looking at magazine pictures of house decorations one day, she is charmed by the New England towns—Falmouth, Concord, Stockbridge—and once more by the "fairy-book suburb of Forest Hills on Long Island" (130), the latter an early example of new town planning in the United States. Her dreams take shape:

> She saw in Gopher Prairie a Georgian city hall: warm brick walls with white shutters, a fanlight, a wide hall and curving stair. She saw it [as] the common home and inspiration not only of the town but of the country about. It should contain the court-room (she couldn't get herself to put in a jail), public library, a collection of excellent prints, rest-room and model kitchen for farmwives, theater, lecture room, free community ballroom, farm-bureau, gymnasium. Forming about it and influenced by it, as mediæval villages gathered about the castle, she saw a new Georgian town as graceful and beloved as Annapolis or that bowery Alexandria to which Washington rode. (131)

But the Thanatopsis Society is unequal to the demands Carol would place on it, and these images of a high civilization in the Midwest remain dreams. The ideal, as *Main Street* shows, is unattainable, given Lewis's realism, and we are left not with the solution but instead with an understanding of the problem, in all its complexity.

Lewis allows the accumulation of discontent, alienation, and disillusionment that Carol feels in Gopher Prairie to drive her ultimately to escape to the East, which can only seem, to a midwesterner, to be the origin and epitome of "culture." This last movement of *Main Street* imitates the typical denouement of the "revolt from the village" plot in the early decades of the twentieth century, where the hero or heroine, a misfit in the small town by virtue of his or her artistic inclinations and sense of difference, escapes to the happiness of the eastern city, usually New York. Lewis revises the convention, however. In Washington, D.C., to which Carol moves, leaving her husband behind, she finds herself in the thick of a political society that is nothing if not cosmopolitan and where, yet again—note Lewis's careful calibrations—she feels somewhat out of place. She is too old to pass as a brilliant young "new woman" and too conventional, try as she might, to pass as a "defiant philosopher." She is, rather, "a faded government clerk from Gopher Prairie, Minnesota" (431). When Will visits her in Washington, he brings photographs from home, just as, before their marriage, he had lured her to Gopher Prairie through photographs. In this second virtual seduction, the images show Carol "the sun-speckled ferns among birches on the shore of Minniemashie, wind-rippled miles of wheat, the porch of their own house where Hugh had played, Main Street where she knew every window and every face" (435). The familiar becomes irresistible, and Carol succumbs once more to the idea of Main Street, an idealized image yet one that is, thanks to her immersion in the community, now significantly edged with realism.

IN RETURNING CAROL to Gopher Prairie, Lewis forces a resolution to the story of his heroine's rebellion which is, for her, neither defeat nor victory: her experience of the political culture of the capital, where people will risk jail to demonstrate for their beliefs, has emboldened her against the Grundified culture of Main Street.[35] She may even have the temerity to invite the town radicals to dinner, though Lewis is careful to insinuate a measure of doubt ("I could invite a Miles Bjornstam to dinner without being afraid of the Haydocks. . . . I think I could" [442]). But it is not simply her resistance that has been strengthened; it is also her tolerance for what she had previously despised—a "toiling new settlement" with "pretty good folks, working hard and trying to bring up their families the best they can. . . . I've come to a fairer attitude toward the town. I can love it, now" (442).

Readers of *Main Street* debated the meaning of this ending, and with good reason. Did Carol's return to Gopher Prairie—even loving it, to a degree—show us a character who had matured, or one who was defeated? Had she achieved a measure of sagacity, or was she simply a fool and the object of Lewis's satire, accepting the drearily unacceptable?[36] Distancing herself from those who create the myth of the perfect small town, she still appreciates, for better and for worse, the sense of community: "After a week she decided that she was neither glad nor sorry to be back. She entered each day with the matter-of-fact attitude with which she had gone to her office in Washington. It was her task; there would be mechanical details and meaningless talk; what of it?" (444).

In Carol's carefully constructed equivocation is the measure of Lewis's own ambivalence toward Main Street.

One way to get behind the facade of Main Street that bears the brunt of Lewis's satire is to examine the issue of heroism and the small town—a conjunction that appears at first highly unlikely. Yet Lewis portrays Gopher Prairie as a place where seriously purposeful lives are led, lives that approach the heroic. Will Kennicott's as a country doctor is one such heroic life, at least as seen by Carol (and remember that Lewis's own father, grandfather, and brother were doctors): while she sleeps comfortably in bed, in the middle of a frigid night, Will leaves the house: "He went out, hungry, chilly, unprotesting; and she, before she fell asleep again, loved him for his sturdiness, and saw the drama of his riding by night to the frightened household on the distant farm; pictured children standing at a window, waiting for him. He suddenly had in her eyes the heroism of a wireless operator on a ship in a collision; of an explorer, fever-clawed, deserted by his bearers, but going on—jungle—going" (177). Carol romanticizes Will's heroism, which is to say that Lewis "corrects" Carol's impulse to romanticize by exaggerating her view of heroism, but it is there, as an icon, nevertheless. Another personification of small-town romance is the night telegraph operator, who, along with the conductors, is part of the high adventure of the railroad that comes through the town: "The night telegraph-operator at the railroad station was the most melodramatic figure in town: awake at three in the morning, alone in a room hectic with clatter of the telegraph key. All night he 'talked' to operators twenty, fifty, a hundred miles away. It was always to be expected that he would be held up by robbers. He never was, but round him was a suggestion of masked faces at the window, revolvers, cords binding him to a chair, his struggle to crawl to the key before he fainted" (235). To Carol, the train engineers, "scratching frost from the cab windows and looking out," are likewise figures of romance: "inscrutable, self-contained, pilots of the prairie sea—they were heroism, they were to Carol the daring of the quest in a world of groceries and sermons" (236).

These are examples, one might say, of the heroism of the commonplace, and Lewis celebrates it, yet not without a touch of irony toward Carol and her romantic vision. Lewis is responding, in *Main Street*, to a question that had vexed critics of American culture for at least two decades: What had been gained and what had been lost in a culture that had become progressively and complacently middle-class, a culture in which the ideals of Chautauqua seemed to be the only ideals? William James, in an 1899 essay called "What Is the Significance of Life?," reflected precisely on a visit to Chautauqua that he had found entrancing, seeing in the place a kind of cultural utopia, a beautifully laid-out town, filled with music, sport, and religious services, "perpetually running soda-water fountains, and daily popular lectures by distinguished men," and the utter absence of poverty, crime, and drunkenness.[37] What is missing from it, James realizes on reflection, is, well, everything—the whole outer world of human drama, savagery, primordial energy, sin, suffering, and heroism, "of strength and strenuousness, intensity and danger."[38] The whole world, he fears, is coming to resemble "a mere Chautauqua Assembly on an enormous scale."[39] Then, looking out the windows of a speeding train, he sees what he had missed, the heroism that is evident in the lives of the laboring classes—who are constructing bridges and buildings, working on freight trains and ships, in cattle yards and mines, or as day laborers and policemen. "The common life of common men," he realizes, possesses the unconscious virtue that he has been looking for.[40]

James's essay, for all its self-consciousness and worldly scope, cannot escape a certain romanticizing of the heroic laborer. Lewis puts these romantic sentiments into Carol's perceptions, making the same point—but then takes us inside the scene of labor, letting us see that the worker's life may seem "heroic" from the perspective of a comfortable winter bed or a speeding train but is for the laborer a daily and unrelenting grind. Persistence makes the heroism of the commonplace, a point Lewis drives home unambiguously in a chapter toward the end of the book, when Carol receives the wise counsel of her Washington friend, the suffragette, with

The Great Northern Railroad Depot, Sauk Centre, Minnesota, ca. 1900. The depot figures in many small-town novels of the period as the point of entry into and escape from the small town. Minnesota Historical Society.

whom she is working to effect social change, and who explains the nature of heroism and self-sacrifice, pointing out that the conquerors must not conquer, or their success will ruin themselves and gain the contempt and suspicion of the people they want to help. Instead, she offers a terse, commonsense view: "Not a matter of heroism. Matter of endurance. . . . There's one attack you can make on it, perhaps the only kind that accomplishes much anywhere: you can keep on looking at one thing after another in your home and church and bank, and ask why it is, and who first laid down the law that it had to be that way. If enough of us do this impolitely enough, then we'll become civilized in merely twenty thousand years or so, instead of having to wait the two hundred thousand years that my cynical anthropologist friends allow" (441). Going back to Gopher Prairie is Carol's act of "endurance," and asking questions is, for Lewis, all that one can do.[41] Lewis ends *Main Street* on just that note of endurance amid the banality of everyday life that is the common lot, even of heroes. "I may not have fought the good fight, but I have kept the faith," Carol tells her husband, to which he replies, "Sure. You bet you have. . . .

Well, good night. Sort of feels to me like it might snow tomorrow. Have to be thinking about putting up the storm-windows pretty soon. Say, did you notice whether the girl put that screwdriver back?" (451).

WE MIGHT BE LULLED into thinking that the small town is a static entity, a cocoon into which Carol returns, an unchanging place, for better or worse, of persistent values: "A savorless people, gulping tasteless food, and sitting afterward, coatless and thoughtless, in rocking chairs prickly with inane decorations, listening to mechanical music, saying mechanical things about the excellence of Ford automobiles, and viewing themselves as the greatest race in the world" (265). But that would be only part of the story Lewis tells, for the town acts as a reagent on its inhabitants, an especially effective and harsh one for the foreigners who enter its orbit, in particular the first-generation Scandinavians. In the process, the novelty and richness of the Norse culture—the farmhouses, folk costumes, and foods—are gradually erased. Carol "saw these Scandinavian women zealously exchanging their spiced puddings and red jackets for fried pork chops and congealed white blouses, trading the ancient Christmas hymns of the fjords for 'She's My Jazzland Cutie,' being Americanized into uniformity, and in less than a generation losing in the grayness whatever pleasant new customs they might have added to the life of the town" (265–66). Dreiser would make such characters, coming with excitement to the town, the center of his own interest, and portray their lives—given the tragic mode of his work—as ending in catastrophe, as he does in the 1926 tale, "Typhoon," in which the teenage Ida, daughter of German immigrants, succumbs innocently to the allure of a young man of dubious integrity. Her susceptibility to him is conditioned by the dreamlike consumer's world she inhabits: "She lived in a mental world," Dreiser writes, "made up of the bright lights of Warren Avenue which traversed the great mill district known as Kensington. The cars, the moving picture theaters of which there were three matinees within a mile of each other on this great commonplace thoroughfare, with its street cars and endless stores side by side. The movies and her favorite photographs of actresses and actors (some of the mannerisms of whom the girls imitated at school)."[42]

But the town itself is part of a larger process of change, subject to the dynamic forces of culture that are sweeping down Main Street. For Gopher Prairie, as Lewis sees it, is firmly in the grip of the twentieth-century consumer age and thinks only of "kodaks, phonographs, leather-upholstered

Morris chairs, bridge-prizes, oil-stocks, motion-pictures, land-deals, unread sets of Mark Twain, and a chaster version of national politics" (264). We can see behind this process the even larger process of modernization, by which the habits, sensibility, and entire sensorium of the American are transformed under the pressure of a commodity-based civilization that sells things, dreams, and idols all at once. Thorstein Veblen, himself born in the Midwest of Norwegian immigrant parents, described the broader relationship between the small town and the ineluctable forces of capitalism in his 1923 book *Absentee Ownership and Business Enterprise in Recent Times: The Case of America*. In it he inveighs against the machinations of big business: "In a way the country towns have in an appreciable degree fallen into the position of toll-gate keepers for the distribution of goods and collection of customs for the large absentee owners of the business. Grocers, hardware dealers, meat-markets, druggists, shoe-shops, are more and more extensively falling into the position of local distributors for jobbing houses and manufacturers."[43] In the interlocking consumer economy of the twenties, the farmer is in debt to the town merchants, and the merchants are in debt to the national manufacturers.

THE ECONOMIC STRUGGLE for the soul of the consumer that was taking place on Main Street was paralleled by a political struggle, which is the focus of Sinclair Lewis's own retrospective on *Main Street*, from the perspective of the 1924 presidential elections (a three-way contest, with Republican Calvin Coolidge vs. Democrat John W. Davis vs. Progressive Robert La Follette), in a piece written for *The Nation*. Pretending to revisit Gopher Prairie after an absence of ten years (though only four had passed since the novel's publication), Lewis encounters several of his major characters—Dr. Kennicott, Carol, and Guy Pollock. Carol, interestingly, is marginalized in this new report. She is seen here as tired, timid, and oddly childish, as if Lewis is no longer interested in her as a character; yet he does show Carol as still keeping faith with highbrow, or at least middlebrow culture. What does Lewis think is the "dernier cri" right now? she asks. "Was it Marcel Proust or James Joyce or 'So Big' by Edna Ferber?"[44] Dr. Kennicott, however, receives most of Lewis's attention, perhaps because he wants to understand the mentality of the midwestern conservative Republican, the quintessential Coolidge supporter. In fact, Will Kennicott comes alive in this narrative, evincing a more aggressively intelligent mentality than anything we saw in *Main Street*: calling Lewis a "limousine socialist," Dr. Kennicott teases the author mercilessly, repeatedly puncturing his "highbrow" pretensions—assuming that Lewis would want the good doctor to make his house calls on foot rather than in his Buick coupe, noting the affectionate first-name relationship "all you hoboes and authors and highbrows" have with Gene Debs, and so on.[45] As to La Follette, Dr. Kennicott is respectful but suspicious of his activist mentality, preferring the passivity of Coolidge as a safer bet, given the volatility of the world and generally celebrating Coolidge as a man who "can pull the wool over everybody's eyes."[46] Opposing Dr. Kennicott, in Lewis's political jeu d'esprit, is Guy Pollock, who is supporting La Follette and is tired of being bullied by the Doc Kennicotts.

Most significant, Lewis's return to *Main Street* affords him the opportunity to draw clearly the connecting lines between the consumption culture of Gopher Prairie and its political culture. Many improvements to the town are immediately visible to the returning author—the lawns are improved; stucco coating has been put over some of the larger clapboard houses; a new "Commercial and Progress Club" has been erected, with a banquet room and pool hall; a new train station has a flower-bordered park; and Main Street has new cement pavement (for three blocks) and electric lights. But the prosperity of Gopher Prairie has solidified its conservative politics. Wealth has not brought a more liberal culture but a more conservative one. From Dr. Kennicott's point of view, the supporters of the progressive La Follette fall into the three categories: There are, first, "a lot of crank farmers that because they don't want to work and keep their silos filled want to make up for it by some one who, they hope, will raise the price of wheat enough so they can get by without tending to business!" Second, there are enthusiasts of any "crazy movement," and third, there are city workmen "that think if some crank comes into office they'll all become federal employees and able to quit working."[47] In short, the class divisions of Gopher Prairie seem more entrenched than ever, with increasing prosperity, and the division between conservative and progressive forces has grown even sharper. From the conservative perspective, Lewis's highbrow culture is the sign of socialism, Greenwich Village, experimental literature, and other Bohemian aberrations. With democratic pride, Dr. Kennicott celebrates the assimilation of the farmers' immigrant children into the new mass culture of clothing, hairstyles, movies, and radio. Meanwhile, from Guy Pollock's perspective—as town intellectual—Gopher Prairie has become, with increasing prosperity, both more conservative and less interesting: "There's more talk, about automobiles and the radio, but there's less conversation, less people who are interested in scandals, politics, abstractions, gallantries, smut, or anything else save their new A batteries. . . . They sing of four-wheel brakes as the Persian poets sang of rose leaves."[48]

The extraordinary celebrity of Lewis's novel of 1920 transformed the original of Gopher Prairie—Sauk Center, Minnesota—in the succeeding decades, into a place of major symbolic significance: given its exhaustive anatomical exposure, and given its geographically representative quality as a midwestern town, an emblem of the heartlands, it became a barometer of American culture, a way of measuring where the country had come from, where it was presently, and where it might be going. It seems only natural that *Life* magazine should offer its readers, following the conclusion of World War II, a profile of Main Street, U.S.A., dominated by the question of how Sauk Centre had changed in relation to its own prior history and in relation to the changing world brought about by the cataclysmic war. The author of the piece, "Main Street 1947," was Henry Anatole Grunwald, twenty-five years old at the time, but on his way to becoming the managing editor of *Time* magazine and the editor in chief of all of *Time*'s publications. The son of an Austrian playwright who had emigrated to the United States during Hitler's Anschluss, Grunwald would become U.S. ambassador to Austria in his later years. Not surprisingly, given the trajectory of Grunwald's career, his essay on *Main Street* makes the most of the opportunity, turning Sauk Centre into a microcosm of postwar American society.

As the emblematic small town, Sauk Centre represents, for Grunwald, America itself—"the most powerful country on earth, the only really powerful defender of the democratic faith." The rest of the world, he argues, now depends on the United States, and so Lewis's foundational irony ("Main Street is the climax of civilization") becomes, for Grunwald in 1947, "close to simple truth."[49] And Main Street itself, as Grunwald discovers, realizes that isolationism is dead, that war-torn Europe and Asia are the necessary concerns of the United States. Outwardly, Grunwald discovers much that is consistent with Lewis's Gopher Prairie and some things that have changed—new civic buildings, new materials, new commercial signs. Continuing the process that Lewis had observed in its infancy, Sauk Centre is more and more a consumer's world, with outside products—"bottles, cans, movies, books, motorcars, philosophies and radio programs"—now brought into the town, transforming the local into the national.[50] In other respects, however, Sauk Centre in 1947 is still Gopher Prairie circa 1920—most notably in the gendered divisions of society (not noted by Grunwald but visible in the photographs accompanying the article), with the males governing the business world and the women the world of "culture." More depressing, Grunwald notes the narrow-mindedness of the high school youth, shockingly ignorant, pathetically complacent. Still, what Grunwald finds most healthy and hopeful about the town in 1947 is its self-doubt, embodied in the town "radical," a New Deal Democrat (rare in the Republican town) who also happens to be president of the Bankers' Association and a voracious reader. Grunwald concludes by celebrating Sauk Centre, in all its contradictions, as an emblem of the open society, with productive farmlands, comfortable homes, and "a stupendous lack of fear."[51] Looking at it from outside, "the world would realize that while Sauk Centre is neither well-informed nor articulate about this business of Western civilization, it is, by virtue of its freedom, an inextricable and priceless part of it."[52]

Lewis himself looked back on Sauk Centre frequently over the course of his career, returning there to visit family and friends and to conduct research for later novels. Asked to contribute to a high school annual in 1931, he wrote "The Long Arm of the Small Town," a memoir looking back with fondness at his boyhood and filled with sentiment to the same degree that *Main Street* had been filled with satire. By then, Lewis was feeling somewhat apologetic to his hometown for the severity of his criticism and was, moreover, beginning to receive the accolades that had not been part of his growing up in Sauk Centre. Leaving aside his excoriating satire, he wrote, in a 1931 reminiscence, "I am quite certain that I could have been born and reared in no place in the world where I would have had more friendliness." Thinking of the swimming and fishing in Sauk Lake, the picnicking and hunting in the area, recalling the fun of stealing melons, Lewis—now turned Tom Sawyer—looked back on his childhood small town with a nostalgia that erased all negativity. He concluded, "It was a good time, a good place, and a good preparation for life."[53] Granted, Lewis was always ambivalent about the town, an ambivalence reflected in the conclusion of *Main Street*; but his frank nostalgia in 1931 captures what would become a pervasive mood of the 1930s and 1940s—and the subject of my next chapter—when Main Street, in a dramatic reversal of symbolic meaning, began to acquire a new magical glow, replacing the jaundice of the village virus.

Even as the dust was settling on Sinclair Lewis's demolition of Gopher
Prairie, the author was moving on to a critique of the small city, the Zenith
of his 1922 novel, *Babbitt*. Now it was not the dullness of the small town that
provoked Lewis; it was the very effort to move it forward under the sign
of "progress." Businessman Vergil Gunch of Zenith offers this uplifting
summary of the small town's effort to raise itself, literally, out of the mud:
instead of wooden sidewalks, "you find pavements and you don't want to
just look at what these small towns are, you want to look at what they're
aiming to become, and they all got an ambition that in the long run is
going to make 'em the finest spots on earth."[1] As for Zenith, like many small
cities in the United States, it was rapidly embodying "modern ideals," visible in such places as the fourteen-story Reeves Building, the downtown
location of Babbitt's real estate business: "The entrance was too modern to be flamboyant with pillars; it was quiet, shrewd, neat. Along the
Third Street side were a Western Union Telegraph Office, the Blue Delft
Candy Shop, Shotwell's Stationery Shop, and the Babbitt-Thompson Realty
Company."[2]

Babbitt was a harbinger of things to come, for the small town was
changing dramatically during the late twenties and thirties as the winds
of modernization blew through it. In the face of these changes, for the
America of the thirties and forties, fundamental questions were being
posed and gradually answered within the discourses of intellectual and
popular culture: Could the innocence of the small town be preserved, and
was it even worth preserving? What, after all, did the innocence of small-
town America represent in a culture committed irrevocably to the machine and mass media? (See Plate 4.)

Consider first the actual town: the process of modernization that Lewis
describes in early twenties Zenith continued well into the thirties, with
downtown Main Streets across the United States being updated, their

storefronts modernized. If the most basic needs of the small town were satisfied by the grocery, the drugstore, the clothing store, and the gas station, its miscellaneous needs were met increasingly after the turn of the century by variety stores. The most successful were those operated by the national chains in the larger towns and small cities—F. W. Woolworth, Kresge's, Newberry's, McCrory's—which brought with them modern techniques of marketing and advertising, including their regularly updated facades. The art deco influence that could be seen in the twenties and early thirties was giving way to a broadly used stylistic vocabulary associated with streamline design, which was changing the appearance of everything from vacuum cleaners to automobiles. And just as industrial designers were streamlining their products to increase sales in the face of the Great Depression, architects were changing the storefronts of the shops along Main Street, covering the older Victorian brick structures with newer contemporary materials like plate glass, steel, aluminum, and glass blocks. And again, it was the chain stores that were better able to afford to make these changes, thus putting even more pressure on the struggling local merchants. Though the federal government was not directly effecting these changes, it was encouraging them, as Gabrielle Esperdy has argued, through the 1934 National Housing Act, which created the Federal Housing Authority, which in turn—under a Modernize Main Street campaign—insured lenders against loss from modernization projects for both residential and nonresidential properties. In short, Main Street during the Depression, despite the struggles of merchants to survive, was casting itself as forward looking, with the high turnover of merchants signaling persistent failures but also persistent renewal and optimism.[3]

As long as the country seemed to be living under the sign of success—a level of prosperity that guaranteed the bland Calvin Coolidge's popularity—there seemed to be no looking back. Indeed, by 1925 the Progressive fever of the previous decade seemed to have burned out, and Main Street, far from being suspicious of big business, identified its own interests with Wall Street's.[4] The *Saturday Evening Post*, which catered to a Main Street readership, celebrated the rising cultural level of the small town in a 1931 editorial: "The average man of Main Street reads magazines and books, drives a car, has an opportunity to keep in touch with world progress, and so sees and hears more in a fortnight than his ancestors did in a lifetime."[5] In other ways, too, there were visible signs of change: by the mid-thirties, many small towns were becoming the beneficiaries of the Roosevelt administration's New Deal programs, such as the Federal Arts Projects

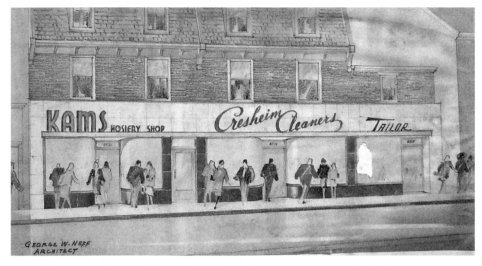

Germantown Avenue, Chestnut Hill, Pennsylvania, ca. 1940, a typical effort to modernize Main Street during the late 1930s, in the newest streamlined Art Moderne style. Chestnut Hill Historical Society.

that installed painted murals in public buildings across the country and developed community arts centers and music and theater programs. The cultural stock of the small town, reviled in the early twenties, was looking better and better a decade later.

Another agent of change, rolling through the small town like a juggernaut, was the automobile. For farmers, it meant getting to the town or to nearby cities in less time than it might have taken to drive the horse and buggy to the nearest crossroads. But the auto ran in two directions—taking people away from the town and bringing others into it. As author R. L. Duffus put it, reflecting on the small town in a 1938 book, *America Now,* "The town is no longer self-contained. Invention and change have let the inhabitants out, the outer world in." All of these changes, part of the larger modernization of Main Street, had palpable consequences, in many cases changing the traditional character of the small town, entailing loss as well as gain. Of his own Vermont town, Duffus wrote, "As a community, economic or social, my old home has lost much of its significance."[6]

Yet even as it was undergoing these changes, the American small town during the 1930s was gaining a larger symbolic dimension, a crucial function in the moral and spiritual economy of the Depression, reversing the stigma that Sinclair Lewis and others had attached to the small town. Admitting the pettiness and meanness of the small town (and the legitimacy of the critiques of the 1920s), Duffus maintained that its enduring appeal would be its offer of stability and intimacy, as against the impersonality of the city. He prophesied that the small town would continue to exist "because it meets a spiritual, a cultural, or if one likes, a psychological need."[7] It was, he concluded, "a reservoir from which creative energy can be drawn."[8] Written in the midst of the Great Depression, when disintegrating forces were pervasive, Duffus's affirmation of sanity on Main Street confirmed sentiments that were ubiquitous in late thirties and forties culture and that picked up on the binary opposition between city and small town that had been given its first authoritative expression by German sociologist Georg Simmel in 1903.[9]

THE CLEAR REVERSAL of polarity among intellectuals from the twenties to the thirties can be explained, as I have suggested, largely by the salient fact that dominated the latter decade: the Great Depression. With the stock market crash of 1929, the Hoover years brought profound uncertainty about the future, eventuating in the election of Franklin Delano Roosevelt in 1932. The drought in the Great Plains regions in the early thirties only made things worse, putting one out of five farmers on relief by 1937. With the economy running on empty, with bread lines in the cities, and with the mass exodus of farmers from the Dust Bowl, the very idea of America, let alone the reality, seemed in peril. It is in this context that we must understand the construction of the small town as an icon of American democracy, yet an icon that contained within it this paradox: During the very period that many actual small towns were undergoing an irreversible modernization, the idea of the small town was taking on a new aura, revered for its tradition and insulation from the onrushing changes of modern life, idealized as the foundation of stability and the unchanging values that made "America" what it was. In effect the small town became, as poet Robert Pinsky suggests, a version of pastoral, and he invokes William Empson's insight "that the need to invent untroubled perfection always springs from anxiety," and that it "may be a denial of the nightmare, and therefore by implication a shadowy acknowledgment of it."[10] The nightmare was, of course, the Great Depression that was destroying the material and social foundations of American life.

But if the small town was imagined as a paradise lost during the thirties, it was also a paradise that might somehow be repossessed. During this decade, running into the forties, the small town took on its mythical dimensions in American culture, and this strongly positive image would then provide the foundation for the popular image of Main Street that emerged after the Depression and World War II.

THE THIRTIES IDEALIZATION of the small town was evident across American culture—from mainstream journalism to literature to film—but was most notably obvious in the visual culture of mainstream America. One of the main sources of this positive image was the vast archive of still photographs—160,000 black and white plus some 1,600 in color—produced by the Farm Security Administration (FSA) from 1935 to 1943, an archive that became gradually visible in newspapers, magazines, books, and exhibitions. Funded as part of Rexford Tugwell's Department of Agriculture, the FSA contained within it a remarkable group of documentary photographers (including Walker Evans and Dorothea Lange, among others) who were directed by Roy Stryker. Stryker took it on himself to interpret the pictorial mission of the FSA broadly, seizing the opportunity not only to represent the ongoing programs of the Resettlement Administration (as the FSA was first called) but also to compile a visual encyclopedia of American life, from the rural farm to the city, from the field to the factory, from Maine to Alabama to California to Oregon. Photographers captured people going to the movies or going to church; in school or waiting for a bus; sitting in their makeshift tents, in their homes, or on their porches; or simply strolling on Main Street. (See Plate 3.)

The main focus of the FSA photographers during the first year or two of the project was rural poverty, for the initiative's ostensible rationale was to provide a propaganda base for the agricultural policies of the Roosevelt administration—spreading knowledge about farming conditions in one part of the country to voters in other parts of the country. Only by expanding the range of information and sympathy to something like a national consensus, it was believed, would the reform policies of the Roosevelt administration win popular and political support. Most of these early images, emphasizing farm life and rural conditions, show drought, soil erosion, and Dust Bowl sandstorms, conditions that were forcing so many off the land and onto the roads west. The farmers are depicted as confused and impoverished, eking out a living amid impossible surroundings—hence the need for the government to assist them through resettlement programs and farm support. To the extent that small towns are pictured, they are places of desolation, backwaters of idleness. Archibald MacLeish's Land of the Free (1938)—the first photo-documentary book to make extensive use of the FSA collection—has but one image of a small

Photograph by Dorothea Lange, "Main street during 1936 drought. Sallisaw, Sequoyah County, Oklahoma" (FSA caption). From Archibald MacLeish, Land of the Free (1938). Library of Congress, Prints and Photographs Division, FSA-OWI Collection.

town, a Dorothea Lange photograph captioned "Main street of Sallisaw, Oklahoma, during the 1936 drought: the farmers in town on the sidewalk." The long view shows a street crowded with farmers, some of whom are walking, with many others leaning idly or squatting against storefronts.[11]

A very different image of the small town, much more positive, emerges in the work of the other FSA photographers—Walker Evans, Russell Lee, Ben Shahn, Marion Post Wolcott, and John Vachon—and especially in the volume by Sherwood Anderson that climaxes the FSA representation of Main Street—*Home Town.* This more positive representation reflects Roy Stryker's growing sense of the ideological and political importance of the small town, as well as the core emotions that colored his attitude. To Stryker, the small town was "the cross-roads where the land meets the city, where the farm meets commerce and industry. It is the contact point where men of the land keep in touch with a civilization based on mass-produced, city-made gadgets, machines, canned movies and canned beef."[12]

Stryker, who came from a small town in Colorado, loved Main Street, but one can hear a slight uneasiness slipping into this characterization: Was all this canned beef a good thing? Would the values of the town hold against the encroachments of mass society? These were the issues at stake for Stryker, as they were for Robert Lynd, the coauthor of the acclaimed *Middletown* (1929), who met with Stryker in 1936, soon after completing the sequel, *Middletown in Transition*, which appeared in 1937.[13] Lynd, concerned about what he perceived as the erosion of the home and family in the face of the automobile, radio, movies, and the other signs of a changing culture, saw the small towns represented in the FSA file as a possible antidote. Stryker, responding to Lynd's narrative, imagined a representation of small-town America that would show these traditional values—home, family, community—as still intact in the small town. The result was a memo urging the dozen or so photographers in Stryker's team to incorporate the small town into their work on a regular basis, and inviting them to carry with them at all times, or better yet keep in their heads, a "permanent small-town shooting-script." Stryker was in the habit of giving his photographers a list of possible subjects to cover when they went into particular areas on assignment, and for the small town, the list included places and people that would visually affirm the values and sentiments Stryker held dear: "Stores, theaters, garages, barber shops, town hall, jail, firehouse. . . . Men loafing and talking. Women waiting for the men, coming out of stores, window shopping, tending children. . . . The church, the cemetery, the railroad station, bus terminal." All of these subjects are visible in the FSA archive, yet with vast differences among the various towns depicted, for as Stryker recognized, there were inevitably regional differences to be observed. Still, it was the common character that Stryker was ultimately after, and he felt sure that the images gathered would "accentuate the similarities of a national rather than a regional character."[14]

Underlying Stryker's attitude toward the small town was the need for a sense of rooted order and tradition that would serve as an anchor in the storms of Washington and the Depression. Reflecting in later life on the meaning of these images, Stryker said, "Through the pictures the small town emerged as a thing possessing emotional and aesthetic advantages: kinship with nature and the seasons, neighborliness, kindliness, spaciousness—plus some certain disadvantages: laziness, pompousness, narrow-

Photograph by Walker Evans, Main Street, Macon, Georgia, 1936. Library of Congress, Prints and Photographs Division, FSA-OWI Collection.

ness, lack of economic and cultural freedom." One image struck a particular chord for Stryker, Walker Evans's photograph of a train depot in Edwards, Mississippi, taken from above the scene, looking down onto the tracks, which are framed on either side by the station buildings. On the right, a small group is in conversation; on the left, a few cars are parked. For Stryker, it was an evocative scene: "The empty station platform, the station thermometer, the idle baggage carts, the quiet stores, the people talking together, and beyond them, the weatherbeaten houses where they lived, all this reminded me of the town where I had grown up. I would look at pictures like that and long for a time when the world was safer and more peaceful. I'd think back to the days before radio and television when all there was to do was go down to the tracks and watch the flyer go through. That was the nostalgic way in which those town pictures hit me."[15]

Stryker's nostalgia is in the same key as Evans's own feeling for the small-town past, not only in the photographs that so impressed themselves on Stryker's mind, but elsewhere as well. In 1948, Evans published an article in *Fortune*, "Main Street Looking North from Courthouse Square," that featured a portfolio of anonymous picture postcards "from the trolley-

Photograph by Walker Evans, view of the railroad station, Edwards, Mississippi, 1936. From Sherwood Anderson, Home Town (1940). Library of Congress, Prints and Photographs Division, FSA-OWI Collection.

era." Though making the obligatory connection between postcard collections and investment for *Fortune* readers, Evans is at bottom evoking the same innocence that had appealed to Stryker, though with a harder edge of irony: "The mood is quiet, innocent, and honest beyond words. This, faithfully, is the way East Main Street looked on a midweek summer afternoon. This is how the country courthouse rose from the pavement in sharp, endearing ugliness."[16] What had been an insufferable ugliness for Carol Kennicott in *Main Street* has now become something endearing, something to hold on to. Indeed, these images of Main Street—which the photographer collected by the hundreds in his immense collection of postcards from the first two decades of the twentieth century—shaped Evans's own head-on, direct depiction of the material constructions of small-town America, in a mode he called "lyric documentary."[17] And though he often self-consciously denied any nostalgic sentiment regarding these images, Evans clearly found them evocative of a time that was otherwise lost, preserved only in these naive views, a product of industrial folk culture.

Evans himself had included three images of small towns in his 1938

Photograph by Walker Evans, county seat of Hale County, Alabama, 1935 or 1936. From Sherwood Anderson, Home Town (1940). Library of Congress, Prints and Photographs Division, FSA-OWI Collection.

American Photographs, placed at the center of part 1. Coming after images portraying the extremes of the urban bourgeoisie and rural indigents, these portrayals of the small town have a normative quality, though they are quite different from one another and in effect offer three versions of Main Street, America: the first shows the Main Street of the county seat of Hale County, Alabama, an active town in a rural farming region on a sunny day; the second, portraying the more upscale resort town of Saratoga Springs, New York, is a carefully composed diagonal shot of a deserted Main Street with wide sidewalks in the rain and elegant bare trees; the third offers a long view down a western Pennsylvania Main Street, mostly deserted, with a prominent statue of a soldier from the Great War (World War I) standing on a pedestal at the crossroads. Presented one after the other, these three dissimilar Main Streets underline the regional variety and particularity of the American scene, yet together they capture a sense of the town's central place in the country's social and cultural economy.

Russell Lee's 1940 photographs of a small town in New Mexico, Pie

Town, have a far more deliberate and consistent ideological cast. Taken at Stryker's behest, Lee's Pie Town photographs were meant to portray the persistence into the present of the virtues that defined the American West, the frontier virtues of individualism and self-reliance, as described by historian Frederick Jackson Turner in his famous 1893 essay "The Significance of the Frontier in American History."[18] Turner himself was drawing on John Peck's *New Guide to the West* (1837), which outlined the stages of civilization, beginning with the pioneer who breaks the new land, builds log houses, practices the rudiments of agriculture, and then moves on when the settlers come in behind him; the settlers in turn purchase land, clear roads, construct bridges, and build mills and schoolhouses; and they are followed by a third wave of settlers who bring in even greater refinements and a wider range of occupations. Pie Town, according to this phylogenesis, is in the second stage, yet with some remnants of the first still visible in the woodsmen and log cabins still being built.

Lee's Pie Town images were published in *U.S. Camera* in a 1941 article addressed in part to professionals interested in the process of making pictures in the field and constructing stories. Yet where Turner had declared the frontier "closed," Lee's camera was showing that it was still open, that the historical process of frontier settlement that had begun three hundred years earlier was still going on. Thus nearly a third of the images show the people's relationship to the land—their logging, woodcutting, rudimentary farming, and building of crude dugout homes. Lee's purpose was also to show the social character of the people, both their individuality and their mutual dependence. Balancing the many shots of individuals at work are the images of group gatherings—town meetings, community sings, children's band, square dances, and games. In fact, the images portray a remarkably cohesive community—albeit a relatively homogeneous one in ethnic terms, owing perhaps to the nearly complete isolation of the place, with the nearest railroad sixty-five miles away.

Pie Town's representative place in the historical mythos of the small town was a big part of Lee's story. Yet it was a story told in terms of a single place, far from the beaten track.[19] We can get closer to the meaning of the small town during the Great Depression by looking at a 1940 book that is in many ways the culmination of the efforts by the FSA and Stryker to mythologize Main Street—Sherwood Anderson's *Home Town*. Working with Edwin Rosskam, who had been hired by Stryker to coordinate exhibitions and publications for the FSA photography project, Anderson found in the FSA file a variegated record of American life, and the 142 pic-

Photograph by Russell Lee, "Helping [sic] the plates at dinner on the grounds, all day community sing" (FSA caption), Pie Town, New Mexico, 1940. Library of Congress, Prints and Photographs Division, FSA-OWI Collection.

tures ultimately published in *Home Town* portray the visual particularity of place. The photographs in *Home Town* form an accompaniment to the text, with illustrations clustered around Anderson's general themes and with occasional groupings that take on the character of distinct photo-essays; regional differences are muted in the images, however, as they are pulled into the more general national argument of the text.[20]

Photographically, *Home Town* encompasses a broad sense of "small town," with the first image a Georgian town hall in a prosperous Vermont town, and offering a few pages later a barely inhabited North Dakota Main Street. The next image is Evans's railroad depot in Edwards, Mississippi, followed a few pages later by his "Moundville, Alabama," which had also appeared in *American Photographs*. There are some quiet images of Main Street, but for the most part the images portray town centers that are vibrant with pedestrians, streets lit up with movie marquees, and a courthouse square on a Saturday afternoon.[21] Meanwhile, the social life of the town is pictured in photographs that feature men at town meetings and women at tea parties, an appreciative audience (men and women) applauding a performance, religious gatherings, market days, and clusters of townsfolk chatting along Main Street. And a fair number of images illustrate the rhythm of farming, from sowing and harvest to winter, in

Photograph by Ben Shahn, Middlesboro, Kentucky, 1935. From Sherwood Anderson,
Home Town *(1940). Library of Congress, Prints and Photographs Division, FSA-OWI*
Collection.

harmony with Anderson's text, which is structured broadly to portray the generic small town under the aspect of the changing seasons.

Anderson was past the peak of his career when he wrote the text for *Home Town,* and certainly no one has claimed it as a masterpiece. But it is a revealing and important book, nevertheless, in part because it reflects a mentality about the small town that not only was shared by Stryker and the FSA but was shaping and summing up a national attitude. In some ways this is the same Anderson who wrote *Winesburg,* with chapter 8 of *Home Town* devoted to the "small town individualist," who had been known as a "grotesque" in the earlier book. Thus, *Home Town* comprises the "lonely man who seldom leaves his own house" (82), the town practical joker, the man who loves an argument, the schoolteacher who never marries (83), the young girl who goes wrong, the town philosopher (86), the mystic, the town bully, the kept woman (87), and the town's own Carrie Nation (94). But unlike Winesburg, where the deformities are in some way produced by the insulation of the town, here Anderson avers that "the characters of the towns give the towns their color," and that life in the town "is a test of man's ability to adjust himself. . . . You have to go on living with your neighbors. If they are sometimes queer it may be that they also think of you as queer" (95).

In other ways, too, the tenets of *Winesburg* are reversed in *Home Town*. Where George Willard's salvation was to flee the confines of the town and find his fortune in the big city (along with a generation of others who could not tolerate the strictures of the town), now Anderson counsels the young man who has written him (as the book opens) to stay put. The young man "has a burning desire to remake life, the whole social scheme" (3). But to Anderson, the "big world outside now is so filled with confusion" that our only hope is "to try thinking small" (4). Anderson is suspicious of "false bigness, men speaking at meetings, trying to move masses of other men" (5). Rather, he advises living fully "in a small way"—understanding the house in which you live, the street, the town. MacLeish had ended *Land of the Free* with just the opposite point: masses of men are pictured, yearning for a change that the poet advocates, though diffidently; Anderson's celebration of the virtues of the small town does not deny the reality of the world outside, but it does promote a kind of stoic realism, as it observes the many young people who have tried to make it in the city only to find unemployment. If this reversal of movement, from the cities back to the towns, is a necessary result of prevailing economic conditions, it is one that Anderson sees now, twenty years after *Winesburg*, as filled with virtue.

For the town is not merely a refuge; it is a place that has itself changed over the years, becoming what to Anderson is a model of American democracy and a place that is not a backwater of staid tradition but a part of the flow of modernity. Unlike the cities, where immigrant groups band together in enclaves of like ethnicity, Anderson sees the towns as places where such segregation could not happen, where new arrivals "became a part of the town life. The new America was being made there. It is still being made" (9). One cannot say that Anderson is blind to social inequality in the small town, for he does observe the town slums (72), and he notes the role of the church in fixing social standing in a town (117); moreover, he observes the special character of the "Negro section of Southern towns" (37), reinforcing the point in four illustrations (44, 45, 101, 123) that portray African Americans in settings that are clearly separate from white people. Yet these observations do not seem to qualify Anderson's idealistic vision; on the contrary, they become part of the argument that the townsfolk, for all their internal differences, must also solve their problems together. That the FSA photography division, with its massive propaganda effort on behalf of the federal government's transforming programs, should be supporting a book that espouses a politics of quietism is an irony that nobody noted, including Rosskam, who wrote an afterword on the photographs.

Of chief importance in Anderson's view of the small town circa 1940 is the rapid change it had undergone in the preceding decade. "The people dance more" and the puritanical "fear of play" and joy has gone; there is a "new opening up of life" and the "breaking up of the old isolation." In a word, the machine—from the automobile to the linotype machine to the phonograph—has changed everything: "Modern machine-driven life has brought the land and the people of the land closer to the towns" (142). And chief among these agents of change were the mass media (movies, radio, and magazines), which were changing the consciousness of Main Street.

Stryker's growing picture archive was appearing regularly in magazines and newspapers across the country, including the new picture magazines that were defining popular American culture during the mid- to late thirties. *Life*, the chief force among them, had its own staff photographers and consequently used relatively few of Stryker's images, but given the magazine's extraordinary influence, its treatment of the small town is worth a closer look, on two occasions especially. In 1940, the same year *Home Town* appeared, *Life* sent photographer Bernard Hoffman to record the "typical small town" for history, focusing on Franklin, Indiana: "Among America's great institutions, none is more remarkable than Saturday night in a small midwestern town," *Life* asserted.[22] Hoffman's camera catches the crowds, the barbershop, the movies, the general store, the bowling alley, and the "Cut Rate Drug Store," a popular teen hangout. The social harmony portrayed by *Life* in 1940 supported the ethos of small-town utopia that Anderson was promoting in somewhat more complex form: Main Street represented social harmony.

In short, by the end of the thirties, the harmony of the small town was something that *Life*'s readers wanted to believe in; and it was also an image that would underlie the definitive representation of small-town life during the 1930s—Thornton Wilder's play *Our Town* (1938). This drama about the transcendence of time has itself transcended time, having become the most frequently produced play in U.S. history. I do not think anyone today would claim, as some did when it opened, that it is the greatest American theatrical work ever written; but it may well be the most popular one (it won the Pulitzer Prize in 1938), and the reasons for

Photograph by Ben Shahn, street scene showing movie theater, probably in the vicinity of Lancaster, Ohio, 1938. From Sherwood Anderson, Home Town *(1940). Library of Congress, Prints and Photographs Division, FSA-OWI Collection.*

its enduring popularity bear consideration, especially given its consecration of the image of the small town.

OUR TOWN IS A DRAMA of sentiment and abstraction, with little action in the conventional sense. It begins with the Stage Manager introducing the town of Grover's Corners, New Hampshire, where the play takes place. It is 1901, and the main action of act 1 takes place within two families—the Gibbses and the Webbs. As we learn about the town and its inhabitants, we also meet Emily Webb and George Gibbs, teenagers who are discovering they are in love. George and Emily do marry in act 2 (it is now 1904), and their wedding day, including the ceremony, is "performed" before us. Act 3, which takes place in 1913, is set in an imagined cemetery, where the dead, characters we have met previously, are now present as their deceased selves, conversing about life and death. On this day, a newly deceased Emily (who has died giving birth to her second child) has just arrived to be buried and takes her place among the dead interlocutors. She wishes to return to the past, and she chooses her twelfth birthday. As she looks back on that day, now from the perspective of the dead, she tells her mother of the future and of all those who will die, and she says to her

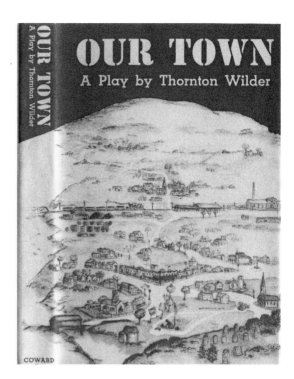

Cover of Thornton Wilder's
Our Town (1938), first
edition, published by
Coward McCann. Library
of Congress, Rare Book
and Special Collections
Division.

mother, urgently, "But, just for a moment now we're all together. Mama, just for a moment we're happy."[23] The Stage Manager has the last word, putting the town to sleep for the night as the Albany train goes by.

Wilder's reputation as a novelist, enhanced by the Pulitzer Prize for fiction that he won in 1928 for *The Bridge of San Luis Rey*, was firmly established by the time he wrote *Our Town*, but his interest in theater was longstanding, and in 1931 he had written two one-act plays that employed some of the same "experimental" devices of *Our Town* (bare stage, narrator, characters drawn from ordinary family life).[24] Central to the initial and continuing success of *Our Town* is Wilder's exquisite balancing of innovative form against traditional theme, and of an everyday, realistic texture against a grandly universal significance. *Our Town* attempts to engage the audience's deepest feelings (regarding love, marriage, family, death, ambition), yet it also allows the audience to view these most basic issues from a lofty perspective. At a time when the daily struggle for existence was on everyone's mind, Wilder took his audience back to a time when things were simpler, providing an escape into a world that seemed lost. Yet he also affirmed the ineluctable fact of death, consoling us with the bitter truth of its universality. Wilder softened the blow of even that

Scene from Our Town *(1940), directed by Sam Wood. United Artists/Photofest.*

pessimistic message, however, for the dead who take the stage in act 3 seem fully adjusted to the long view of things and distanced from, if not indifferent to, all earthly struggles. (These qualities also account for the play's continuing appeal, indeed its international appeal.) In short, Wilder puts the American small town under the lens of eternity, applying the perspective that Spinoza favored for viewing all earthly matters—*sub specie aeternitatis.* Like all great works of middlebrow culture, *Our Town* offers a mix of the familiar and the exotic, taking the members of its audience beyond where they usually go, but not so far as to be truly disturbing.

In a 1946 letter to their older brother Amos, Isabel Wilder, Thornton's sister, who lived and traveled with him for many years, wrote of the response to the play in post–World War II East Germany: "The Russian authorities stopped it in 3 days. Rumors give the reason it was 'unsuitable for the Germans so soon,—too democratic.'" Meanwhile, in Japan, U.S. authorities were translating it into Japanese for performance in native theaters, as a showcase of "the American and democratic way of life" (170). It is not surprising that *Our Town* should be taken as an epitome of democracy—given the characters in the play, all of whom are "average" types of humanity. And the "average" quality of Grover's Corners is in fact one of the Stage Manager's reiterated points: "Nobody very remarkable ever come out of it, s'far as we know" (6), he says early in the play. And in concluding the wedding of George and Emily, he again subsumes this special day for the play's characters in a broader conceit of the reiterations of such moments in life: "M . . . marries N . . . millions of them. . . . Once in a thousand times it's interesting" (82). We are not interested in these characters because they are special (which is why theatergoers expecting otherwise can be disappointed by what appear to be unexciting characters and lack of action); rather, we see these types of humanity, although specified by place and time, as representative of the "common folk" and the common lot of humankind. In this sense, *Our Town* is a meditation on that favorite construction of thirties culture, the common man.

In other ways, too, *Our Town* is an exemplar of the period, not least in its innovative theatrical construction. Although conventional staging—with the curtain as the fourth wall that opens when the play begins—was (and is) the norm in American theater, there had been a strong current of experimentation in the American stage, from the avant-garde Provincetown Players of the teens and twenties to the left-oriented Group Theater of the thirties. Even more experimental—and more politically radical—was the Federal Theater Project (FTP), which was created by the New Deal in 1935 and which presented a range of productions nurturing such talents as Elia Kazan, John Houseman, Arthur Miller, and Orson Welles. The FTP included as well the Living Newspaper, productions that focused on current social and economic problems (e.g., housing, agriculture, health) and used a variety of documentary techniques to dramatize these issues. Wilder's removal of the stage's walls and his elimination of scenery in favor of barely suggestive props was thus in line with this current of experimentalism, as was his use of a "Stage Manager" to introduce and manage the presentation.

Wilder's dramatization echoed as well the period's fascination with facts, which pervaded the visual, literary, and dramatic arts of the time. (John Dos Passos had used newsreel headlines and biographies in *U.S.A.*; John Steinbeck had inserted documentary chapters in *The Grapes of Wrath*; the Federal Writers Project's regional guidebooks had doted lovingly on local particulars.) So we learn from Professor Willard, a "rural savant" from the State University, that "Grover's Corners lies on the old Pleistocene granite of the Appalachian range" and other guidebook facts, such as the town's population: 2,640 (21–22). But Wilder steers clear of any literal realism, not only in staging but also in characterization. "When the theater pretends to give the real thing in canvas and wood and metal," he says, "it loses something of the realer thing, which is its true business." Where realism had earlier been promoted by Henrik Ibsen and Anton Chekhov, now, Wilder says, "the camera is carrying it on and is in great 'theoretical peril' of falling short of literature" (156).[25] Wilder's own response was to shape a hybrid aesthetic, fusing minimalist staging and documentary embellishments with characters drawn from the commonplace tradition of realism, all within a framework of philosophical and religious abstraction.

Given that Wilder's play is the portrait of a town, its setting is critical, and Wilder offers us a clear and typical picture of a New England small town: the Stage Manager's opening geographical description of Grover's Corners moves from the town's longitude and latitude to gesture toward an imagined Main Street and railway station. A demographic sketch then follows: "Way back there is the railway station; tracks go that way. Polish Town's across the tracks, and some Canuck families." The Congregational and Presbyterian churches occupy the center of town, with Methodist and Unitarian nearby. "Baptist is down in the holla' by the river. Catholic church is over beyond the tracks" (4). Grover's Corners is, we assume, a typical New England town, and its geography is a mirror of the town's social structure, dominated by the Protestant establishment—with immigrants and non-Protestants safely on the other side of the tracks.

Like all great works of popular art, *Our Town* lets its audience have its cake and eat it, too. We can identify with the establishment perspective, but we can also identify with a dissident view of the town. If we are feeling uneasy about the social arrangements of Grover's Corners, so is Belligerent Man, who rises from the audience and says, "Is there no one in town aware of social injustice and industrial inequality?" To which, the bland editor of the town newspaper, Mr. Webb, replies, "Oh, yes, everybody is— somethin' terrible. Seems like they spend most of their time talking about who's rich and who's poor." (Thus does Mr. Webb reduce questions of social equity to questions of personal jealousy.) But when challenged by Belligerent Man—"Then why don't they do something about it?"—Mr. Webb offers a more abstract response, based on principles of Platonic justice: "I guess we're all hunting like everybody else for a way the diligent and sensible can rise to the top and the lazy and quarrelsome can sink to the bottom. But it ain't easy to find. Meanwhile, we do all we can to help those that can't help themselves and those that can we leave alone.—Are there any other questions?" (25–26). These simple rules of the community leave the larger questions of injustice unanswered, of course, but they allow us to think that Mr. Webb and Grover's Corners are, well, doing their best in a difficult world, and that this is the American Way.[26]

Mr. Webb is equally unworried about "culture" in Grover's Corners. Lady in a Box (also rising from the audience, on cue) asks, "Is there any culture or love of beauty in Grover's Corners?" Mr. Webb replies, "There ain't much—not in the sense you mean." The main pleasures are those of nature—"the sun comin' up over the mountain in the morning." As for the rest—"*Robinson Crusoe* and the Bible; and Handel's 'Largo,' we all know that; and Whistler's 'Mother'—those are just about as far as we go" (26). Wilder lets these examples represent the simplicity and strength of American culture—oriented nevertheless toward European touchstones; yet withal Grover's Corners is within the broad range of middlebrow culture, at the small-town end of the spectrum. Mr. Webb's is a perfectly calibrated response, allowing the audience to feel superior to Grover's Corners, but in a sympathetic way, unlike the satiric treatment of Gopher Prairie in *Main Street*, where Sinclair Lewis placed his reader on a far higher plane.

In thus enjoying a culture of limited aspiration, Grover's Corners is plainly not a place for genius or even for any significant aberration from the norm. Wilder makes the point through the character of Simon Stimson, a choirmaster and church organist (read: artist), whose repeated drunkenness is the subject of gossip, if not scandal. We do not know the cause for all this (Mrs. Gibbs refers to "the troubles he's been through" [39]), but Dr. Gibbs's pronouncement acknowledges the misfit with a sense of fatalism: "Some people ain't made for small-town life. I don't know how that'll end; but there's nothing we can do but just leave it alone." In the end—act 3—Stimson is among the dead, having committed suicide at some point in the intervening years, and leaving as his gravestone epitaph "just some notes of music" (91). But Wilder takes it all in stride, as we are meant to do. Unlike his predecessors—Cather, Lewis, Anderson—who lamented sharply the loss of genius in such circumstances, Wilder sees the extinction of the artist as sad but unremarkable. And in general, the acceptance of limitation is one of the central qualities of life in Grover's Corners. Mrs. Gibbs dreams of going to Paris for a vacation, but she is resigned to accompanying Doc Gibbs, who, like a happy Ixion tied to his wheel, instead revisits the Civil War sites every year. George thinks of going away to college but persuades himself easily that it is better to stay put, take over his uncle's farm, and marry Emily.

In fact, the overall tone of *Our Town* is stoic acceptance of the way things are, of fate, of chance, of death, of life. Springing originally from Wilder's admiration for the New Hampshire hill towns, it is an attempt, as Wilder put it, to place "the life of a village against the life of the stars" (156). Like Edgar Lee Masters's *Spoon River Anthology*, which retells the constrained lives of the midwestern townsfolk who now sleep restless in their graves, *Our Town* looks back on the passions of human life from a distance, but Wilder's philosophical aloofness is more complete. In comparison to the contemporaneous *Grapes of Wrath*, which argues for the urgency of change, albeit within the framework of the American political tradition, *Our Town* is quietist and stoic. Its consolatory message, in a time of economic, political, and social upheaval, was that in the gradual evolution of life in Grover's Corners, amid the births and deaths, one finds the core meaning of American life. We must take joy in what we do have and place our lives in the broadest possible spectrum of life on Earth.

A similar message, also employing a perspective from beyond the grave, informs one of the most popular films ever made in America—Frank Capra's *It's a Wonderful Life*. Released in 1946, the film carries Capra's characteristic vision of a divided America that he was able to translate into a populist affirmation of an ideal community in which small-town values triumph over the values of the powerful moneyed interests. In centering on the small town, *Wonderful Life* follows a strong current in American film of the period, yet one containing surprisingly contradictory elements, from the sharply critical to the celebratory.

At bottom, Capra is interested in big themes—the contingencies of happiness and the fragility of the social contract. He uses Bedford Falls as a microcosm to explore these themes, by looking at the social and political forces that divided American culture in the thirties and forties—the common man versus the privileged; the integrity of the small town versus the duplicity and powers of the city; the values of community versus the values of money. Some of these same themes had been explored in other Capra films, as early as *Mr. Deeds Goes to Town* (1936) and as late as *State of the Union* (1948). *Mr. Deeds* featured an idealistic altruist, played by Gary Cooper, and pitted him against the big-city lawyers and financial predators who would take control of his newly inherited fortune and quash his plans for social betterment. In *Mr. Smith Goes to Washington* (1939), Capra puts another unlikely hero, a scout leader played by James Stewart, on the floor of the Senate, where he discovers the will to resist the controlling forces of the media and big business by hearkening finally to his own values of fair play and opportunity for all. And in *Meet John*

Doe (1941), Capra again showed a man taken from the crowd (Gary Cooper again) who finds himself leading a mass movement founded on the values of neighborly love and compassion, in defiance of the powers of media and business (this time in a fascist guise) who would use him as their tool. The power of money and the media to create their selected tool is again the subject of *State of the Union* (1948), with Spencer Tracy as the hero and would-be presidential candidate.

In each of these films, Capra's heroes are reluctant, surprised by their good fortune and nearly overwhelmed by the predicaments that flow from it. *Wonderful Life* breaks from that pattern in giving us a hero whose life does not change as a result of a series of "accidents"—which is precisely his dilemma. George Bailey's fate is *not* to leave town, *not* to have the adventures he had dreamed of as a youth.

Like *Our Town*, Capra's film takes place under the aspect of eternity, in this case under the eye of the Lord, who dispatches Clarence, an angel trying to earn his wings, to rescue our hero George, who on Christmas Eve is about to jump to his death off a bridge. Unlike the somber Wilder, Capra has a comic ending in view, as George decides—at the end of the movie—that his life in Bedford Falls is wonderful after all, and he races home to his wife and kids. As the plot unfolds, going back to George's childhood, we learn that his youthful ambitions—to leave Bedford Falls and find adventure traveling, along with his dreams of building cities, bridges, skyscrapers—all have been put aside by a series of events that have prevented him from leaving his hometown. First, he cannot resist falling in love with Mary, a hometown girl; then he cannot serve in the army because of partial deafness (the result of his rescue of his younger brother from an ice pond when a child); then he is compelled to take over the family savings and loan when his father suddenly dies.

In a sense, *Wonderful Life* deals with the perennial question in the American representation of the small town: Do I stay or leave? Like the hero of the early-twentieth-century small-town narrative, George Bailey wants desperately to escape the strictures of his native town. But the dramatic situation in *Wonderful Life* negates that possibility. In *Mr. Deeds* and *Mr. Smith*, the hero is explicitly from a small town, while John Doe, a vagrant, finds himself by promoting the small-town value of kindly neighborliness. Only in *Wonderful Life* does the story itself take place in a small town, and Capra portrays a setting that is somewhere between a town and a small city. Physically, the town seems prosperous, with an active Main Street, busy with foot traffic and automobiles, small stores, larger stores, cafés and bars, and two banks. In fact, Bedford Falls has to be large enough to contain the Bailey Savings and Loan and the bank owned by Bailey's nemesis, Henry F. Potter, who views the townsfolk as "riff raff." These two forces define the conflict between good and evil that Capra imagines in *Wonderful Life*, with the Bailey Savings and Loan offering affordable credit to its patrons so they can build their own homes and stop renting from Potter, whose goal is to destroy the savings and loan and hold the town more completely in his financial grasp. (Potter, who is confined to his wheelchair, is a crabby Scrooge-like figure made powerful and malevolent in his portrayal by Lionel Barrymore.)

George is proud of his family's business, and loyal to the town folk who have invested in the savings and loan: when there is a run on the institution during the Depression, Bailey, about to depart on his honeymoon with his private savings, instead saves the S and L by dispensing his own funds to the clamoring customers. But his proudest accomplishment is the new development of homes that he is building for the town, Bailey Park, which is in its rudimentary stage (dirt roads, rough curbs) but boasts a steady stream of new homeowners moving into modest split levels and bungalows. George had dreamed of being a builder of cities and bridges, but he has happily settled for being a builder of first homes for the town. The population of Bedford Falls, when massed together on Main Street, seems to consist largely of average white Protestants, but interestingly Capra chooses to focus on an Italian immigrant family in whom Bailey takes a special interest and who are saving in order to buy a house in the new development. In short, Bailey is bringing the "American Dream" to Bedford Falls and helping the struggling underclass to rise. One of the ironies of *Wonderful Life*—which Capra does not seem to have acknowledged—is that a film that enshrines the small town in the hearts of the American viewer is at the same time showing us a model of suburban development that seems to contradict it. We shall return to this paradox—a central fact of post–World War II development—in the next chapter.

It's a Wonderful Life moves to its climax when George's Uncle Billy loses a huge cash deposit at the very moment the bank examiner is inspecting their books. (Billy has let his cash fall into the greedy hands of George's nemesis, bank president Potter, who conceals his find and calls in the police when he hears of George's bank problems, even encouraging George to commit suicide to redeem his life insurance.) George, thinking he is ruined, is indeed on the verge of suicide, when the angel Clarence intervenes, showing him the world as it would have been without

Scene from It's a Wonderful Life *(1946), directed by Frank Capra, showing Bailey Park, a suburban development outside of Bedford Falls.*

Scene from It's a Wonderful Life *(1946), directed by Frank Capra, depicting a moving day celebration in Bailey Park.*

Scene from It's a Wonderful Life *(1946), directed by Frank Capra, showing Bedford Falls as Pottersville, a town of vice and disorder.*

George and his good works. It is Christmas Eve, and the two visit the town's Main Street—only now the town is called Pottersville, after the evil banker. George's friends of course do not know him and greet him with blank stares, provoking his shocked and belligerent response; his mother and wife do not know him, and the latter runs in fright. Also shocking to George is that the town is not the happy place it had been but instead a seedy amalgam of nightclubs, strip joints, pool halls, and honky-tonks. And there is no Bailey Savings and Loan. Capra films the new Main Street as a night scene, with quick cuts suggesting the phantasmagoria of a dystopia, a Walpurgisnacht, crowded with spontaneous fights and disorder.

Waking from this nightmare of possibilities, George realizes that his life has had much happiness and value, and he races back to his family, even at the cost of going to jail. The bank examiner and constable are waiting for him at his home, but within moments his wife returns and with her the entire town, or so it seems, whose residents have been contributing funds to make up the lost $8,000. Even the bank examiner, warmed by this show of community, kicks in. Only Mr. Potter is absent, removed from the joyous affirmation of fellowship. The whole of George's Pottersville experience may seem like a fantasy to the viewer, easily explained as part of George's delusion, but Capra leaves us with a final image that makes it all "real": a copy of *Tom Sawyer* inscribed from Clarence to George. Clarence has been carrying Twain throughout the movie, and it is the perfect book to connect the viewer, and George, to an enduring image of small-town America that was already looking backward to a simpler time when Twain published it in the Gilded Age America of 1876.

Capra's vision of the dystopian small town may be placing too heavy a burden on one man—George Bailey—as the sine qua non of the successful town. Surely there were small towns that lacked a Bailey and still fared well. Nevertheless, Capra seems to have drawn on real fears during the 1930s about the dangers of ideal small towns losing their charm and going to the devil. As early as 1925, Frank R. Kent, a political journalist for the *Baltimore Sun* who was on the cover of *Time* magazine a few years later, toured small-town America observing the uniformity of opinion, custom, and business methods, and observing also the pervasiveness of radio, movies, cars, golf, lipstick, and so on. "In the smaller towns," he wrote, one can see more clearly "the speed and direction in which national habits are forming." What shocked Kent was "the truly extraordinary extent to which the country is drenched with smut by the steadily increasing stream of pornographic periodicals and dirty fiction magazines."[27] Not only pornography, but gangs as well, were threatening Main Street, as an article in the *North American Review* argued in 1932. Prohibition had led to slayings in small towns as well as in cities, the author wrote, "and so the gangs are emerging in Main Street."[28] Even if gangs were relatively rare, a more enveloping change was noted in a 1934 article by journalist and novelist Irving Bacheller, who wrote of his flight from the noisy sidewalks of New York to what he expected would be the peaceful hills of a New England town and a "small, restful hotel on the shore of a lake." What he found instead was mayhem on Main Street, in the form of snorting and roaring engines, trucks, and buses.[29]

In opposing Bedford Falls to Pottersville, Capra was posing the dilemma of the small town during the thirties and forties: Could small-town America become part of a changing world—which was bringing into it the national media, automobiles, and all associated vices—and still maintain its innocence? If the changes were already taking place, as many had observed casually and as the Lynds' Middletown studies were showing exhaustively, then the ideal of Capra's Bedford Falls could at least show how vulnerable the small town was to inimical social, economic, and moral forces. Coming in 1946, *It's a Wonderful Life* also reminded viewers of what America had been fighting for all along—the Main Street values that lay at the center of American life, as Capra saw it. Unlike many of his professional associates, Capra had joined the armed services during the war and spent those years making films for the Army. His documentary series, *Why We Fight*, comprised seven films that were shown to soldiers and subsequently to the general public, detailing the history of the conflict and its crucial importance to the American people—whose isolationist tendencies had to be overcome. In a sense, *Wonderful Life*, made soon after the war was over, completes that series, showing Americans what they had fought for. But it also may mirror to some degree Capra's own feelings about his wartime experience: like George Bailey, Capra was the guy who stayed at home, doing what he had always done (though officially commissioned in the U.S. Army). In the film, it is Bailey's brother who goes to war and comes home a war hero, though as things go, it is George/Capra who earns the eternal thanks of Bedford Falls for being who he is and doing what he has done.

It's a Wonderful Life also represents a benevolent and restorative view of small-town society as a microcosm of America. When the whole town crowds into the Bailey house at the end of the film, offering their dollars to Bailey, the viewer's faith in human goodness and the power of collective good is restored. It is a perfect Christmas ending. And for anyone watching the film when it first came out, it is the essence of comedy—the reintegration of the hero into society—an ending that likewise occurs in Preston Sturges's wartime comic satire of small-town morality, *The Miracle of Morgan's Creek* (1944). Significantly, these comic films reverse the depiction of the mob as a hive of resentment, irrationality, and combustible anger in earlier thirties films like John Ford's *Doctor Bull* (1933) and Fritz Lang's *Fury* (1936), which reflected the uncertainties of the early Depression, and the fear of mass unrest. By the forties, the nostalgic recovery of the small town had been accomplished, and Capra's work would epitomize the new view of the small town.

But Capra's romantic rescue of the hero—and the town—at the end, is nothing compared to another 1944 film that took nostalgia for the town to a new level: Vincente Minelli's musical comedy *Meet Me in St. Louis*. A Technicolor, syrup-drenched confection, the film looks back on St. Louis at the turn of the century as a heaven of richly furnished Victorian houses, clanging trolley cars, tennis parties, horse-drawn phaetons, romance, and Christmas balls. At about the same time that Walt Disney was dreaming up Disneyland, Minnelli put it on film, rendering residential St. Louis (we do not see the downtown area) as the perfection of small-town America. When the paterfamilias is invited to head a new office in New York City, it appears that the family is about to leave the Garden of Eden; but he decides in the end to refuse the job offer and instead affirm the virtues of small-town life, which include, somewhat anomalously, the St. Louis World's Fair (1904), grand but—in the film—more like a state fair than a world expo. The recuperation of the small town that had begun in the mid-thirties in the work of the FSA photographers was now complete, and the caustic satire of Lewis's *Main Street* could be safely distanced now as part of another culture and sensibility.[30]

CODA: THE GLOW OF nostalgia surrounding the small town would continue into the popular culture of the post–World War II period, especially in the 1970s, when a generation of younger writers and directors began to look back on Main Street in the fifties with bittersweet memories. *The Last Picture Show* (1971), a film based on the novel by Larry McMurtry, is set in the tiny town of Anarene (though it was actually shot in Archer City) located in northwestern central Texas. As portrayed by director Peter Bogdanovich, Anarene is claustrophobic and practically deserted, with the wind blowing through empty streets, a pool hall with a dozen regular customers, and a movie theater on the verge of closing its doors. For each of the two central characters, about to graduate from high school, the world beyond beckons vaguely, but in the end only one escapes to military service, while the other, drawn back irresistibly, stays on to operate the town's pool hall and take the place of the town's moral center, who in dying had bequeathed him the business. The hero's loyalty to the small town offers little materially, but it serves the heart's reason. *American Graffiti* (1973) is, one might say, the converse of *The Last Picture Show*, for in this film the hero leaves the town. George Lucas's re-creation of his Modesto, California, youth, set in pre-Kennedy-assassination 1962, offers a time capsule of a much richer small-town life, also from the narrow perspective of teen culture—with rock and roll forming a continual accompaniment to, and comment on, the film's action. Here, too, a pair of close friends are graduating from high school and planning their escape to college in the East, and here, too, only one, in the end, can escape the cocoon. As he looks down from the airplane on his flight east, his small-town Northern California existence seems a thing of the past, enshrined forever in a jukebox glow of nostalgia. The hero escapes, but the memory of the town is, we feel, the best thing that he is carrying into the next phase of his life. That glow—which began in the late 1930s and continued through the 1970s—would infuse the whole of post–World War II American culture, lasting into the twenty-first century and shaping the way Americans thought about and imagined the new communities they would build for years to come. But that same glow of nostalgia also obscures some of the harsher realities of life on Main Street, realities of social division in the small town that we must next address.

Chapter Five

Main Street

Belonging and Not Belonging

When the new Park Forest development thirty miles south of Chicago was marketed in the late forties as the first postwar planned suburban community, the brochure addressed the reader in terms of the bifurcation between city and small town that had become an accepted convention of American culture: "Many of you reading this story come from smaller cities in the Midwest. Recall for a moment the friendly, heartwarming, social life that was so much a part of your everyday experience. If life in a big city has denied this enjoyment of human companionship to you and your family, here is an opportunity to regain these privileges."[1] There may be a postwar innocence about these stereotypes of urban anomie and small-town bonhomie, but they are still very much with us: the heterogeneous city, made cold and unfriendly, a place of social avoidance, by the diversity of populations; the homogeneous small town, communal, warm, and friendly, "a nurturing extended family," as John Jakle puts it.[2] Yet beneath the myth of harmony and democracy in the typical American small town is a counternarrative of exclusion and discrimination.

The mythic image of Main Street as a place of communal harmony—with townsfolk greeting one another on the street, tipping their hats, and with friendly shopkeepers and a general trust and good feeling—was attacked in the twenties by Sinclair Lewis and restored in the thirties by Frank Capra and others. Yet it has always concealed a far more complex social reality than what first meets the eye, one that I want to explore in this chapter. My aim is to look at the small-town community historically, focusing mainly on the period before World War II, and especially the crucial 1930s, when Main Street was becoming enshrined as an icon of social harmony. Beneath the surface narrative of benign community, a darker story of ambiguities and contradictions can be told, a story of disharmony that is still troubling us in the twenty-first century. More particularly, I want to explore the question of what makes a community tolerant—or intolerant—of difference. Or, to put it even more simply, who belongs and who does not? Much has been claimed on behalf of small towns and the dream of community; it is my purpose in this chapter to explore these claims and to assess that dream.

Going back historically to the first English settlements in North America, one finds the history of social cleavage beginning almost simultaneously with the history of the town in America when Roger Williams was expelled from Salem, Massachusetts, on the grounds of religious heterodoxy in 1635. That expulsion was soon followed by Anne Hutchinson's banishment from Boston in 1638 on charges of heresy, the result of her advocacy of women's rights and free grace. Hutchinson joined Williams in Rhode Island, where Williams had declared a state of religious tolerance; and Rhode Island's broad and official tolerance eventually became the official model for American society, as affirmed by the First Amendment of the Constitution, which drew a line between church and state.

But the broad tolerance of religious difference within the United States as a whole conceals the intolerance that is often at the heart of individual communities, where the desire for purity and homogeneity has led inexorably to the long-standing practice of excluding the "other" on the grounds of religious, political, ethnic, or racial difference. The lesson was not lost on Arthur Miller, who—while Park Forest was promoting the joys of community—was writing his critique of America in the McCarthy era, in the guise of a play about Puritan New England. *The Crucible* (1953) shows us a village destroyed by its own hysterical suspicion of difference—the witches in Miller's Salem were typically on the margins of society—just as powerful elements in postwar American society were attempting to create a monolithic political culture by punishing the remnants of the Communist Left from the 1930s.

Perhaps it is enough to say that the small town has always been ruled by a powerful elite at pains to conceal the practices of exclusion through hearty proclamations of the principles of community. William Allen White, in one of the first celebrations of small-town life, admitted in *In Our Town* (1906) that "we had known in a vague way that there were lines of social cleavage," but it took an acute and fearless social columnist to point out all the nuances between the "best society" and lesser beings, thus giving the lie to the "official" belief in the town's "democratic" nature. If the small town has been a cultural symbol of "friendly, heartwarming, social life," it has also been—often at the same historical moment—a symbol of prejudice, segregation, and hostility to the stranger. Sinclair

Lewis captures the repressive political authority of the small town in Go-pher Prairie's reaction to Carol Kennicott's daring declaration, "We want our Utopia *now*," a utopia that encompasses "the industrial workers and the women and the farmers and the negro race and the Asiatic colonies." That is precisely the social mix that the town does *not* want, and it decries this vision as dangerously socialistic and egalitarian, a "world reduced to a dead level of mediocrity."³ At a more dramatic pitch, the films of the mid-thirties also depict the small town's enforcement of conformity: its lack of tolerance for eccentricity, as in *Doctor Bull* (1933); its eager ex-clusion and calculated murder of the ethnic outsider, as in *Black Legion* (1937); its potential for homicidal mob violence on the merest suspicion of the outsider, as in Fritz Lang's *Fury* (1936).

This vein of criticism continued after World War II in American lit-erature and popular culture. Philip Roth's 1959 acerbic parable, "Eli the Fanatic," shows us a town whose secular Jews observe with uneasiness a community of Hasidic Jews that moves into their largely Protestant town soon after World War II; they fear that the ultrareligious Jews, in their extreme and visible form, will arouse the town's hostility toward their own moderate Jewish community, which is trying to blend invisibly into the town's fabric, and they go to absurd extremes to police their brethren. Roth focuses on the fears of the assimilated town Jews—close to being outsiders themselves—who want to be accepted by the community. But the more consistent picture in our popular culture is of the town's para-noia, as in Rod Serling's *Twilight Zone* episode "The Monsters Are Due on Maple Street" (1960), which features a mob, crazed by the strange behavior of some neighbors, that then turns violently on an otherwise accepted member of the town, a "Mr. Goodman," presumably a relative of Hawthorne's earlier hapless character, Young Goodman Brown. Vio-lence is also at the center of Norman Mailer's extravagant vision of the small town in *Armies of the Night* (1968), especially the southern small town, which Mailer imagines haunted by insanity, possessed by hatred and alienation from urban America, and finding its ultimate fulfillment in a lust to slaughter: "The true war party of America was in all the small towns, even as the peace parties had to collect in the cities and the suburbs."⁴

Some thirty-five years after Mailer's dark vision, filmmaker Lars von Trier unmasked the evil folk of *Dogville* (2003), who first embrace and then imprison the captive stranger in their midst; meanwhile M. Night Shyamalan's *The Village* (2004) reverses the convention in revealing the desperate and paranoid effort of a small community to live outside of time in order to insulate itself against the stranger and remain immune to the evils of the outside world, all the while incubating its own pathologies. These works are obviously at the opposite affective pole from the Norman Rockwell image of small-town life that was a part of late thirties and forties popular culture, an image brought to life in Disneyland's vision of Main Street in the late twentieth century. Yet in tapping into the layers of paranoia in American culture, these films revealed the exact complement, the flip side, of Main Street as utopia, and they raised the question at the heart of this chapter: Is the peace and harmony, the friendship and warmth of the small town bought at the expense of keeping out the stranger, muting the dissident, expelling the oddball, purifying the community of its contaminants of whatever stripe?

The chronicle of small-town "purity," achieved through acts of violence, has been most vividly recounted by Sherrilyn A. Ifill in *On the Courthouse Lawn: Confronting the Legacy of Lynching in the Twenty-First Century* (2007). Lynching was, as Ifill affirms, a major instrument for enforcing the town's identity. In addition to detailing the statistics of lynching in the United States and the thousands of places where these acts of sadism were committed, Ifill makes the important point that lynching was a public act in which "public spaces were used to enforce the message of white supremacy."[5] Most lynchings were not carried out in secret in the woods; rather, victims were often dragged through the streets of black neighborhoods before they were lynched in full view of the town's white citizenry at such prominent spots as the courthouse square, bridges, and parks. The point was to establish a rule of terror outside of the rule of law but also to compel citizens of the town, in general, to witness these events and thereby to become accomplices in them, binding them together.[6] Mob actions were not officially sanctioned, of course, but police, hospital workers, and town officials would turn a blind eye to what was happening, keeping away from the mob's deliberate fury.

In addition to such violent punctuations of daily life, long-standing practices in many towns obtained the force of law, as has been told recently by James W. Loewen in his revealing study *Sundown Towns: A Hidden Dimension of American Racism.*[7] A "sundown town" is one where African Americans (or other minorities) were compelled, by force of law, written or unwritten, to leave town at sunset or, typically, at 6:00 P.M. If there were any blacks in town at that time, they could leave voluntarily, often in response to some signal—siren or whistle—or they might be forcibly escorted out by the police. (In his 1938 autobiographical essay "The Ethics of Living Jim Crow," Richard Wright observes that "Negroes who have lived South know the dread of being caught alone upon the streets in white neighborhoods after the sun has set," a point he illustrates in a vivid anecdote in which he is threatened by police while making a bicycle delivery in a white town.)[8] Loewen estimates that between 1890 and 1930, there were between 3,000 and 15,000 sundown towns and that another 2,000 to 10,000 suburban towns initiated a similar practice between 1900 and 1968.[9] (In Illinois, he estimates, 70 percent of towns excluded blacks.)[10] Loewen's main emphasis is on the forced removal of African Americans from small-town America, but, as he acknowledges, Asian Americans and Jews were also subject to nativist ethnic cleansing, along with gays and lesbians.[11]

The sundown towns Loewen describes are not principally in the South, which he claims has for the most part tolerated the mixed-race town, but a first-person account by a black man growing up in Natchez, Mississippi, during the 1950s speaks directly to a kind of segregation in the southern town that drew the lines with extreme clarity:

> It was the movies, the only place I remember where whites and blacks came together. We didn't play baseball together. We didn't play football together. We'd play black schools in Mississippi. White schools played white schools. There's no other time I remember [when we'd be together], unless we were meeting on the street or something, or shopping at a place downtown. You weren't supposed to be in their neighborhoods. If they caught you, you were going to jail. They would question you and they would beat you. I heard people tell, what are you doing there, you stealing something? So you ain't got no business being in their neighborhood.[12]

If blacks were tolerated in the southern town, they were restricted by Jim Crow practices to their own distinct places. In the small towns of the Midwest, North, and West, there was more typically no place at all for blacks. The variety of towns encompasses the full range of population and the full range of socioeconomic levels; what these towns share is a racist attitude that was, during the early twentieth century especially, naturalized to the point that it was virtually invisible to residents. Sundown towns, as Loewen explains, evolved rapidly during the Jim Crow years, from 1890 through the 1930s, when segregationist policies were widespread in the U.S. following *Plessy v. Ferguson* (1896), which upheld

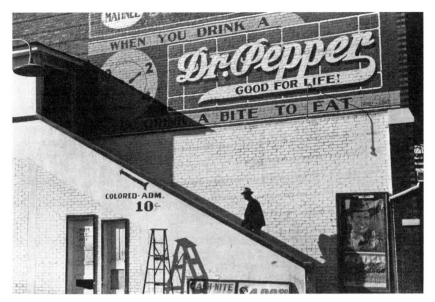

Photograph by Marion Post Wolcott, "Negro going in colored entrance of movie house on Saturday afternoon, Belzoni, Mississippi Delta, Mississippi" (FSA caption), 1939. Library of Congress, Prints and Photographs Division, FSA-OWI Collection.

Photograph by Marion Post Wolcott, "Rex Theatre for Colored People. Leland, Mississippi Delta" (FSA caption), 1939. Library of Congress, Prints and Photographs Division, FSA-OWI Collection.

the constitutionality of "separate but equal" accommodations. And these continued in practice, even after the U.S. Supreme Court's declaration in 1917 that segregationist housing policies in Louisville, Kentucky, were unconstitutional (*Buchanan v. Warley*).[13] Not only did segregationist residential patterns persist, in defiance of that ruling, but the federal government itself, beginning in the 1930s, virtually required separatist housing patterns, through the advocacy of local restrictive covenants by the Federal Housing Authority (FHA): "If a neighborhood is to retain stability," the FHA declared in 1938, "it is necessary that its properties shall continue to be occupied by the same social and racial classes."[14] Of post–World War II loans to homeowners, 98 percent were available only to whites.[15] The result of these policies was what Loewen calls the "Great Retreat," the migration, during the twentieth century, of blacks from small towns to big cities, where their presence in the inner city produced an accelerated migration of whites outward to the suburbs.[16]

The tide of segregationist housing patterns began to reverse itself only after 1968, with the civil rights legislation of the Johnson administration, including the Fair Housing Act (Title VIII of the Civil Rights Act), though, as has become increasingly clear, discrimination simply went "underground," with realtors engaging in the more subtle steering of black clients away from white neighborhoods.[17] Indeed, one can argue that the widespread creation of gated communities throughout the United States since the 1980s—with estimates of 40 percent of new housing behind gates in some areas—is simply the latest form of racial exclusion, though it may be technically based on income.[18] The fact that the model originated in South Africa and Latin America—with their polarized societies and security forces—does not bode well for the United States. As the inhabitant of the gated subdivision purchases community and supposed safety, the larger community of American society is increasingly fractured along race and class lines, and the social contract is threatened, if not ruptured.[19]

Gated communities represent, by their obvious and declared symbolism, the creation of an exclusive community, and while their popularity has ominously accelerated in the last twenty years, their antecedents stretch back to the mid-nineteenth century in America. The first such community in the United States was Llewellyn Park, in New Jersey, twelve miles west of New York City, and within commuter distance by a rail line nearby. There wealthy businessman Llewellyn Haskell, advised by landscape architect Alexander Davis, built a villa park, about the size of Central Park, with picturesque landscaping and spacious homes. The fact that

Photograph by Dorothea Lange, "Fish restaurant for colored in the quarter cotton hoers are recruited. Memphis, Tennessee" (FSA caption), 1937. Library of Congress, Prints and Photographs Division, FSA-OWI Collection.

Photograph by Ben Shahn, "Sign on restaurant, Lancaster, Ohio" (FSA caption), 1938. Library of Congress, Prints and Photographs Division, FSA-OWI Collection.

it was private, as John Stilgoe argues, may well have diminished its influence on later development.[20] Another closed society for the rich, Tuxedo Park, New York, evolved in the 1880s out of a hunting and fishing preserve owned by Pierre Lorillard IV. The fenced area grew into a vacation retreat and ultimately (in 1952) into a privately incorporated community of more than 300 houses.

IF THE CONSTRUCTION of defensive barriers to keep out the stranger represents one extreme of American social practice, compromise is at the other extreme, as embodied in the town meeting. The town meeting—which allows all registered voters in a town to vote directly in an annual meeting to decide on issues affecting the entire community—has a celebrated, even mythical, place in American political culture. Yet Frank M. Bryan's study of the institution in Vermont, *Real Democracy: The New England Town Meeting and How It Works*, reveals the degree to which this purest form of democracy, as it has been called, is in fact a limited form of participation, with only about 20 percent of a town's eligible voters typically attending the yearly meeting.[21] Although Bryan concedes that the town meeting has not successfully integrated the disadvantaged into its ritual of self-government, he nevertheless argues that it has been a uniquely educative and beneficial institution, an instrument for civic engagement, teaching responsibility, cooperation, and civility, and for balancing self-interest against the common interest.[22]

Yet Bryan does not deny the difficulty of self-government in the town meeting. And these same political virtues—and political challenges—can likewise be observed in the writings of intellectuals about the small town in the thirties and forties. Abandoning the theory of the grotesque that had encapsulated his view of small-town life circa 1920, Sherwood Anderson later called the small town, in his nonfiction study *Home Town* (1940), "the test of man's ability to adjust himself. It tells the story of his skill in living with others, his ability to go out to others and to let others be a part of his own life."[23] A similar note is sounded by Granville Hicks, one of the leading Marxist intellectuals of the 1930s, who himself had retired to a northeastern small town (more like a village) in 1932 and wrote a memoir, at the end of World War II, affirming that towns like his own had much "to teach us about the American character."[24] Turning his back on "city intellectuals" and their alternate mockery and celebration of "the common man," Hicks sought to portray the actual varieties of human character as he saw them. Being viewed as a red when he arrived at a place in which "anyone who is not a Republican is an oddity," Hicks found himself a divisive force, not so much for his political beliefs as for his being an intellectual. His reading of small-town democracy is anything but sanguine, learning as he does that "most public issues are confused by factionalism, prejudice, or stupidity, and a most unenlightened selfishness."[25] In the end, however, he comes to see the small town as "an experiment station for new democratic processes," a place where working with others—the essential premise of democracy—is a necessity.[26]

Hicks's realism about the politics of the small town, colored by optimism, reflects its moment of composition—the end of World War II, when democracy had triumphed over fascism, and its virtues needed to be recalled, something best done with a hardheaded pragmatism. A more complex sociological approach to small-town society was undertaken by Robert and Helen Lynd in their Middletown books. These studies of Muncie, Indiana—the most exhaustive studies of small-town life ever undertaken—tell us a good deal about the mentality of exclusion that governed Main Street and the traditional small town in the early twentieth century.[27] The Lynds chose Muncie precisely because it had a relatively homogeneous population, allowing the sociologists to focus on general characteristics without what they considered to be the distraction of interracial conflict or religious difference that might be found elsewhere.[28] The omission of any substantial discussion of the Jewish and African American communities of Muncie—which seems in hindsight to be oddly blinkered, to say the least—would be corrected some seventy-five years later. Nevertheless, the Lynds' examination of Muncie revealed several points worth our consideration: first, the degree to which the harmony of the small town was an artifact of public rhetoric; second, the existence of fissures in the community along class lines, made worse by the Depression; and third, the degree to which minorities in the town were marginalized—allowed a particular place and function but not full acceptance into the community.

The Lynds' chapter "The Middletown Spirit" in their second study (*Middletown in Transition*, 1937) is a compendium of the small-town belief system, with quotes gathered from the public discourse of Muncie (chiefly the editorial pages of its newspapers) and including such tenets as these:

That "radicals" ("reds," "communists," "socialists," "atheists"
—the terms are fairly interchangeable in Middletown) want to
interfere with things and "wreck American civilization." "We con-

demn agitators who masquerade under the ideals guaranteed by our Constitution. We demand the deportation of alien Communists and Anarchists." . . .

That people should have community spirit.

That they should be loyal, placing *their* family, *their* community, *their* state, and *their* nation first. "The best American foreign policy is any policy that places America first." "America first is merely common sense." . . .

That "big-city life" is inferior to Middletown life and undesirable. . . . "[Middletown] is still a 'Saturday-night town,' and if big cities call us 'hicks' for that reason, let 'em."

That most foreigners are "inferior." "There is something to this Japanese menace. Let's have no argument about it, but just send those Japs back where they came from."

That Negroes are inferior.

That individual Jews may be all right but that as a race one doesn't care to mix too much with them. . . .

That the fact that people live together in Middletown makes them a unit with common interests, and they should, therefore, all work together. . . .

That there isn't much difference any longer between the different Protestant denominations.

But that Protestantism is superior to Catholicism.

That having a Pope is un-American and a Catholic should not be elected President of the United States.[29]

The list of Middletown beliefs is fifteen pages long; the list of what Middletown is against is shorter and can be summed up in the following point: "Any strikingly divergent type of personality, especially the non-optimist, the non-joiner, the unfriendly person, and the pretentious person."[30] The Lynds observe that the Depression, in heightening insecurity, has also "brought with it greater insistence upon conformity," but the basic lines of Muncie's thinking were already laid out in the earlier study, from the twenties, when the Lynds observe the advent of the Ku Klux Klan in Muncie, brought to town by a group of wealthy businessmen.[31] Hostile to Catholics, Negroes, Jews, and anything foreign, and with torchlight parades, cross-burnings, and white-sheeted rituals, the Klan saw its vitriolic influence peak in the early twenties, though the sulfurous fumes lingered on into the thirties.

The unity of Muncie, as the Lynds describe it, is to a large degree an artifact of the news media and the official language of public leaders, who created a credo based on the promotion of business values and loyalty to power. The Depression and its insecurities deepened hostility to outsiders at the same time that it seemed to widen the distance between workers and businesspeople, whose fiction of a classless society, the "American way," worked hard to deny social class difference, proclaiming the community to be "one big happy family."[32] On the contrary, as the Lynds observe, the divisions in Muncie grew not only between the business class and the working class but also within the middle class, between a dominant business class and a more modest class of salaried employees, divisions that mirrored those in Lewis Corey's contemporaneous broader study of American society, cited by the Lynds, *The Crisis of the Middle Class*.[33]

MUNCIE, THE MOST STUDIED of American towns, offers yet another angle on small-town community during the twenties, thirties, and forties in the form of two postscripts from the perspectives of its Jewish and African American residents, which further complicate the picture of Middletown held until the 1970s. The Jewish narratives were collected in 1979 by Dwight Hoover and C. Warren Vander Hill, who were commissioned by a Muncie Jewish businessman concerned that the struggles and achievements of the earlier years would be forgotten. Muncie by 1979 had lost many of its Jewish merchants and many of the restrictions on Jewish life had disappeared, but the narratives looking back on the twenties and thirties revealed lives that were increasingly prosperous but largely isolated from mainstream American Jewish life, especially in cities like New York. Muncie's Jews were restricted in terms of where they could live, they were barred from business and professional associations, and they were excluded from Muncie's only country club. And for many of these years, they endured the frightening racket of anti-Semitism coming from the Klan and some of the public media.[34] A similar story is told by Ewa Morawska of other midwestern towns during the first decades of the twentieth century, where, despite integration in the workplace, especially in Jewish-owned stores that employed non-Jews, there was little social mixing. In Terre Haute, the separation of the population after work hours was called "the five o'clock shadow," the "tacit understanding between local Jews and the dominant group that at sunset social integration ends, and life resumes within ethnoreligious boundaries."[35]

Our understanding of Muncie's African American population is likewise the result of a Muncie native who was responding to the Lynds' omissions, in this case Hurley Goodall, an African American who had collected materials on the history of his community for many years and engaged Ball State University faculty and students (along with outside anthropological consultants) in the creation of an ethnographic history. *The Other Side of Middletown: Exploring Muncie's African American Community* tells the story of a black community that, in the early twentieth century, was only about 5 percent of the total Muncie population but that was nevertheless larger proportionally than those in most larger cities in the United States. Blacks in Muncie mainly worked at the bottom of the employment ladder—as janitors, domestics, and low-level factory workers—until the industrial boom of the 1940s, which helped African Americans obtain better employment as part of the war effort. Following the civil rights conflicts of the sixties, Muncie blacks began moving into medicine and other liberal professions and eventually into positions of commercial and civic power. Muncie's African American population lived chiefly in a separate part of the city, a distinct geography where blacks had their own clubs, associations, and medical and professional services. But the marginal position of African Americans in Muncie through most of the twentieth century, which had not registered in the Lynds' Middletown studies, concealed a community with considerable pride and stamina, surviving the Ku Klux Klan of the twenties and the Depression of the thirties to achieve eventual civic respect.[36]

The Lynds do report on Middletown's generally negative attitude toward African Americans, who are never far, in the white mind, from the possibility of criminality and immorality. Given the town's endemic suspicion of blacks, the Lynds write, "Middletown shuddered and felt confirmed in its views when two Negro boys were lynched in a nearby city."[37] This particular story is rather more complicated than that, however, when seen from the black perspective, as we learn from *The Other Side of Middletown*:

> The next morning a determined black mortician, Muncie's Reverend J. E. Johnson, drove to Marion. He intended to bring the bodies back to Muncie so that he could embalm and prepare the bodies, then return them to Marion for burial. As word of his plans swept through Muncie, a white mob began to form. The mob planned to take the bodies from Johnson's Whitely funeral home and drag

them through the streets of Muncie. Muncie's Negro community, aided by principled white law enforcement officers, gathered up arms, rallied at nearby Shaffer Chapel Church, and held an all-night vigil at the church, vowing to protect Reverend Johnson and the two bodies. The white mob, no doubt surprised by the strength of black Muncie's reaction (and by the sheriff's support of black Muncie), never fully formed. Johnson finished his work and returned the bodies, under police escort, to Marion the next day.[38]

The pride the community felt was tempered by their fear of some future reprisal, and when a black man was, the next year, arrested for murdering a white woman, the African Americans in Muncie were much relieved when the prisoner was taken to prison in another town.[39]

The Lynds were not interested in the African American perspective and were likely unaware that this had been a traumatic event for the black community. They were also unaware that Muncie was at that moment on the edge of violence and close to repeating a pattern already common in towns across America: the white community, in response to some catalytic event—a murder, a lynching, a rape—would seize the opportunity to riot, burn the houses in the African American neighborhood, and drive the black population from the town. In virtually all cases, these actions had no legal consequences for the white community. That indeed is one means by which towns in the United States became all white.

If we assume that Muncie was representative of the American town before World War II, then it seems fair to say that race, social class, ethnicity, and religion were all factors determining who belonged on Main Street and who did not. But even granting the Lynds' premise—which was an essentially white Muncie—we must still acknowledge that the lines between inclusion and exclusion were drawn within the white community itself. Muncie, in other words, was a highly stratified society, and no novelist was as meticulous in describing the small-town social structure as the Lynds were in their Middletown books. With Olympian irony, they discerned the six layers of Muncie society (chapter 12, "The Middletown Spirit"), in descending order of power and privilege: (1) an upper class of wealthy local manufacturers and bankers; (2) a group of smaller merchants and professionals; (3) a "middle class" of sorts, including retailers, minor professionals, and civil servants; (4) the "aristocracy of labor"—foremen, craftsmen, and machinists; (5) semiskilled or unskilled laborers; and (6) the "poor whites," the ragged bottom margin, not employed regularly.[40]

But if social lines were firmly drawn, they were rarely acknowledged, and Muncie's official rhetoric portrayed a society in harmony with itself at all levels. Where the Lynds show us the distinct strata of society, the myth of community affirms a unified society. And that is precisely the view anyone would take away from a major feature in *Life* magazine's May 1937 issue, a lavishly illustrated article designed to coincide with the publication of the Lynds' *Middletown in Transition*, with images of Muncie, Indiana, by *Life*'s premier photographer, Margaret Bourke-White.[41]

Bourke-White portrays Muncie "at work and at play," with pictures of leisure activities, clubs, residential sections, and domestic scenes. She also gives us a gallery of Muncie portraits, including the waitress still smiling at 1:00 A.M. and the "tycoon" George A. Ball, who, the caption explains, "began with a little glass factory in 1888" and came to own railroads, thus confirming the "reality" of the American dream. Muncie comprises, in Bourke-White's lens, a cross-section of social classes, though a society where everyone knows his place, typified by the full-page photo of the barber (vice president of Muncie's Central Labor Union) happily shaving a member of the "rich and philanthropic Ball family." Obviously, this is not Melville's *Benito Cereno*: though wielding a razor, the barber smiles benignly, and it seems out of the question that labor, as pictured, would ever dream of cutting the throat of big business.

Life presents Muncie as Muncie would want to see itself portrayed and as *Life*'s readers might expect it to be portrayed: as the "typical U.S. town," each of its inhabitants as "the average 1937 American as he really is." *Life*'s conflation of the diverse white population, so carefully distinguished by the Lynds, is staggering. Where is the "average" American in the cross-section of Muncie portraits, given the full range of social classes represented? And what does "average" mean? What we in fact see, what the photographs show us, in full-page layouts, are the contrasts between Muncie's wealthiest neighborhoods and its working-class homes—47 percent lacking running water, 20 percent lacking an indoor toilet. *Life* shows us pictorially as "typical" families the home of the mayor, who "collects old American glass," and the home of a man who is missing one leg and collecting twenty-six dollars every two weeks on relief. Can both be "typical"? We see a one-room clapboard shack papered with cardboard cartons, and we see the luxurious parlor, fireplace, and grand piano of the Ball family. Each of these, the text tells us is "a typical Midland home." And so it goes: contradictions of class and lifestyle are elided, treated as if they are part of the same coherent society. And this theme is carried to its

PLATE 1. *Main Street, Geneva, New York, a classic late-nineteenth-century main street as an idealized vision of the past. Photograph by Sandy Sorlien.*

FOURTH of JULY
in FOREST HILLS GARDENS

PLATE 2. *Forest Hills Gardens, New York, the planned community as the center of American values, ca. 1917. Illustration by Herman Rountree. Forest Hills Gardens Corporation.*

PLATE 3. *Photograph by Russell Lee of Main Street, Cascade, Idaho, celebrating the United States on the eve of World War II, 1941. Library of Congress, Prints and Photographs Division, FSA-OWI Collection.*

PLATE 4. *Gale Stockwell, Parkville, Main Street (1933), WPA painting portraying the peace and quiet of a Missouri town, with a mother and child as the sole pedestrians. Parkville is nevertheless alive with color, vitality, and industry (the smokestack), against the unpeopled Missouri River valley beyond. Smithsonian American Art Museum, transfer from the U.S. Department of Labor.*

PLATE 5. *Norman Rockwell,* Home for Christmas *(1967). Norman Rockwell's painting of the Main Street of his hometown, Stockbridge, Massachusetts, on a cold and gray New England day nevertheless portrays the warmth of the town, glowing with light and alive with holiday shoppers. Norman Rockwell Museum Collection, Stockbridge, Mass.*

A Main Street favorite is a ride on the Disneyland Fire Department's old-fashioned hose and chemical wagon.

Main Street's musical Keystone Cops provide sidewalk entertainment for Disneyland guests.

Disneyland guests find tempting meals in the beautiful surroundings of Grandfather's day at this restaurant on Main Street's Plaza.

Disneyland's horseless carriage takes some happy visitors for a ride down Main Street.

9

PLATE 6. Main Street, Disneyland, brochure with photographs of street entertainment, an old-fashioned horse-drawn fire engine, a horseless carriage, and the Plaza, 1956. Author's collection.

PLATE 7. *This welcoming sign, designed by Robert Venturi and Denise Scott Brown, evokes a fifties graphic style, celebrating the ordinary values of the Philadelphia community, Manayunk, where the world-famous architectural firm of Venturi Scott Brown happens to have its main office. Photograph by author, 2011.*

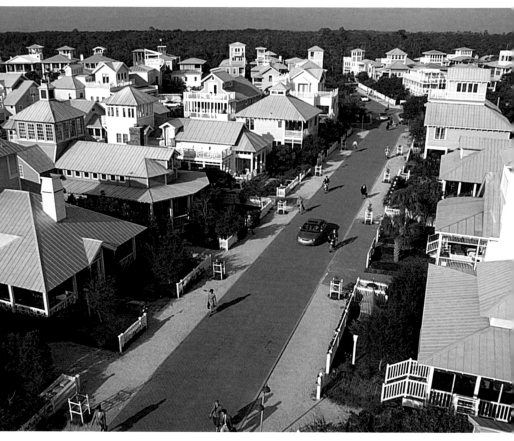

PLATE 8. *Film still from* The Truman Show *(1998), directed by Peter Weir, which was set in Seaside, Florida, the birthplace of the New Urbanism. Seaside was built by Robert and Daryl Davis, with architects Andres Duany and Elizabeth Plater-Zyberk.*

PLATE 9. *Michael McCann was commissioned by Disney and Robert A. M. Stern to do several renderings of the town of Celebration, outside of Orlando, Florida, before any construction in the town commenced, in order to create the feel of the imagined space, ca. 1990. Courtesy of Michael McCann.*

PLATE 10. *This North Philadelphia mural, with its vision of the new public housing that was replacing the dismal earlier buildings, imagines a new beginning for the inner city. Photograph by author, 2010.*

PLATE 11. *Quincy Market, Boston, a festive market created within the historic district of the city as a new urban solution: town center, outdoor mall, and Main Street combined into one, 2009. Photography by GoLeafsGo. Wikicommons.*

PLATE 12. *Detail from Skeet McAuley's* Plasticville *(1990), a photograph of a miniature playscape (manufactured by the Bachman Brothers beginning in 1947) that portrays ironically the nostalgia and banality of the small-town plastic world, capturing the post–World War II dream of community. Courtesy of Skeet McAuley.*

At the bottom of Muncie's social strata live Scott and Liza-belle Brandenberg. Scott is the second husband of Lizabelle, who hails from Fiat, Ky. Their home, lined with paper car-tons, is a one-room clapboard shack in "Shedtown." In a homemade brooder, consisting of a wooden tray, an oil lamp and a paper box, they are raising chickens "fer eatin'," not for sale. Mrs. Brandenberg talks with the Kentucky hill-billy drawl heard in many midwest industrial towns from southerners migrated north to work in the great auto plants.

At the top of Muncie life is the Ball family. Here is the West End home of William H. Ball. Son of one of four hardy brothers who founded Muncie's dominant glassworks, he typi-fies, for Dr. Lynd, a significant new development. This is "the emergence of an upper class to whom certain leisure activ-ities have value, not in relation to work, but quite independ-ently as a symbol of status." The first pink-coated fox hunt ever to astonish an Indiana landscape was held on William Ball's Orchard Lawn Saddle Horse Farm in April (turn page).

Photographs by Margaret Bourke-White of Muncie, Indiana (Middletown), showing the bottom social level and the top. From "Muncie, Ind. Is the Great U.S. 'Middle-town,'" Life, May 10, 1937. © 1937 Picture Collection Inc. Reprinted with permission. All rights reserved.

Symbol of many Ball philanthropies is Ball State Teachers College. This Bourke-White air view shows only a part of its $2,500,000 plant. The college's experimental school (*inner right*) and the Ball Memorial Hospital (*centre*) will probably soon receive more Ball millions. For early in April Philanthropist George A. Ball turned over the 28,000 miles of Van Swer- ingen railroads he bought for $3,000,000 in 1935 to a new foundation. On April 26 he sold them, in the name of the foundation, to Wall Street brokers (*see p. 28*) for $6,375,000.

Far across town from the college are homes like these. Depression years have made them shabbier, but the people in them, like all Middletown, have resisted fundamental change. New streets may strike out through the cornfields, new houses arise, new faces emerge. But year in and year out, these earnest midland folk still steer their customary middle course, still cling to their old American denominations. Middletown, say the Lynds, may relocate this course slightly to the left, but the new path will become the "American way."

Photographs by Margaret Bourke-White of Muncie, Indiana (Middletown), with an aerial view of Ball State Teachers College and a view of dilapidated housing in another part of town. From "Muncie, Ind. Is the Great U.S. 'Middletown,'" Life, May 10, 1937. © 1937 Picture Collection Inc. Reprinted with permission. All rights reserved.

conclusion in the article's ending: below a photograph of shabby homes, in the process of disintegrating, the caption reads, "Year in and year out, these earnest midland folk still steer their customary middle course, still cling to their old American dream. Middletown, say the Lynds, may relocate this course slightly to the left, but the new path will become the 'American way.'"

In the textual framing of the *Life* essay, one can see how hard America's most popular magazine was struggling to create a positive and harmonious image of small-town America, despite the far more complicated image the Lynds' text presents and most remarkably despite what the pictures themselves seem to represent. Whatever force the photographs might embody as pictures of reality was suppressed through the greater power of the captions in *Life* to shape our reading of the images.

From another perspective, however, one might say that *Life* succeeded in representing Muncie according to the accepted public image of the town, roughly the same image promulgated by the local media. Class consciousness, as the Lynds explain, remained scarce in Middletown, with some slight advance among the poor and the lower middle class, who saw some of the rewards of organized labor and generally voted for Roosevelt in 1936; at the same time, there was a hardening of attitudes among the wealthy, who were pulling away from the middle class yet whose rhetoric of egalitarianism grew correspondingly more solid. Editorials, voicing the rule of big business, declared that from the rich down to the poor, all were part of the "working class," and the only real dangers to democracy in America were class hatred and higher taxes. Yet there was a difference between private and public speech, as the Lynds observe: in public, the upper class affirms that class differences are largely imaginary, and that business and labor are partners. Yet privately they are contemptuous of the poor: "They are more incapable, stupid—just a crummy lot, biologically inferior, with a lot of these dopes from Kentucky and Tennessee." Or consider a remark like this one, also recorded by the Lynds: "Did you ever see such a sight as the Saturday evening crowd on Walnut Street?" a woman of the business class asked. "I never walk down there Saturday evening. It makes you feel like a three-penny piece. It's so cheap. I don't like it any time after noon Saturday."[42]

What impedes class consciousness for Middletown—and it is a legacy of the thirties that we have inherited into our own time—is the generally accepted belief that we are all on the social ladder, and that one can always climb upward. The small-town American, coming from a farming background, tends to see things in terms of individual responsibilities rather than the larger forces that may be constraining human action. Yet the working-class poor were only too painfully conscious of their status during the Depression at the bottom of the ladder and were happy not to mingle with the upper classes in school or shopping, where they found themselves on the receiving end of disdainful looks.

In short, careful readers of *Middletown in Transition* would recognize *Life*'s version of the Lynds' study as a gross distortion, forcing an optimism where the Lynds saw doubt and uncertainty; forcing an image of social cohesion where the Lynds saw increasing disunity; forcing an affirmation of the "American Way" where the Lynds saw at best a middle-of-the-road expediency and at worst an embrace of fascism by the business class that would be endorsed by the working class and publicized in the name of Americanism and prosperity (509–10). It could happen here, the Lynds were saying, and it could happen because the business class felt the New Deal had gone too far and the working class thought it had not gone far enough. In short, Main Street as meeting ground of the rural and urban, the new and old, looked to the Lynds like a space filled with conflicts to be negotiated, and not the happy juncture of complementary forces that *Life* habitually and programmatically pictured for its millions of readers.[43]

Small-town life would obviously be different from one place to another, but insofar as we can generalize, it seems safe to say that lines of social demarcation were clearly drawn on Main Street, and that such distinctions and submerged conflicts have marked towns in the United States from the beginning to the present. One could extend this narrative of exclusion to encompass the dividing lines not only between classes and ethnicities but also between straight and gay, and these stories also have more recently—in the past twenty years—begun to be told.[44] Main Street was in reality a place where some belonged and some were excluded, and a place where even among those who belonged the lines of hierarchy and status were clearly drawn and well understood. The only thing surprising about such a conclusion is that it stands opposed to the countertendency we have already observed, in which small towns were often represented in the media and in film, theater, and literary works as places of harmony.

The reality of disharmony and class conflict also stands opposed to the utopian impulse, itself a strong element in American culture from the early nineteenth century to the present, the impulse to build a world of community that would serve as a model for the perfect society. That utopian project is the subject of the next chapter.

Chapter Six

Utopian Dreams
From Forest Hills to Greenbelt

Sitting in a small airport in the Florida Panhandle, following a week spent looking at Florida's New Urbanist developments of the past twenty-five years, I see a large sign directly opposite me advertising newly built properties in the area: "Preserving nature's beauty and tucked inland just enough to be off the beaten path, we're building communities where small town living means quality of life, not lack of choices."[1] It is the perfect conclusion to my trip. The billboard, with enticing photographs of unpeopled spaces, sums up an ethos that has been widely appealing, if not dominant, in the late twentieth and early twenty-first centuries: the value of the small-town community. Yet the ad makes a careful distinction between the positive and negative connotations of "small town," acknowledging that "small town" might mean "lack of choices," claustrophobia, a cultural provinciality that no one would want to buy. Instead, what is being sold is the small town as enhanced "quality of life," summed up in the word "community."

At the distinctive core of the New Urbanism has been a devotion to the concept of community as embodied in an image of the small town drawn from the collective American mythical memory: the New Urbanists want their towns to *look like* the archetypal small town (modeled on the Platonic ideal of Disneyland's Main Street) and they explicitly invoke that standard. What the developers have been creating, out of bricks and mortar, earth and fresh plantings, is, in a word, tradition. And this is in fact the name of a town in Florida that makes its appeal unabashedly, in an online promotional video, to the warm and fuzzy memories of the past. How many of the prospective residents of Tradition actually grew up in a small town we cannot know, but Tradition markets itself to a collective sense of that happy past in the most predictable of ways, with sepia-tinted visuals, clips from 1950s home movies showing a happy nuclear family, a couple dancing, kids riding their bikes, a parade of Boy Scouts, boys with a dog, little girls in ballet tutus, and so on. Meanwhile, the narrator intones: "The past provides us with lots of great memories. And for most of us the past is where we lived once upon a time. That was where we learned the things that still guide us today—the importance of family, the sharing, the special feeling of belonging to a community. That's when we learned about 'our town.' That's when we learned about 'home.' And by reaching into our past, to those things about a town that made life warm and welcoming, vibrant, Core Communities has drawn on some of the best memories of home, to create a town for today and for generations to come. Tradition."[2] We cannot miss the allusion to Thornton Wilder here and the nostalgia that has colored postwar attitudes toward the small town ever since.

But how, we might ask, can the New Urbanists be talking about creating ideal towns and ideal communities in the face of the history we have just looked at—the history of Main Street's social boundaries and exclusions, of social class stratification and snobbery, the history of discrimination and marginalization, the history of lynching even, that is the actual story of small-town life? The answer is not simply that hope and utopian aspiration die hard; it is also, more practically, a matter of exactly who would be living in these new planned communities. The actual historical small town comprises a population that grows organically, with all of the accidents of fortune and misfortune that result in real communities. The planned community, an ersatz creation, an artifact of the social and spatial imagination, selects its own society along far more consistent and homogeneous lines than any actual community. To the degree that it is homogeneous—by virtue of ethnicity, color, income, social habits, customs, and religion—issues of difference and conflict are less likely to arise. In looking at the impact of the Main Street idea on planned communities of the twentieth century and beyond, we are considering communities that have struggled with just such issues. Who should be living there? Is homogeneity good, or is diversity better? How much diversity can be tolerated? How can diversity be achieved?

The effort to create the ideal community as planned space has, of course, a much longer tradition in North America, going back to the seventeenth century even, when settlements were established not only as material constructions but as social worlds. I am speaking of the design of space, the design of towns, and of the simultaneous effort to create the kind of social community traditionally associated with Main Street America. What lies behind the invention of the contemporary community in the United States? What traditions of planning did the late-twentieth-century New Urbanist planners have to draw on as they pursued the project of creating the utopian space of community? Can the good place even be planned?

The roots of the New Urbanism go back at least 100 years to the ideas of an Englishman—a visionary and amateur planner—Ebenezer Howard. Howard's concept of the garden city in his 1898 *Tomorrow: A Peaceful Path to Real Reform*, later published as *Garden Cities of To-morrow* (1902), has had a pervasive influence through the entire history of planning in the twentieth century and on into the New Urbanism of our own time, demonstrating the continuing power of the idea of the small town. True, an abundance of planned communities existed in the United States before Howard—from the utopian experiments of the mid-nineteenth century to the company towns of the late 1800s—but these examples tend to be somewhat detached and insular;[3] with Howard, in contrast, we can draw a line from the early twentieth century to the present.

Because Howard's chief labors and greatest results were in England, we tend to forget that he spent several early years in the United States. While in the Chicago area, for example, Howard doubtless visited Frederick Law Olmsted's suburban garden community, Riverside, as well as the company town of Pullman.[4] Not coincidentally, perhaps, Chicago itself was known before the great fire of 1871 as "The Garden City." But it was Edward Bellamy's American utopian romance, *Looking Backward* (1888)—so popular in its day as to spawn numerous Bellamy Clubs—that was likely the strongest catalyst for Howard in forming his own "garden cities" in England.[5] In *Looking Backward*, the main character looks back from an imagined utopian future in which the myriad social problems and unjust economic arrangements of the nineteenth century have been solved; the greed of private wealth has been banished, and the polity as a whole can now enjoy the splendor of an earthly paradise, embodied in the public architecture and spatial plan of the city that has come to replace nineteenth-century Boston: "At my feet lay a great city. Miles of broad streets, shaded by trees and lined with fine buildings, for the most part not in continuous blocks but set in larger or smaller enclosures, stretched in every direction. Every quarter contained large open squares filled with trees, along which statues glistened and fountains flashed in the late-afternoon sun. Public buildings of a colossal size and architectural grandeur unparalleled in my day raised their stately piles on every side."[6] Although Bellamy was influenced by the phalansteries of Charles Fourier, which had been translated to America in the mid-nineteenth century, Bellamy's is essentially an urban vision, carrying elements of Boston as well as Pierre-Charles L'Enfant's Washington. And it looks forward to the 1893 Chicago World's Columbian Exposition, which was being planned shortly after Bellamy's book appeared, and which likewise evinces the Victorian assumption that the function of the aesthetic is to provide moral and social discipline.

Like Bellamy's, Howard's thinking was on a grand scale, and his planned communities—with expected populations of about 30,000—were designed to be satellite cities, far enough away from the central city (London, for example) to be independent, yet close enough to allow for a degree of commerce and cultural association. Bellamy inspired Howard on another level as well: the imagined society of the future—despite its regimentation, consumerist mentality, and slight regard for the meaning of work—was in its day a vision of cooperative social equality and of the rational distribution of society's goods. Howard was not a communist, but his vision of a cooperative society was at the bottom of his thinking and has colored, in very general terms, the vision of community that Howard's followers would pursue. More concretely, the imagined future society was the physical embodiment of those ideas, the material incarnation of the community, most significant for twentieth-century planning. Howard's own book, *Garden Cities of To-morrow* (1902), would far surpass Bellamy's in its influence, especially in creating a template for the creation of planned communities in both Britain and the United States.

The influential urban theorist Lewis Mumford—who wrote an introduction to a 1965 reissue of Howard's book—saw him as the progenitor of the regional approach at the core of Mumford's own thinking from the 1920s on. Howard, for Mumford, solved the complementary problems of rural desolation and urban congestion in one concept: The garden cities were to be designed in multiple clusters around larger cities, with easy access to one another and to the major city via trains. Metropolitan growth, by this plan, would proceed in an orderly and planned way, avoiding the overcrowding of cities and the sprawling haphazard development of the suburbs. Surrounding the cities would be green land, thus preserving a needed agricultural base; and within the cities would be manufacturing zones, thus allowing for needed production.[7] Most important, these were self-sufficient communities, not bedroom adjuncts to the metropolis, and they were organized around an economic plan that made residents renters who were gradually paying off the mortgage debt of the company that would found the community. Howard's success in England—Letchworth

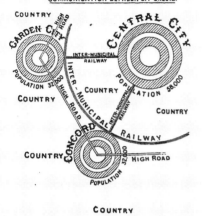

"Illustrating Correct Principle of a City's Growth," with circular cities interconnected by rail and roads and rural country zones in between. From Ebenezer Howard, Garden Cities of To-morrow *(1902).*

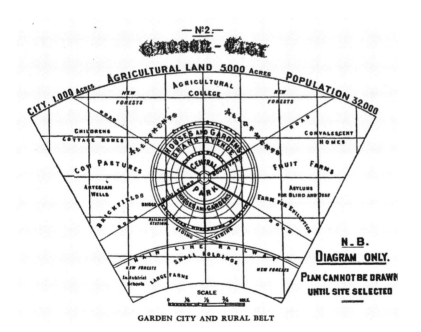

"Garden City and Rural Belt," showing the central park of the town surrounded by houses and gardens, with farm fields and pastures beyond. From Ebenezer Howard, Garden Cities of To-morrow *(1902).*

Garden City (1903) and the later Welwyn Garden City (1920) were out-growths of his thinking—gave substance and legitimacy to his utopian ideas and were touchstones for American planners.

The garden city idea has had a long life in America, though never coming close to achieving the concrete embodiments produced in England, where government-sponsored new towns built after World War II accommodated at least 10 percent of Britain's population growth.[8] With the Garden City Association of America founded in 1906 by Howard and other like-minded church and civic leaders, the road was paved for the new vision. And what Howard's idea came to represent was a way of thinking about space, on two levels—the level of regional planning, where the community's place in a larger geography that preserved agricultural green land could be envisioned; and the level of the community itself, where the incorporation of green space within a geometric plan was variously interpreted to fulfill the basic principle that man and nature should live in harmony, restoring a connection broken by the industrial age. More specifically, it translated into two principal design ideas: that communities should be planned with a hierarchy of roads, so that traffic through residential areas could be limited and controlled; and that communities were best conceived as bounded spaces, having a limited population and an optimum size.[9]

If Robert Fishman is right in arguing that the years 1890 to 1930 witnessed "the most fundamental global transformation" of our century— "the change from a world still centered on the rural village to a world dominated by the 'mega-city'"—then we might view the planned communities of the early twentieth century as intentional responses to that transformation, an effort to counter the dystopian aspects of urban civilization as it was evolving on the inhuman scale and in the monolithic verticality of the modern city.[10] (In like manner we could view the planned communities of the post–World War II era as an effort to counter the dystopia of suburbia.) There were piecemeal solutions to the problem, at the local level, as for example in the popular bungalow courts built in Southern California, beginning around 1910, by Arthur S. Heineman and others, consisting typically of ten to twenty attached dwellings and featuring a well-kept harmonious aesthetic environment, shared garages, and a community "playhouse" where guests could organize their own entertainments.[11] But even while bungalow courts were spreading across the country from the West Coast, a stronger and more ambitious model was already well under way on the East Coast, built under the direct influence of the garden city idea.

One of the first communities inspired by Ebenezer Howard to be built in the United States was Forest Hills Gardens, begun in 1908 in the borough of Queens, New York. Where Howard labored hard to come up with investment plans for his communities in England, Forest Hills was the creation of the philanthropic Russell Sage Foundation, which brought in the extraordinary team of landscape architect Frederick Law Olmsted Jr. and architect Grosvenor Atterbury. The Sage Foundation aimed initially to construct model housing for the working class, but land costs quickly made this goal unworkable, and the target audience for Forest Hills mutated from the worker to the middle-class professional—clerks, merchants, managers, salesmen, architects, artists, teachers, and engineers.[12] There were some small apartment houses placed close to the town center, but otherwise, the houses were attractively Tudor in style, evoking an old English feel, yet filtered through an arts and crafts sensibility. In the initial conception, there were few freestanding homes, as Atterbury was striving for picturesque groupings, with some houses at right angles to others and with varying lot arrangements, so as to create quaint clusters rather than the usual emplacement on a rectilinear lot.[13] Olmsted's street plan, with wide central avenues and narrower secondary roads, favored gentle curves and pleasantly winding streets that interwove common open greens and private yards. As Olmsted wrote, "The monotony of endless, straight, windswept thoroughfares which represent the New York conception of streets will give place to short, quiet, self-contained and garden-like neighborhoods."[14] Olmsted Jr. was doubtless influenced by the strong example of his father's signature design element—the gently curving roads the senior Frederick Law Olmsted built in Manhattan's Central Park, which slow down vehicular traffic and express the ideal of a leisured and humane appreciation of nature. (Riverside, outside of Chicago, was an early suburban community designed by Olmsted senior along these same curving lines.) Also, Olmsted Jr. had traveled to Europe the year before designing Forest Hills Gardens—visiting Howard's first garden city, Letchworth; Hampstead Garden Suburb outside of London; and German models of town planning and medieval villages—and brilliantly synthesized what he had absorbed in the New York plan.[15]

Built on land adjacent to the Long Island Railroad, Forest Hills incorporated the commuter line train station into the town center, a coherent

Bird's-eye view of Forest Hills Gardens, New York, showing housing clusters with miniparks and common lawns in between, ca. 1915. Frances Loeb Library, Graduate School of Design, Harvard University.

design of shops and a hotel with a clock tower. In this sense, at least, Forest Hills Gardens was following the example of countless American Main Streets, built alongside railroad lines. But the town center did not have the simple linearity of an American Main Street, although it did embody the same sense of a commercial center that was also a center for the community. Built of reddish stucco and evoking a romantic storybook village, part English arts and crafts and part German medieval village, the town center was like a fairytale of Europe, magical, yet derivative. Despite the European inspiration—or rather precisely because of it, given the cultural predominance of Europe at the time—Forest Hills was to be an American garden city, an exemplar for future suburban development. As a program for Independence Day 1915 proclaimed, the community "will help to make the nation great by illustrating the greatness possible to a small village."[16] (See Plate 2.) The greatness intended was above all based on the idea of community as opposed to individualism, and Forest Hills was seeking in its design qualities the creation of a community spirit that was secular but based on a homogeneous population.[17]

Two major principles embodied in the design of Forest Hills Gardens would prove foundational for subsequent American planning: the grouping of houses and the consistency of design. These features had been found previously in company towns or utopian communities, where members of the community had basically given up their individual rights by virtue of either their allegiance to an idea (the utopia) or their consent to conditions of labor (the company town). Forests Hills was neither company town nor utopia. It was a planned development where residents bought property that they individually owned, yet by virtue of their ownership they were agreeing to give up some of their own individuality; they were buying into a community. Atterbury and Olmsted had designed a place where the individual house might be clustered in an arrangement of houses, rather than standing entirely on its own; where outside spaces could accordingly be shared in common; and where housing styles were either initiated by the original architect or could be added only with the approval of the architect or an architectural review board.

In thus aiming for a coherent aesthetic environment, Forest Hills Gardens was following the principles already formulated in Parker and Unwin's Hampstead Garden Suburb, conceived a couple of years before Forest Hills, where roads and spacing were carefully planned to achieve an overall effect. Behind Hampstead, as Unwin made clear in his comprehensive *Town Planning in Practice*, lay the broader idea of cooperation:

> However much we may strive to improve the individual cottage, to extend its accommodation, and enlarge its share of garden or public ground, it must for a long time, and probably for ever, remain true that the conveniences and luxuries with which the few rich are able to surround themselves cannot be multiplied so that they can be added to every house. It is possible, however, and indeed easy, by co-operation to provide for all a reasonable *share* of these same conveniences and luxuries; and if we once overcome the excessive prejudice which shuts up the individual family and all its domestic activities within the precincts of its own cottage, there is hardly any limit to be set to the advantages which co-operation may introduce.[18]

Clearly, the basic principle of cooperation, of shared common resources, was in the air, and the Russell Sage Foundation and Olmsted and Atterbury were exemplifying it in this first American garden city. Yet it was, for Americans, a revolutionary (even an "anti-American") idea that was being sold here: instead of the primacy of the individual and the individual house, Forest Hills as garden city was to represent the possibility of sharing space, sharing luxuries: cooperating, not competing.

Station Square, Forest Hills Gardens, New York, with the railroad connection to New York City and shops and a hotel at the town square, ca. 1915. Frances Loeb Library, Graduate School of Design, Harvard University.

But the term *garden city* in its American incarnation was certainly far different from the English model that Parker and Unwin, based on Howard, had realized. Whatever it was, Forest Hills Gardens was not a place for residents to work (in fact, virtually every industry was forbidden in the place); nor did it house anywhere near the population of Howard's new towns; nor was there the mix of income levels originally envisioned. (This mutation from an intended diverse socioeconomic mix to a more homogeneous one has more than once been the consequence of planned communities whose attractiveness created a strong enough market to displace the lower-income population.) Instead, it was a model for neighborhood development, an adaption of the British planner's theories to the more modest needs of an expanding metropolitan area where amassing land to build on was a huge challenge. It was, in short, a bedroom community, yet still a small town, one in which the physical plan—the street layout, local shops, shared public spaces, the town's size and boundaries—created a sense of insulation from the rest of the city. And the commercial town center, though not a linear Main Street, functioned as a hub for the residential areas, thus anticipating a crucial aspect of New Urbanist design. As a new

Station Square, Forest Hills Gardens, New York, view of the street and tower, ca. 1920. Frances Loeb Library, Graduate School of Design, Harvard University.

community, Forest Hills needed services and recreation, creating thereby a sense of common purpose among the residents. "The plan, in most of its aspects, either compelled association or made it easy and enjoyable."[19]

In short, the Russell Sage Foundation had built a neighborhood from scratch, an idea that would have far-reaching implications for town planning in the twentieth century. In fact, the major theorist of neighborhood planning in the United States, Clarence Perry, lived in Forest Hills for years and credited his surroundings as a major inspiration in his thinking. Perry's experience at Forest Hills, with its quaint town center, its mix of apartments and single families, its winding streets and open green spaces, its community theater, its Christmas Eve caroling, its Fourth of July celebrations, and special events like the 1917 speech by Theodore Roosevelt, who hopped off the Long Island railroad at Forest Hills for the occasion, on his way to his home on Long Island—all of this was deeply influential on Perry's thinking, and Perry's thinking in turn strongly shaped the evolution of neighborhood and community development in the first half of the twentieth century.

CLARENCE PERRY posited that community was a defining social agency, creating moral health, happiness, and collective welfare within groups that met face-to-face for decision and discussion, whether casual or formal. What the neighborhood represented as well, as Shelby M. Harrison wrote in introducing Perry's *The Neighborhood Unit* (1929), was "the physical basis for that kind of face-to-face association which characterized the old village community and which the large city finds it so difficult to recreate."[20] Perry saw the city in the machine age as a magnet for the arts and education but also, with its overcrowded neighborhoods, as a place of misery, insanity, and suicide.[21] The city was the essential background, the negative force, against which the neighborhood concept evolved (which explains why the utopian communities of the non-urban nineteenth century never gained traction on a national scale), and the city meant, at this point in time, mass society, where individual identity was all too easily erased by the sheer size and complexity of urban life. (Perry's study came out one year after King Vidor's classic cinematic depiction of the problem of the individual in a mass society, *The Crowd* [1928].)

Seeking a way to duplicate the success of Forest Hills, Perry concentrated his attention on recreation spaces, community centers, and shopping districts, in relation to residential areas and population.[22] The ideal neighborhood, as Perry saw it, would cover a radius of approximately one-half mile from a central elementary school and town center, encompassing about 1,000 families, with a population of about 5,000.[23] (Perry had learned from Ebenezer Howard's mapping of neighborhoods in his garden cities.) Assessing the needs of families with children, especially, Perry saw the distinct disadvantages of large metropolitan areas like New York City, where schools might be far from home and playgrounds too few and too small. But even if playgrounds—the essential meeting place for children and an essential of community life—were large enough and close enough, there was still the special consideration of who was there. Parents "need a school, a playground, groceries and drug stores, and perhaps a church. They want their children to associate with children from homes which hold standards similar to their own." Or again, the playground "may be both accessible and safely reached and not be satisfactory if it must serve classes of people who will not mix or allow their children to play together."[24] Social homogeneity underlay this early conception of the ideal neighborhood: at Forest Hills, references were required of prospective buyers "with a view to discovering whether they would make congenial members of the colony."[25] Needless to say, African Americans and other minorities would not fit into this congeniality model. In short, Perry makes a twofold assumption as to what is essential for community: while his main energies are focused on the physical and material structures that shape community and character, he is also taking for granted and articulating unashamedly that sameness of population is a key factor in establishing community. As Perry wrote in conclusion, Forest Hills "constitutes an excellent illustration of a new type of urban local community. The fine quality of neighborly social life it has produced obviously has its roots in a real estate plan which brought people of somewhat similar standards into proximity, and then promoted acquaintance-ships and congenial groupings through the mere routine of caring for common values and facilities."[26]

Forest Hills has sustained its air of exclusivity into the twenty-first century, with houses and surrounding grounds well maintained. And while there are freestanding private homes, there are also many attached and semiattached units, whose residents have happily given up their private yards, front and back, to the greater good of shared space and a shared aesthetic appearance. The difference between houses within the visible borders of the neighborhood and those outside is immediately palpable: outside, there is a looser standard of maintenance along with aesthetic chaos, with new houses in a variety of styles, some seemingly invented on the spot, often with absurdly palatial ambitions though built on tight lots. Compared to the aesthetic consistency of Forest Hills Gardens, the world outside is either drably conventional or over the top. But the gain of aesthetic consistency within the Gardens is purchased at the price of mandatory conformity: residents are governed by a host of restrictions on streets and buildings, resulting in a community that is charmingly photogenic but also, according to critics, unaccommodating to change (ignoring the automobile, for one) and having, paradoxically, the air of a company town.[27] The past visitor to Forest Hills Gardens might have felt like an interloper in a land of fantasy and privilege, but today's caller might as well be visiting a gated community, for all the welcome it affords the outsider. Signs are ubiquitous warning that the streets are "private" and that parking is prohibited except with a proper sticker; even larger signs, such as one sees on the walls of convenience stores, are placed at intervals reiterating that warning, with the additional proviso that cars will be towed, with the usual extravagant sum required to liberate them. Meanwhile, the larger neighborhood of Forest Hills—surrounding the Gardens—is, like all of Queens, a new world in the twenty-first century, with a fair share of ethnic residents, especially Asian Americans, who have moved into what was previously a neighborhood with strict ethnic policing.

THE CONCEPT OF THE NEIGHBORHOOD as the foundation for growth within the large city became the foundation for later efforts to build communities along less exclusive lines, and the decades after Forest Hills—until the Great Depression—saw several significant and successful experiments in community planning. Arguably the most notable during the two decades following Forest Hills were Mariemont outside of Cincinnati; Sunnyside, in Long Island City, Queens; and Radburn in northern New Jersey.

Like Forest Hills Gardens, John Nolen's Mariemont had the financial backing of a philanthropist—Mary Emery, a visionary who was not embarrassed to align her own inspiration with Edgar Allan Poe's in his fantasy "The Domain of Arnheim," a visionary tale that describes a perfect landscape, the fulfillment of the landowner's utopian dreams. (Nolen gave Emery a volume of Poe, himself inviting the parallel with Arnheim.)[28] Emery's agent in enacting her dreams was Charles J. Livingood, who arranged for the purchase of the land and hired Nolen as master planner. Livingood and Nolen coordinated the various architects who were designing homes for the community, which featured housing at various income levels, including workers' apartments. (In keeping with the English village influence, the architecture followed Norman, Tudor, Queen Anne, and Georgian styles.)[29] Mariemont was within easy distance of Cincinnati, but Nolen was prescient in anticipating the problem of sprawl as cities spread planlessly outward, and he modeled his town on Howard's Letchworth Garden City, imagining it as a "national exemplar" for the United States. Planned as a self-sufficient community, Mariemont had its own schools, church, farm, hospital, commercial town center, and a community governing structure; anticipating New Urbanist principles, Mariemont was planned as a walking community, with a mix of residential and commercial property housed in a town center; streets were interconnected and the neighborhood had a defined edge.[30]

Also a product of the forward-looking 1920s were the planned communities of Sunnyside and Radburn, both designed by Clarence Stein in association with the Regional Planning Association of America (RPAA). By the 1920s it was becoming clear to these regional planners—a group that included Stein, Lewis Mumford, Benton MacKaye, Henry Wright, and Alexander Bing—that America was at a turning point forced by the ever growing popularity of the automobile. MacKaye's 1928 *The New Explora-*

tion posited four stages, corresponding to patterns of migration: the first migration was the initial westward expansion into the frontiers; the second was the migration via the railroads, which allowed for the establishment of industrial centers; the third was the migration back to the city, with its skyscrapers and financial centers. All of these migrations were still in progress, MacKaye argued, but the fourth, a function of the automobile age, was the most momentous for the twentieth century and marked the movement out from the city to the suburbs and the surrounding metropolitan region. The solution, as MacKaye argued in *The New Exploration*, was not to expand existing towns into larger entities, for that degraded the integrity of the towns' distinct cultures. Instead, MacKaye advocated the village as a kind of ideal community, with its definite limitations of physical scale and population (about 2,500). The New England village was the archetype, with its common ("the nucleus of the village life")[31] and its five main structures, each embodying a crucial sphere of human activity—the church (religion), the town hall (politics), the schoolhouse (education), the general store (commerce), and the dwelling houses. But with the village ideal long in the past, what was needed now, MacKaye argued, along with Mumford and others, was regional development that allowed for expansion out of the city into planned communities separated from one another by green zones yet tied together by limited-access highways. In a 1930 article, MacKaye termed these the "Highwayless Town" and the "Townless Highway." The example he pointed to was Stein's Radburn, New Jersey.[32]

Radburn was actually the second invention of Stein and Wright. Their first was the community of Sunnyside, in Long Island City, established in 1924 by realtor and RPAA member Alexander Bing, who founded the nonprofit City Housing Corporation (CHC) and was able to secure land in Queens that was available and inexpensive (thanks partly to a city tax break), but that had to be developed in conformity with the city's grid system. On seventy-seven acres zoned for industrial use and thus offering flexibility in terms of housing groupings, Stein and Wright constructed 1,200 units on only 28 percent of the land, thus leaving plenty of open space for backyards, a community park (members only), and, most important, a common area within each city block. Many of the houses were two-story row houses, but there were also two- and three-family houses (allowing for rental units) as well as apartment houses. All fronted the streets on four sides of each large block, with the interior court serving as community space that would beautify the grounds, allow playing space

Sunnyside Gardens

A HOME COMMUNITY

*"Sunnyside Gardens: A Home Com-
munity," Long Island City, New York,
promotional brochure, ca. 1920s.
Greater Astoria Historical Society.*

for children (who could be observed from the house), and symbolize the ethos of community that lay behind the conception of Sunnyside Gardens. Sunnyside had, as Richard Ely wrote in 1926, two aims: to promote individual homeownership ("a home owner is almost invariably a good citizen") and to advance community values ("encourage and develop cooperative methods of home ownership").[33]

   Aiming for a middle-class community, the early residents were about one-third blue-collar workers and two-thirds white-collar, with a number of artists and writers as well, for whom Sunnyside was seen as an inexpensive and pastoral outpost of Greenwich Village.[34] Unlike the more professional class of Forest Hills, Sunnyside Gardens had a more mixed population: about a quarter of Sunnyside's population in 1928 comprised intellectuals—artists, writers, and teachers—with the great majority identifying themselves as mechanics, office workers, small tradesmen, and salesmen.[35] With a median income at the time of $3,000, residents clearly were not the very poor, who would later be housed under government-supported public housing programs. There were many rental units as well, and Stein was happy with the resulting environment in which renters and

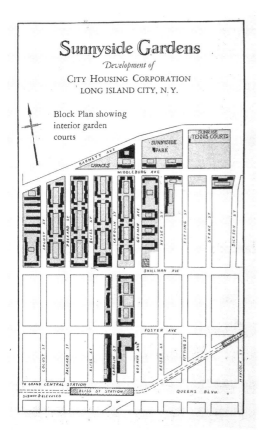

Sunnyside Gardens

Development of
CITY HOUSING CORPORATION
LONG ISLAND CITY, N. Y.

Block Plan showing interior garden courts

Sunnyside Gardens, Long Island City, New York, block plan showing interior garden courts, ca. 1920s. Greater Astoria Historical Society.

owners had an equal voice, however different their backgrounds and interests: one main motivation for Sunnyside was the creation of a "democratic community," combining individual homeownership with a communitarian, socialistic ethos.

Lewis Mumford, perhaps the leading intellectual of the time with a major interest in urbanism, lived there for eleven years (1924–35), moving from a small apartment to a larger house. For Mumford, Sunnyside offered space on a human scale, with "gardens and courts [that] kept that friendly air," as the trees and gardens grew.[36] Sunnyside represented, for Mumford, "the essential idea of community," which came not only from the physical design of the place, with its common areas, but even more from the diversity of the community, the mix of professional and working-class residents, an attraction equal to the charm of its architecture and plan. In the early thirties, Mumford recalled, all were imbued with a community spirit that manifested itself in social activities and parties, local

Sunnyside Gardens, Long Island City, New York, photographic views of the inner courtyards with common areas for playing and walking, promotional brochure, ca. 1920s. Greater Astoria Historical Society.

politics, and meetings on community maintenance. To Mumford, the local meetings proved "that with a little leeway for experiment, the democratic process would still function provided the local unit allowed a mixture of political, religious, and social beliefs—and of occupations, too."[37] Sunnyside was diverse, as Mumford notes, but its population was all within a middle-class range and was also self-selecting, since its residents had chosen the experimental community partly because of what it stood for.

Sunnyside Gardens was thus envisioned as a social experiment, balancing the value of homeownership and the value of community. With a supporting economic structure that would make it all work, buyers needed only a 10 percent down payment to purchase property, which came with certain easements allowing community access. Covenants governed what homeowners could and could not change, thus limiting individual freedom but ensuring a common and consistent aesthetic environment. And

Sunnyside Gardens, Long Island City, New York, community garden, with children gardening, ca. 1920s. The billboard in the background reads "Sunnyside Gardens: A Home Community." Greater Astoria Historical Society.

generally, the experiment of Sunnyside Gardens as a community of common interest was sustained through the first generation of residents.

But the relative unity of Sunnyside Gardens began to fracture as early as the 1930s under the weight of the Great Depression, when many of the homeowners were forced to abandon their dream of community. Ironically, the struggle to remain in their homes offered perhaps the last unified cause worth fighting for, when many of the residents, unable to pay their mortgages, went on strike against the City Housing Corporation. But the mortgages were now held by various other lending institutions, and the CHC, which had organized Sunnyside's financing, was by now the wrong target and powerless to help.[38] As Stein saw it, this was the beginning of the end for the community ethos that the corporation was trying to build, with increasing conflicts among residents. What he could not foresee were the even greater challenges that lay ahead for Sunnyside Gardens as the distance grew between the original communitarian ethos and a later-twentieth-century spirit of individualism, resulting in a conflict over the essence of what Sunnyside Gardens means, or meant, as a planned community.

Present-day Sunnyside retains the basic structure of the original design, with taller trees and more lavish landscaping in some of the inner courtyards. The private park still serves the Sunnyside Gardens community, with tennis courts for adults and play areas for small children. But the population has changed somewhat over the years: by the forties and fifties Sunnyside had, along with the Irish, a significant Jewish population, but by the sixties, the Jews were moving out, and Sunnyside generally began to assume the multicultural diversity typical of Queens. (A *New York Times* reporter could write in 1983 of the increasingly "Korean, Spanish, German and Armenian" populations, with "just a scattering of blacks.")[39] African Americans, in the early twenty-first century, remain a minority in Sunnyside, with increasing numbers of Central American immigrants and Asian Americans.

Given the idealism of the founding generation, with its faith in community and diversity, it is not surprising that Sunnyside has always attracted a certain number of politically progressive types, and as new residents move in, many have appreciated the historic importance of the development and have sustained its aesthetic unity as a cultural value. Yet in other ways, the community has suffered the ravages of "improvement," begun in 1964, when the original easements expired, thus allowing owners to claim the individuality of their property. Stein's assumption, of course, was that Sunnyside would sustain its aesthetic integrity: "The brick exteriors remain more harmonious than wood because they are not painted. Therefore there is no danger of assertive souls expressing their individuality, to the dismay of their neighbors, by coloring their dwelling with an inharmonious pigment. The natural quality of the brick eliminates the need of one expensive item of upkeep."[40] Yet in other, subtler ways, Stein seems to have tacitly allowed, if not approved, certain other changes to the original design, visible in the 1949 photographs of the place, included in Stein's *Toward New Towns for America*. The original 1926 *Declaration of Easements and Restrictions* had forbidden fences or hedges in the common backyards, which were three and a half acres large; when Stein wrote *Toward New Towns for America*, his illustrations reveal that some inner yards had hedges separating the common area from small, private backyards.[41]

In succeeding years, Sunnyside Gardens would change more drastically. Following the termination of the easements in the mid-sixties, the inner courtyards now were violated by the installation of chain-link metal fences and a variety of other fencing to separate the private from the public. Within the private fencing, owners were free to use the space as a garden, a patio, a wooden deck, or, if they chose, a junkyard. On the street side, where once the brick facades had had a pleasing uniformity and coherence of design, owners began constructing enclosed vestibules, faced with every conceivable variety of building material; others built bay windows, or balconies, or vertical additions, or cut curbs for driveways, putting their cars in their frontyards. Seeing these changes, and feeling they were destroying the original concept of the community, a group of residents challenged the renegade home improvers in court, eventually achieving a victory that resulted in 1974 in the designation of Sunnyside Gardens as a Special Planned Community Preservation District. But since the law was not retroactive, the visible "damage" could not be undone, and the community's division between preservationists and property-rights advocates became more entrenched, with one group favoring community history and the other favoring individualism and property rights. The chain-link backyards in many of the courts and the incongruous modern "improvements" to the red brick Georgian facades still testify to the history of the conflict. (In 2007, New York City's Landmarks Preservation Commission recommended landmark status for Sunnyside, writing guidelines for any future changes residents might make.)[42] Meanwhile, the private Sunnyside Gardens Park is still private and closed to outsiders, and, like all private parks, a source of pleasure for those inside and resentment for those outside.

Does the history of Sunnyside Gardens demonstrate, as some might argue, the irrelevance of the "master plan" to contemporary political and social behavior, the failure of the original planners, Stein and Wright, to build in enough flexibility to accommodate individual taste and changing values? Or does it demonstrate a clash of values between American individualism and a socially conscious respect for community values? Or does it demonstrate simply a failure on the part of the realtors marketing Sunnyside Gardens? If someone moves into Sunnyside expecting and desiring a planned community that will remain faithful to the original design, then we have no problem; but if someone moves in who is really only interested in finding a house and not a community, then the imposition of community rules governing backyards, paint color, additions, and so on will seem like a restraint on individual choice. Of course the solution is for the individualist to move to a community that allows such choices

"Radburn: The Town for the Motor Age. Safe for Children," Radburn, New Jersey, promotional brochure, ca. 1920s. From the personal collection of Jane Lyle Diepeveen, Fair Lawn Borough Historian.

and let the others live in their planned community, but the complexities of circumstance often make that resolution difficult. The post-1960s battles in Sunnyside Gardens, while a paradigm of the conflict between individual rights and communal values, were rooted in the ambivalence of the founders, an ambivalence expressed in the expiration of the easements and covenants that governed the original deeds.

STEIN AND WRIGHT'S next major project was the community of Radburn, New Jersey, built in 1928, a few years after Sunnyside, and it represented an even bigger step toward the garden city ideal. Instead of being forced to conform their plan to the city grid, as in Sunnyside, Stein and Wright could create a street plan that would freely express the design and intent of the community, and the result was the highly influential "Radburn idea," as it came to be known. If Sunnyside had the advantage of a nearby elevated train that took residents to Manhattan in twenty minutes, Radburn had a commuter rail line to New York City, with a station within easy walking distance. In fact, lacking industry in the area, Radburn's residents were mostly commuters, with New York sixteen miles away. But

Photograph by Carl Mydans of Radburn, New Jersey, with fronts of houses facing an interior common with walkways, 1935. The street and motor vehicles were accessed behind the houses. Library of Congress, Prints and Photographs Division, FSA-OWI Collection.

the founding idea was to make Radburn a town for the motor age, yet what this meant was that the automobile would be virtually invisible, ingeniously kept out of the main public areas in front of the houses (which bordered on the common park lands) and relegated instead to back streets and back doors.[43]

Like Sunnyside, Radburn was intended as a mixed-income community, with rental units and individual homes, though as it evolved, with higher construction costs and a smaller number of units than originally anticipated, it became in reality far more homogeneous—an upper-middle-class suburb of New York, quite different from Sunnyside, with minimum family income of $5,000 required for purchasers (city residents typically earned $1,200), resulting in nearly 60 percent of residents who were junior executives and professionals commuting to the city.[44] Radburn was an all-white community; 86 percent of the men and 75 percent of the women had college degrees; 77 percent of all residents were Protestant; and 16 percent were Catholic.[45] Unlike Sunnyside Gardens, it was far removed from the urban texture of New York City, and the intent of the CHC was to keep it forever as a model community.

Photograph by Carl Mydans, "Underground pass at the Radburn, New Jersey, model housing community which alleviates the dangers of the highway" (FSA caption), 1935. Library of Congress, Prints and Photographs Division, FSA-OWI Collection.

Stein employed a plan of graduated roads, differentiated according to speed and function: the highway led to perimeter roads which led to connecting or "collector" roads, which led to culs-de-sac in the backs of the houses. Moreover, by building under- and overpasses, pedestrian paths were separate from vehicular routes, an idea first embodied in Olmsted's Central Park. The key feature was the superblock: taking an idea from Sunnyside, Stein and Wright created two superblocks (thirty to fifty acres in size), plus the major part of a third, with houses facing a central common area, thus rendering automobiles invisible from the fronts of houses and from the interior grassy common areas. All of the houses had private gardens, but these opened onto a larger common area with ample recreational space and free from surrounding traffic. Pedestrian paths separated the private space from the public common, but the general flow created a sense of community that is still essentially visible, despite the fact that some residents have, over the years, built private fences or grown hedges to fence in their privacy. (The efforts are more modest than in Sunnyside.) Radburn was a comprehensive plan, intending not only to unite the human and the natural but to provide a community that had its own governance, its own schools, churches, and theaters.

Photograph by Carl Mydans, "Commercial Center of the Radburn, New Jersey, model housing community" (FSA caption), 1935. Library of Congress, Prints and Photographs Division, FSA-OWI Collection.

Radburn has aged nicely, with the original brick or frame colonial-style buildings retaining a traditional quality that is echoed in the original town center, a public area comprising shops and a meeting hall—the Plaza Building—situated at the intersection of two major roadways and serving the areas surrounding Radburn itself. The stately original colonial town center still stands, surrounded by more recent commercial development that is out of sync and out of scale with the original plan.

Envisioned for 25,000 residents, Radburn would have been, if completed, close to the ideal size of Howard's garden city, though it lacked the essential greenbelt around it that Howard had sought; Radburn was, and still is, essentially a bedroom community. But in the end, with Radburn's opening coinciding with the advent of the Great Depression, only two superblocks were built before the CHC went bankrupt and homeowners, with spreading unemployment, began to lose their mortgages. (Building continued in Radburn through the 1930s, but at a much slower rate.) Still, Radburn demonstrated the viability of planning a town that could accommodate the automobile, or rather, in keeping with advanced thinking in the twenties and thirties, limit its intrusion into the space for living and playing. It also demonstrated the virtues of the neighborhood plan, with all residences within a half-mile radius of schools; even today, children play as they always have in the playgrounds and grassy common areas within shouting distance of their homes. What it demonstrated above all, to Stein, was the value of community itself, and in writing about Radburn some years later, Stein remarked on "the friendly atmosphere, the relaxed tempo of the community, [which] speak of pleasure in living."[46]

But creating a utopia in the midst of the real world was not without its problems, both external and internal. Looking back at Radburn, Stein noted the friction that developed between the new community, with its luxurious amenities (swimming pools, tennis courts, community center, etc.), and the surrounding borough of Fair Lawn. When Fair Lawn could exert its power over Radburn, it did not hesitate to do so. Radburn residents paid additional charges and taxes, but, as Stein worried, if the new town could not serve a "normal cross-section of American people . . . the bad social effects might easily outweigh the benefits."[47]

Internally, Radburn's peculiar governance structure has proven to be a two-edged sword. In addition to the restrictive covenants governing the appearance of buildings in Radburn, the main innovation of the CHC was the creation of the Radburn Association, incorporated to collect charges, maintain services, and enforce protective restrictions, and governed by a "self-perpetuating Board of Trustees," thus "having the power and functions of a municipal government." Yet the Radburn Association Trustees did not necessarily include, as members, residents of Radburn. It could choose its own successors. As Stein exclaims, in some astonishment at the Frankenstein he and his associates had created, "An American government without public representation! Luckily it was well administered for the good of the Radburn people by one of the ablest town managers in America, John Walker, chosen by the Trustees."[48] (All trustees are now Radburn residents.)[49]

Here was a much admired, much imitated community, spacious, peaceful, orderly, and vital in many ways, yet ruled by a town manager reporting to a board that was not subject to dismissal or free election. One must ask whether it was despite this oligarchy or because of it that Radburn has flourished. When the residents in 2005 petitioned the New Jersey Department of Community Affairs to compel the governing board to allow their representation on it, the community's manager responded, "People in Radburn become wonderful human beings. . . . I don't know why it happens, but it does. And I don't know why we would want to change a way of life that's worked so well. I don't know why people would want to pit neighbor against neighbor and friend against friend."[50] Democracy be hanged—this benevolent dictatorship works! In any case, the first decade of the twenty-first century brought a crisis that would test the strength of the founding principles, as the Radburn Association Trustees decided (without community input) to sell a nondedicated park, formerly a ball-field complex owned by the town of Radburn, to a developer who would create high-density housing, a decision opposed by the Radburn Citizens' Association, which is democratically elected to represent the residents but has little power over the governing Radburn Association.[51]

In addition to becoming an internationally significant model for planned communities, Radburn became a model of how restrictive communities can be governed in the United States, offering the paradigm for future "common interest housing developments." As Evan McKenzie observes, the deeds and governing structures created in the late 1920s for Radburn in effect enabled the creation of "positive ghettos," as he calls them. Until 1948 (when a U.S. Supreme Court decision declared the practice unconstitutional), developers could exclude African Americans, Jews, and Asians. After that, instead of restricting the undesirable to a bounded geography, developers created communities where the requirements were so particular that in effect they restricted entrance to only those few who met the exclusive standard, thus accomplishing "the same purpose as racial covenants."[52] In Radburn from the twenties to the late fifties, community planners, no matter how idealistic in other respects they might be, followed these same exclusionary practices. The government-sponsored greenbelt towns of the thirties—which I turn to next—were no exception, despite their being proud achievements of the New Deal.

DESPITE ITS SUCCESS, as Stein looked back on Radburn, he had come to one firm conclusion: for a new town to succeed it needed financial backing solid enough to weather any national financial collapse; it needed, in short, government support—to buy and hold the land until needed for construction, to assist local government in building schools and other infrastructure, and to provide subsidies for low-income residents.[53] As fate would have it, the very forces of economic collapse that curtailed the fulfillment of the Radburn experiment would lead, a few years later, to the government-sponsored communities built as part of the Roosevelt administration's response to housing—Greenbelt, Maryland; Green Hills, Ohio; and Greendale, Wisconsin.[54] The deepening Depression bankrupted the CHC and brought an end to the Regional Planning Association of America, but the RPAA's members were individually lobbying the Roosevelt admin-istration to take a more active role in government support of housing. The RPAA's last policy statement, in 1933, was directed toward Roosevelt's New Deal and argued that the government should acquire outlying land, rather than urban areas, to solve the nation's housing problems.[55] And the association's efforts bore at least some fruit, as several of its mem-bers entered New Deal agencies and helped bring about the government-sponsored projects that became the Roosevelt administration's principal housing achievements.[56]

This was not the first government effort at constructing housing. The immediate necessity of housing workers during World War I, for exam-ple, had produced some surprisingly successful results—Union Park, near Wilmington, Delaware; Yorkship Village, near Camden, New Jersey—but these fell victim to congressional posturing (they were called "socialistic" after the war ended), and the government ordered the units sold at mar-ket value.[57] It was not until the Great Depression (when cries of socialism were somewhat muted, at least temporarily) that government became that ideal sponsor, as in the 1935 Carl Mackley Houses in Philadelphia, a Bauhaus-inspired design by Oscar Stonorov, sponsored by the Hosiery Workers Union and financed by the Housing Division of the Public Works Administration.[58] But it was under Rexford Tugwell's leadership at the Re-settlement Administration that the federal government sought to solve the problem of affordable housing nationally and at the same time pro-vide a model for planned development on a regional scale.

Tugwell's original conception was to build 3,000 communities that would entice residents to leave derelict urban neighborhoods, which, in turn, could be transformed into urban parks. In the end, which was practi-cally the beginning, so short-lived was the program, only three communi-ties were built, each close to a city and each combining, as Clarence Stein noted, the "three basic ideas of the modern community: the Garden City, the Radburn Idea, and the Neighborhood Unit"—ideas that Stein saw be-ing brought into practice in Europe and Scandinavia.[59] At the heart of the concept was the idea of the neighborhood, articulated by Clarence Perry on the basis of his experience at Forest Hills, with residents living within a half mile (walking distance) of schools and shopping. Greenbelt, with its market, shops, and movie theater in a town center, a gathering spot for children and parents alike, was Stein's best example: "Around the quiet square are grouped the varied functions of one of the finest small town centers of these days. It is both thoroughly functional and architectur-

Photograph by John Vachon, showing residents pitching horseshoes in spacious common yards, Greendale, Wisconsin, 1939. Library of Congress, Prints and Photographs Division, FSA-OWI Collection.

ally of a simple, attractive unity."[60] The communities shared other design features derived from Radburn—superblocks, circular roads, culs-de-sac, and shared open space.

Yet in other ways, the greenbelt towns exhibited striking contrasts in their underlying conceptions: where Greenbelt, near Washington, D.C., employed a stylish European modern idiom, with flat-roofed two-story garden apartments and large glass windows, Greenhills, near Cincinnati, had a more utilitarian cast, with multiple units built in two-story clusters along gently curving streets. Greendale, outside of Milwaukee, was most traditional, the majority of its units consisting of individual houses with a garage in a simplified colonial style, surrounded by a private yard; Greendale also built a smaller number of row houses, duplexes, and apartments, thus allowing for diversified income levels. Yet none of the three greenbelt towns fulfilled the garden city ideal of economic self-sufficiency. Built close to cities, they were essentially bedroom communities, government-sponsored suburban developments.

Despite their democratic ethos, these government-built communities were also based on stringent principles of selection and exclusion. While initially planned for low-income families, the costs of construction and

Photograph by John Vachon, showing lawns near houses that provide playing space for children, Greendale, Wisconsin, 1939. Library of Congress, Prints and Photographs Division, FSA-OWI Collection.

maintenance required raising the rent to the level of "moderate income" (from $1,200 to $2,000 depending on family size).[61] And while Greenbelt's original plan called for the creation of a separate development for black families, in the end, none were admitted to the new development. As Cedric Larson wrote in 1938: "[N]egroes were not admitted as residents, since they have their own low cost housing project in Northeast Washington . . . called Langston Terrace."[62] In following the prevailing suburban prejudices, Greenbelt's creators were following the path of least resistance, fearing the disruption of their "model" town. The resulting community at Greenbelt, consisting mostly of men who commuted to Washington, D.C., to work, and women who stayed at home to do the laundry (with clothesline drying prohibited after 4:00 P.M.), seems to have been happily adjusted to the town council's rules, benefiting from the many cooperative features of the community and protesting occasionally over such restrictions as no bathing suits in the town center.[63] Only when minorities tried to penetrate the community did internal conflicts emerge.[64]

BY 1936, THE COMBINED FORCES of the real estate lobbies and banks, spearheaded by conservative congressmen, successfully curtailed the gov-

Photograph by John Vachon, showing women pushing baby carriages across spacious grounds, Greenbelt, Maryland, 1937. Library of Congress, Prints and Photographs Division, FSA-OWI Collection.

ernment's "socialistic" housing program.[65] The need for expanded housing was evident, but the way to achieve that goal was not. The culmination of this utopian movement to plant the garden city in the United States—at least from a public relations standpoint—was the 1939 film *The City*, which entered the public discourse at a time of intense debate over housing and development. It was shown as one of the most popular features of the New York World's Fair, itself an embodiment of futuristic and utopian thinking, dominated by American corporations like General Motors and Ford that, we can see in retrospect, assumed an endless future of gasoline-powered cars. Sponsored by the American Institute of Planners and the Carnegie Corporation of New York, *The City* was dramatized by the foremost documentary filmmaker in the United States at the time, Pare Lorentz, and directed by two of the era's great cinematographers, Ralph Steiner and Willard Van Dyke. Most important for our purposes, it was based on the conceptual paradigm of Lewis Mumford, and it bears the mark of the RPAA. As both a summation of ideas about community and town planning in the twenties and thirties and an index of what was at stake at that pivotal moment, it bears a closer look.

The showing of Mumford's film could not have had a more auspicious venue: situated in Queens on the marvelously reclaimed ash-heap land-scape of *The Great Gatsby*, the World's Fair offered itself as an artificial paradise, a fusion of City Beautiful vistas and fountains, geometrical abstractions and biomorphic architecture. In addition, two model cities attracted enormous attention: the General Motors Futurama, with its Le Corbusier towers and grand boulevards, its urban separation of automobile traffic from pedestrian; and Henry Dreyfuss's Democracity, housed in the perisphere at the center of the fair, an idealization of the suburban future that was as close to paradise as most people could dream: modeled on Ebenezer Howard's garden city plans, it featured a city of culture, business, and recreation, with streets radiating from a central tower, surrounded by rivers and green, and ringed by twenty-five satellite towns, each residential and industrial, each with its own schools and small businesses.

Running forty-four minutes, *The City* is constructed with a clear, almost syllogistic argument leading to an overwhelming conclusion: we must have garden cities in America. In doing so, it recapitulates the thinking of Mumford, whose analytic approach (influenced by the Scottish ecologist and geographer Patrick Geddes) focused on the interaction of community, place, and work within a regional perspective, beyond the merely metropolitan area.[66] Reflecting Mumford's own theory of history, *The City* embodies a kind of mythos, a sequence of major socioeconomic American paradigms in terms of their spatial construction, from the seventeenth century to the present: First there was the New England village, an idyllic ecology uniting agriculture, small-scale technology, and the power of millstreams, its polity the ultimate in democracy, the town meeting. (This section of the film uses scenes from RPAA member Benton MacKaye's hometown of Shirley, Connecticut.) Next, in a violently abrupt transition, comes the industrial city of the late nineteenth century and early twentieth—smokestacks, giant steel mills, and depressed and maimed workers living in shacks with outhouses and with children playing on railroad tracks: not a pretty picture. Third, the metropolis: skyscrapers, clogged streets, traffic, fire engines, dangerous street crossings, rushing office workers, rushed eating, a vibrant picture but one the film wants us to deplore: "Cities, where people count the seconds and lose the days." Fourth, the city people fleeing the metropolis for their weekend recreation—again clogged roads, crying children in cars stuck in traffic, in short an irrational, unbalanced system. Thus far, we have seen the innocence of America's early settlements overwhelmed by the shock waves of the Industrial Revo-

Cloverleaf and highways connect the garden cities of the imagined planned suburbs in The City *(1939), directed by Ralph Steiner and Willard Van Dyke. Civic Films/ Springer/Photofest.*

lution and the resulting urban chaos. Now we are ready for the solution, act 5 of the drama: the green city, the planner's paradise. Here we return to the ecological idyll of the New England village, only on a larger scale, uniting workplace, schools, and recreation within a landscape of rolling hills, lakes, and garden apartments. Filmed in two of the very few available existing models, Radburn, New Jersey, and Greenbelt, Maryland, this segment shows us auto traffic separated from pedestrians and bicycles, everything clean, wholesome, and happy. In aerial views, we see the city of the future set in a network of interconnecting limited-access highways, blessedly free from traffic.

The point of *The City* is not to escape into the past but rather to embrace a future that demonstrates, with the optimism of that prewar moment and in defiance of the Depression outside the fairgrounds, human mastery over technology: not only the motor parkways and the new cloverleaf intersections but hydroelectric dams and airplanes in the sky: "Science takes flight," the narrator tells us. In short, the Mumfordian synthesis was an ecological vision balancing place, community, and work, all within a structure that united the forces of nature with the controlling rationality of science and technology.

As a vision of place, *The City* is only partly convincing, since the viewer is expected to fall in love with the relative dullness of life in the utopian garden city, where the greatest excitement is the local softball game. (The filmmakers themselves could barely stand the dull, extended vision of the garden city, forced on them by the planners.)[67] There is little sense of a community commercial center or anything like a Main Street atmosphere in the model communities pictured in the film: the closest we come is the shared laundromat. By contrast, the negative images of the metropolis, designed to repel us, are unnervingly appealing in their mix of energies. As a vision of society, the film also has its limitations, for the pictured residents are uniformly white (though at presumably different income levels) and the victims of a rigidly gendered social structure whereby the women stay home with the kids while the men are off in the world of work. Happiness, for the women, is a round of cards while the washing machines do the once backbreaking work of laundering. But the film has a clear point to make, and it comes at the end, with its stark choice, embodied in conflicting images: here is the town as we can create it—a paradise on Earth, fresh air, sun, modern buildings, happy children; and here is the city as we presently know it—disorder, steel, and stone, men forced to live like machines. You take your choice, the narrator tells us.

From the film's point of view, there really is no choice, of course, assuming we are rational creatures. But leaving aside the merits of this vision, there is another question we must pose to the film itself: If we do want the garden city, how do we get there from here? *The City* offers no politics of reality, no plan for the transition to utopia. It is assumed that rational creatures will design and inhabit a rational society when the truth is shown to them. It is assumed that we do have a choice. But the reality of housing development is far more complicated than that—a matter of zoning, of commercial development, of profit, of local incentives, of tax breaks for investors and developers. Most of all, *The City* assumes that the government, if empowered by the will of the people, can bring about these changes. But the history of housing in this country following World War II—which I turn to next—has demonstrated how limited government's power is in actuality, hedged in as it is by real estate lobbies and private developers.

Meanwhile, what the utopian experiments of the early twentieth century demonstrated—from Forest Hills to Sunnyside to Radburn to Green-

Children play in a healthy environment in the garden cities of the future envisioned by The City *(1939), directed by Ralph Steiner and Willard Van Dyke. Civic Films/ Springer/Photofest.*

belt—was, first, that the good place, the ideal community, can be designed in ways that temper the intrusion of the automobile and maximize social contact, and, second, that the community can function in relative social harmony when common interests and backgrounds are shared. In the postwar era, as suburbanization took hold in the United States, these key issues would be the focal points of renewed debate and experimentation: what to do with the automobile and how to balance harmony and diversity?

Chapter Seven

Rethinking Suburbia
Levittown or the New Urbanism?

With the withdrawal of the government from community building follow-ing the Roosevelt years and World War II, the future of new town plan-ning was in the hands of private developers, who stepped into a perceived vacuum in home construction in the United States. And the focus imme-diately shifted from the creation of the ideal community to the creation of individual houses, packed into suburban developments, in short, the kind of tract housing that has become endemic to suburbia for the past sixty years. In doing so, builders were responding to what was perceived as the American's God-given right, the sum total of human happiness, the fulfillment of the American Dream, and what America was fighting for: the single-family home. At the same time, a countermovement was beginning to emerge that would lead, by the end of the twentieth century, to the res-toration of the community ideal in the principles of the New Urbanism. In short, the struggle of the late twentieth century and into the twenty-first has been the struggle between individualism and community, between suburban sprawl and the planned new town, between Levittown and the New Urbanism. Though the term *Main Street* was not always foregrounded in these debates, the concept of community that it embodies was visible in the notion of the village or town center.

The single-family home has always had an iconic significance in Amer-ica, dating back to the mid-nineteenth-century chromolithographs of Cur-rier and Ives—the house surrounded by land, the domain of the individual and his family, bordered by a fence, if possible. And when, in the Great De-pression, the Currier and Ives family farm was auctioned off or, as happens most vividly in John Ford's *The Grapes of Wrath*, obliterated by the bank's bulldozer, that scene of destruction emblematized the end of the world as we knew it. But after the disruptions of World War II, as the U.S. economy began what would become a solid recovery, homeownership resurfaced as an immediate need and a major force in American society. The popular 1948 comedy film *Mr. Blandings Builds His Dream House* epitomized the ethos of that moment, when Mr. Blandings (played by Cary Grant), a middle-class advertising writer, becomes possessed by the need to remove his family from their crowded New York City apartment and buy a house in suburbia. But the old house they have their eyes on initially is in such disrepair that it can only be demolished and a new one built in its place. Thus begins the comedy of the film—with the endless delays, revisions, added costs, and inconveniences of the building process; in the end, of course, it is exactly the house they dreamed of. Yet what is interesting from the present perspective is the relative isolation of this ideal house in the rural countryside; not only must Mr. Blandings endure an arduous commute to work from his dream house, but the house is apart from any neighborhoods—it is in "the country." Suburbia, with its massive developments and identical houses, may be on the horizon, but that is not the location of Mr. Blandings's house.

In fact, it is hard to see Mr. Blandings's dream house—with its abundant space and luxurious appointments—as even close to a plausible aspiration for the postwar middle class. It was simply too expensive; and it would take the much cheaper suburban tract house to answer the mass need for Mr. K-Mart's dream house. But these tract houses were, in effect, the emotional equivalent of the Blandings house. The suburban tract house was not the first low-cost home built for the mass market: the goal of providing an affordable house for the average American has given rise periodically to attempts to lower the price of construction through prefabrication, most notably in the Sears boxed kits sold by mail order in the earlier twentieth century. But the most convincing fulfillment of that promise came in the postwar constructions of Levittown. For that precisely was the genius of William Levitt, the builder, marketer, and company president, and his brother Alfred, who was in charge of design. Together, the Levitts gave the young postwar American family a single-family home it could afford, a house that seemed to exist exclusively for it in its singularity and insularity, despite the fact that it was merely one of thousands of identical houses in a community that was so uniform, so efficiently packed with house after house, that a stranger would be hard put to find his or her way into or out of it.

From its beginnings in 1947, demand for the Levitts' houses far outstripped supply, and when sales were first announced, people camped out overnight to be in line early enough to sign on the dotted line. When William Levitt had completed his Long Island building spree in 1951, he had

"The Most Perfectly Planned Community in America! Levittown, Pennsylvania,"
advertisement in the Philadelphia Inquirer and Public Ledger, *December 9, 1951.*
Although the images depict individual house types, the ad represents the second
Levittown as an improvement over the Long Island original, offering better recreational
facilities, safer streets, "small neighborhood shopping centers within walking distance
of every home," and a new commuter rail station. Temple University Libraries.

Aerial view of a planned prefabricated housing development in Levittown, Pennsylvania, 1950s. Traces of farmlands are visible, as a new pattern overtakes the suburban landscape modeled on the packing crate. Library of Congress, Prints and Photographs Division.

constructed 17,447 houses and was moving on to build a similar development in Pennsylvania and another in New Jersey. It was the start of a suburban building boom that would be fueled by new roads, zoning that favored uniform residential housing, and government-guaranteed mortgages, not to mention by the need to shelter the postwar babies.[1] What made the Levittown house, with its surrounding yard, affordable was the Levitts' innovative construction technique (perfected during World War II, when the brothers built naval housing in Norfolk, Virginia). The Levitts came as close to mass producing the house as we have come: with flat concrete foundations (no basements), precut lumber, and standardized windows and appliances, William Levitt was able to produce thirty houses per day, all in the basic Cape Cod style, resembling the kind of simple, generic house children draw.

Certainly the Levittowner was buying into a community, and the Levitts paid attention to street layout, creating feeder streets and inner

Levittown Center shopping center, Levittown, Long Island, New York, 1957. Photograph by Roger Higgins. Library of Congress, New York World-Telegram and Sun Newspaper Photograph Collection.

streets, curving lines, bends, and culs-de-sac, producing an effect of intimacy. But, unlike Radburn, Levittown put its front to the street, with the family car in front; in the backyards, no fences were permitted originally, leaving a flowing movement from backyard to backyard that was especially engaging to children, playing across a neighborhood with watchful eyes trained on them from the household watchtowers. (Levittown communities, succumbing to the instinct for private space, soon developed fences separating the properties.) In the New York Levittown, there were originally several small shopping centers distributed throughout the community, while in Pennsylvania, the Levittown Shopping Center functioned more like a town center, with shops and chain stores providing a social and commercial center for the community that lasted until the original center—slowly declining since the seventies—finally expired in the face of supermall competition in 2002.[2] In fact, the original Levittowns were creating a collective environment—through shared schools, neighborhoods, recreational associations, common habits, and shared lifestyles—that would give comfort to the suburbanite.

But at bottom William Levitt was not selling the idea of community so much as the idea of the house itself and affordable ownership: more than one couple exclaimed in joy, on moving in, "We have achieved the American Dream!"[3] Moreover, Levitt's gift to the consumer was a house that was sufficiently generic that it could be shaped and expanded over the years according to the owners' whims, with ample yard space to accommodate that expansion. The result, after more than half a century, has

Peg Brennan house, 25 Winding Lane, Levittown, Long Island, New York, 1958.
Photograph by Gottscho-Schleisner. Library of Congress, Historic American Buildings
Survey.

been a community where few of the original Cape Cods remain, replaced
by a plethora of designs bearing little resemblance to the ur-house. A response to the new postwar individualism, the freedom built into Levittown contracts directly contrasted with the design covenants of Sunnyside and Radburn.

Levittown's success inspired a multitude of subsequent developments
along similar lines, and by the mid-fifties the United States was well on its
way to the suburban sprawl that would increasingly characterize growth
outside the city. Americans' investment in their homes was at once financial, spiritual, and political, and William Levitt had it right when he said
famously, reflecting the Cold War's pervasive conservatism, "No man who
owns his own house and lot can be a communist. He has too much to do."[4]
Indeed, fixing up the house would become a major weekend preoccupa-
tion if not recreation for the homeowner, who lived too far from the city
anyway to enjoy the resources of the metropolis, especially after a week
of tedious commuting. (The "do it yourself" ethos would also compensate
perfectly for office jobs that characteristically separated the hand from
the head.)

Levittown may have been created in the image of Cold War America, but it was not created in the image of freedom and justice for all. In 1948, following the participation of African Americans in all branches of the armed forces, President Harry Truman at last ordered his defense secretary to end discrimination and segregation in the military.[5] In American communities, however, integration was not so easily achieved, and when it came, its progress was not easily predictable. In the case of the Levittown communities, new buyers were seeking not only homeownership but also social status, which meant, for the white occupant, a close attention to the social class, ethnicity, and race of the neighbors.

Yet the three Levittowns offer three different case studies. On Long Island, Levitt was so conscious of catering to the perceived values of his potential buyers that he used restrictive covenants to exclude Jews from some of his higher-priced communities, despite the fact that he himself was Jewish.[6] In Levittown, Pennsylvania, built in 1952, some five years after the Long Island town had been started, Jews were admitted and began organizing their own religious and social associations, but they remained a distinct minority. More problematic to the Pennsylvania community was the arrival in 1957 of the first African American family, who had purchased a home directly from the previous owner and appeared suddenly in the midst of a predominantly working-class community that saw black people as a symbol of everything Levittown residents feared and in some cases had fled—the poverty of the inner city, racial conflict, and the degradation of their social status and property values. In the summer of 1957, 500 whites gathered outside the home of the new African American residents, shouting epithets and throwing rocks. The ugly incident made headlines across the country and the world.

The case of Levittown, New Jersey, which opened in 1958, is an altogether different story. In Herbert J. Gans's classic early account of the community, including its eventual integration, he observes that William Levitt had declared in 1958 that he would not sell to African Americans, despite the fact that it was illegal in New Jersey to practice discrimination, and despite being under pressure from national Jewish leaders to integrate. Levitt's defense was the businessman's: "Most whites prefer not to live in mixed communities. . . . The responsibility for this [integration] is society's. . . . It is not reasonable to expect that any one builder could or should undertake to absorb the entire risk and burden of conducting such a vast social experiment." The company would go with the group of builders in New Jersey, if all integrated; but it would not be singled out.[7] Circumstances went against Levitt, however, when in 1960 a suit against the builder by two African Americans was brought to the state supreme court, leading the company to decide that more damage would be caused by fighting the issue (the ugliness of the Levittown, Pennsylvania, riot was still in the air) than by gracefully accepting the inevitable.

William Levitt's handling of integration in the New Jersey town was, as Gans reports, shrewd, with appropriate public relations (supported by the community ministers) and practical management. Black applicants were given their choice of lots, and they naturally chose the most desirable ones—that is, the most private. Most important, no two black families were permitted to buy adjoining houses, thus avoiding the creation of a black "neighborhood" that might discourage white buyers from moving in. Scattered throughout the development, the African Americans' impact and visibility in Levittown was minimal and, for the whites, tolerable. They were not seen as a threat to the whites' status. In fact, few African Americans could afford to buy houses in Levittown in the early 1960s, and perhaps fewer still were willing to move into a virtually all-white neighborhood where they were not welcome. By 1964, Gans concludes, only fifty black families had moved into Levittown, New Jersey, leading him to assume a minimal effect on white residents: "No one knew—or seemed to care—about the exact number."[8]

Yet the subsequent history of Levittown, New Jersey (which changed its name to Willingboro in 1963), seems to have gone well beyond Gans's imaginings. Where the earlier two Levittowns have held relatively steady in terms of their ratios of whites and blacks, Willingboro has become a predominantly black town. Levittown, Long Island, is 89 percent white, with the addition of 5 percent Asian Americans in the 2000 census; Levittown, Pennsylvania, with its legacy of violence, is even more segregated, with a white population of 94 percent and the remainder split about evenly between blacks and Hispanics. The New Jersey community, which is the smallest of the three (33,000 inhabitants compared to more than 50,000 in each of the other two), is by far the most integrated. In fact, 70 percent of the population in the 2000 census was black, with 27 percent white and 2.5 percent Asian American. The tipping point occurred sometime in the 1980s; by the 1990 census, there were already 5,700 black households compared to 5,000 white. These figures suggest that with the rising economy of the late twentieth century, more African Americans could afford to move into the town William Levitt had founded. Moreover, it had increasingly acquired the reputation of being hospitable to blacks, who have made it a community of choice. The figures also suggest that whites have left gradually, and by attrition, as their circumstances have changed, rather than in a hasty flight. The integration of Willingboro has been peaceful, yet the numbers imply that in the absence of some mandatory balance of white and black, the neighborhood has been moving toward homogeneity rather than maintaining diversity.

THE RACIAL INTEGRATION that William Levitt had resisted in the late fifties became, a decade later, one of James Rouse's chief goals as he developed the new town of Columbia, Maryland. Rouse, surely one of the visionary developers of his time—responsible for Harborplace in Baltimore and Faneuil Market in Boston, among many other influential projects—was responding to a cultural moment when government was taking the lead in its efforts to legislate a more just society in many dimensions. Though a businessman, first and always, Rouse's motivations and inspirations in founding Columbia lay deeper than simply financial gain, including at least four other key factors.[9] Rouse was first of all convinced that people are influenced by their environment, that, as he put it, "physical plan matters—in allowing community to naturally come into being."[10] Rouse was also strongly shaped by the idea of the neighborhood unit (see my discussion of Clarence Perry in chapter 6), which had been passed on through the Regional Planning Association of America and Lewis Mumford. Rouse implemented it in his concept of small neighborhoods within clusters of villages, each with its own center, within the larger totality of nearly 100,000 units. In addition, Rouse's natural optimism was encouraged by the successful examples of European town planning, which were developing in the fifties and sixties with much stronger government involvement. Underlying his ebullience was an outgoing Christian faith, inspired by his steady involvement in a Washington group founded after World War II, the Church of the Saviour, which stressed social service.[11]

Rouse was also developing his ideas at a time when, following Levitt's example, suburbia was rapidly changing from farmland to tract housing. Rouse had a clear analysis of the factors that led inexorably to sprawl— chief among them the low-density residential zoning that communities imposed on development, in the belief that low density would preserve their way of life. The results of low density were disastrous environmentally and created communities at once dependent on the automobile and choked by it. With government offering only minimal support (e.g., infrastructure, federal highway funding, and tax incentives for homeownership), Rouse saw the place of the private developer as crucial to an effective response to sprawl.[12]

As it evolved in the 1960s, Rouse's version of the "new town" concept was meant very deliberately to be a new beginning, a needed reimagining of town planning that anticipated an era on the cusp of utopian imaginings, if not revolution. (The term *new town* began to replace the older *garden city* as early as the 1920s, as the latter term came to signify simply a suburban development with flowers and trees.)[13] Inspired by Radburn and the greenbelt towns, Rouse also looked back to the idea of the small town. In fact, it was the idea of the small town that most powerfully motivated Rouse and the Columbia planners. In imagining the ideal environment, Rouse's small-town background—he grew up in Easton, Maryland—was a constant reference point: "I hold some very unscientific conclusions to the effect that people grow best in small communities where the institutions . . . are within reach of their responsibility," he said in a 1963 speech. Moreover, he went on, "a broader range of friendships and relationships occurs in a village or small town than in a city."[14]

Yet Rouse's planned community—more like a planned city—was on a much grander scale than anything that had preceded it, with an expected population of close to 90,000, three or four times the size of Howard's garden city model. It would even include a mall—with department stores, food markets, office buildings, restaurants, and ample parking—that served as a city center. What gave Columbia its small-town character was its division into nine subordinate communities, or villages, each with 10,000 to 15,000 residents and each containing smaller villages of about 2,500.

As early as 1959, Rouse had affirmed the importance of the neighborhood idea and the "human scale," drawing again on his own small-town childhood, a view he elaborated in a 1964 presentation to residents of Howard County, where Columbia was to be built: "The villages permit a scale of life reminiscent of the small towns which form such a rich heritage of America. In place of monotonous, sprawling suburbs stretching in endless ranks across much of the country, the villages of Columbia will offer a vitality and a scale of living too often sacrificed today."[15] The village scale, he believed, promoted a social culture that fostered not only greater self-reliance but also a sense of responsibility, counteracting the anomie of the city and the isolation of the suburbs.[16] Though Rouse was nothing if not a successful businessman, his progressive ideas were rooted

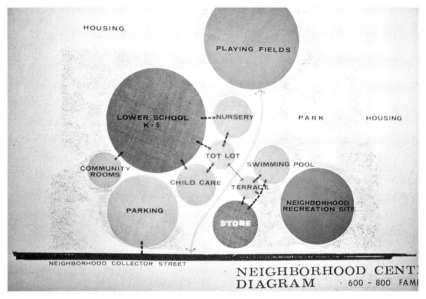

HOUSING

PLAYING FIELDS

LOWER SCHOOL K-5 ----NURSERY PARK HOUSING

TOT LOT

COMMUNITY ROOMS SWIMMING POOL

CHILD CARE TERRACE

PARKING NEIGHBORHOOD RECREATION SITE

STORE

NEIGHBORHOOD COLLECTOR STREET

NEIGHBORHOOD CENT:
DIAGRAM · 600 - 800 FAMI

Early planning diagram of a Columbia, Maryland, village center, showing school, recreation areas, parking, and commercial area, all in a contiguous layout, ca. 1965. Photograph by Robert Tennenbaum. Courtesy of Columbia Archives.

in his Christianity, with its emphasis on serving the world, a belief he shared with his wife, Libby. Inspired perhaps by her early reading of Lewis Mumford on the city, Libby Rouse recalled, in a 1977 talk, how "the design of small residential communities (now cul-de-sacs in Columbia) came to be dreamed of in my head"—through her musing on Jesus and what he would "want for the family": "He would want them to be in small communities, so they could be more loving, sharing warmth and friendships."[17] Her utopian impulse seems inspired not only by Mumford but also by the ideal religious communities of the mid-nineteenth century.

Whatever their inspiration, Rouse's planners at Columbia worked to create a real world for real people, giving each of the village town centers a unique character, so that people would be drawn to the center but also attracted across the community to other village centers, each of which was a small shopping center with public areas and parking that served as a surrogate for a linear Main Street.[18] The city as a whole, with tree-lined streets and lakes, was interconnected by bike and walking paths, as well as by limited bus service. Within each village, townhouses and single-family homes were located on winding roads, while village centers—consistent with Rouse's vision for a mixed-income and racially in-

194 RETHINKING SUBURBIA

Rendering of Columbia Mall, Columbia, Maryland, as an outdoor Main Street, part of the first presentation by Rouse Company to Howard County on November 11, 1964. Courtesy of Columbia Archives.

tegrated community—had rental units for lower-income residents who might not be able to afford cars and would therefore benefit from proximity to the village center and other public transportation. In fact, more than any other planned community in the United States, Columbia has embodied a carefully balanced population of mixed income levels, including the extremes of affordable housing units and luxurious dwellings.

Columbia was indeed as much an experiment in social engineering as it was in town planning. Rouse saw the community not only as the developer's answer to suburban sprawl but also as the answer to the need for new housing at all income levels. Diversity within the overall community was the essence of Columbia, and each village in the new town had homes at a variety of levels, from large single-family homes (about 35 percent)

Wilde Lake Village Center, Columbia, Maryland, with outdoor common areas surrounded by shops. Courtesy of Columbia Archives.

to townhouses (about 27 percent) to apartments and condominiums (38 percent), including government-subsidized affordable housing—about 6 percent in the early years. Rouse's ideal, as he put it, was to have the janitor and the company president be neighbors, though he did not mean necessarily on the same street.[19] Inevitably, the social mix of the community as a whole can be seen at closer inspection to contain social strata. Thus particular neighborhoods within the development have taken on class status, recognizable to residents as more or less "desirable." (The "working poor" below the lower-middle class could generally not afford even the smaller rental units in Columbia.)

Wilde Lake, Columbia, Maryland, aerial view showing groupings of houses of different sizes, attached and single, within the same general area, thus creating zones of contiguous, yet separate, housing levels. Photograph by Morton Tadder. Courtesy of Columbia Archives.

Rouse was aiming for an integrated community, but he did not want to provoke any racist reactions in the process of building it. Consequently, he was walking a fine line between dispassion and advocacy: "We are not going to be bigoted, nor are we going to be crusaders. . . . We are going to be unselfconscious about integration. We are not going to try to develop a new kind of population mix artificially to bring more Negroes into Columbia than would ordinarily come, nor are we going to set up any barriers or frustrations to their coming to live here."[20] But it was, of course, an artificial mix, at least for the suburbs, where whites who were fleeing the inner city had sought a homogeneous community. To avoid calling attention to this effort at integration and to disguise the better part of his moral purpose, Rouse was at pains to prevent having African Americans purchase homes in contiguous lots (an approach Levitt had pioneered). Meanwhile, he was also committed to building housing for the poor—despite some resistance from middle-class residents.[21] Village centers, especially, were designed to afford lower-income housing, thus allowing for proximity to local services and public transportation. These areas have tended over the years to aggregate the lower-income African American community within Columbia. Sadly, occasional incidents of crime in recent years have led to fears among many residents—not all of whom have been imbued with the original progressive zeal for integration—that Columbia is replicating the problems of the inner city that it was designed to overcome.

Columbia has maintained over the years a racial mix not far from its original formula. With a population in 2000 of 88,000, Columbia was 66 percent white and 21 percent black, with about 10 percent of residents being of Asian and Hispanic descent. This represents an increase in minorities that parallels an increase in minority income levels, with a consequent displacement or attrition of white families. Over the years, Columbia has remained remarkably stable demographically and aesthetically, winning many accolades. One reason for the aesthetic consistency has been the power exercised by the Columbia Association (controlled by the developer) over community rules and zoning, including what color one can paint a house, whether a fence can be built, and so forth.[22]

Rouse's experiment in creating a new society was undertaken with the help of architects and landscape designers like Ian McHarg, Frank Gehry, and Anne Spirn. Remarkably enough, also contributing to the effort was a "social planning work group" consisting of Rouse planners plus fourteen urbanists and sociologists, which advised the builder on the prospects of creating a diverse community. The group included such well-known sociologists and urbanists as Kevin Lynch, Christopher Jencks, and Herbert Gans.[23] Rouse's assumption, and a shared premise of the working group, was that "social mix" was desirable: it represented a democratic ideal, the philosopher's stone of progressive social thinkers, in opposition to the more strictly homogeneous subdivisions being built by most suburban developers, where the prices of new houses were within a narrow range. Rouse's ideal society, emulating the small town where he grew up, would allow for random encounters in the village center, creating the bonds and cohesions of the good society: going beyond the traditional white-only small town, it would embody racial and economic diversity, reflecting national progressive goals and serving as a model for a future America.

But a new development was not like an actual small town, which might accrue a variety of building types over many years and at a variety of income levels, all within a small space, thus building into its evolution a measure of diversity (though not necessarily racial diversity). New residential developments consisted of houses in streets (or culs-de-sac) that had to have a certain homogeneity in terms of price, and therefore also in terms of the residents' income level, which accordingly acted as a segregating factor. The theoretical problem for Rouse and his team was to figure out the optimum numbers for the village—how many houses at what income levels, and where to place them—so as to achieve the goal of social mix.[24] One eureka moment came, apparently, with the realization that a supermarket and a high school both needed a population of about 15,000 to 20,000 people, which translated into about 3,500 families as the target number for each Columbia village.[25] (This is a bit smaller than Ebenezer Howard's ideal of 30,000.) Even so, as Herbert Gans argued somewhat pessimistically, social diversity—based on education, income, and race—leads to conflict, and people preferred homogeneity. Yet as Nicholas Bloom observes, the "residential isolation" within the villages seems to have mitigated these conflicts over the years.[26] One aspect of the original plan, however, has been significantly modified: where originally nearly 200 subsidized housing units might be grouped around the village center, the plans for later villages in Columbia allowed for the dispersal of these subsidized units (with a limit of forty in one locale) across a wider geographic area.[27] To this day, the most problematic areas of Columbia are the original, more densely populated subsidized village centers.

The Columbia model, given its scale and complexity, was not broadly imitated, especially during the recession of the 1970s. Only so many people at the upper end of the market want the higher density that comes with the community model, and fewer still are imbued with the egalitarian spirit that inspired the pioneers. As a result, most suburban developments in the decades following Columbia have catered to the demands of a market that for years has desired housing expressing a particular income level, developments that have contributed heavily to the pernicious growth of suburban sprawl, furthered by the muscular efforts of the federal highway program in exurban areas.

With the advent of the New Urbanism in the 1980s, however, all of this began to change—slowly, but persistently, with the aggressive marketing of the ideal of community and the gradual mainstreaming of New Urbanist ideas. How profoundly the New Urbanism has changed the social mix of suburbia is another question.

IN PICKING UP on the Rouse dream of building on the model of the small town, the New Urbanists were affirming the primary value of building community and building for density of population, in contrast to the practices of suburban sprawl. In fact, the word *community* is so naturally appealing—only a misanthrope would not want community—that we may not realize the vast and historic change represented by the effort to sell it. For the idea of community has, in the twenty-first century, displaced one of the strongest drives in American culture, the need to possess one's own, individual home on a separate, private space of land, however small, which was the dream of suburbia. The ideal of the individual house surrounded by a lawn and fence is replaced by that of homes built in some more contiguous arrangement (most obviously as row houses), with the dwellings sharing some proximate collective space in a denser pattern of construction. In short, what is replacing the suburban house is a version of the idea of small-town America, an enormous shift in consciousness that amounts to a rejection of the unplanned development that has come to be known as sprawl.

What does it mean to sell "community"? What does it mean to want to buy into community? The word itself has a long history in the United States, existing at times in competition with the idea of single-family homeownership and at other times as a complementary force.[28] For the New Urbanist planning philosophy, *community* is most certainly a central term, for at the core of the New Urbanism is the assumption that the design of place is essential to the shaping of social behavior. That fundamental idea has been disputed by, among others, Herbert Gans, who is often cited for his opposition to the idea that planned space is necessary to the creation of community, for Gans finds social cohesion in places that are supposed not to function as the material ground of community (e.g., the inner-city ghetto at one extreme and the suburbs at the other).[29] Yet it might be argued, against Gans, that such places, including the street alleys of Washington, D.C.—another example—have indeed provided the needed physical space for social communication, even though they do not look like the traditional small town.[30] In other words, we cannot necessarily use Gans to disprove the general proposition that place affects community.

Design decisions surely do reflect a variety of factors—prevailing aesthetic models, ecological and geographical locus, fiscal constraints, available building materials, and so on—but they also, most consciously in the work of the New Urbanists, reflect the designer's attempt to create a space that directly affects individual and group behavior. Thus, the proximity and contiguity of dwellings to one another, the availability of open space and gathering places, the width of streets, the location of symbolic buildings, and so on, all express the values of a community and all in turn are designed to affect the way people think of themselves and act toward one another, a view that is supported by new research on place and community.[31] What may be just as important—to take the perspective of cultural psychology—is the belief itself that place can inspire community, a view held by both designers and those who buy into the New Urbanism as residents.

UNDERLYING THE NEW URBANIST VISION of community is a critique of suburban sprawl similar to that of Rouse, which focuses on the pernicious effects of single-use development, resulting in segregation by age, income, and function. Absent a regional plan, suburban land is developed in restricted functions and uses: dwellings of a certain type and cost in one area, shopping malls in another area, industrial parks in another area— with the consequent absence of a coherent sense of place and community and a life revolving instead around the automobile and clogged expressways. As Andres Duany and Elizabeth Plater-Zyberk—the two leading New Urbanists—wrote in 1992, the proliferation of isolated "planned communities" has resulted in a radical disjunction between the happy private space of the suburban homeowner and the extreme degradation of the public realm, with "traffic, commuting time, and the great distances from shopping, work, and entertainment" all cause for complaint. "The classic suburb is less a community than an agglomeration of houses, shops, and offices connected to one another by cars, not by the fabric of human life. . . . The structure of the suburb tends to confine people to their houses and cars; it discourages strolling, walking, mingling with neighbors. The suburb is the last word in privatization, perhaps even its lethal consummation, and it spells the end of authentic civic life."[32] This is not far from the motivating critique of the suburbs that Rouse had affirmed in his own vision of the "new town" in the 1960s.

The New Urbanism is not, then, so much a break with the guiding tenets of earlier new town planning as it is a critique of the *inadvertent results* of that movement, whose integrated vision and idealism became caricatured in the hands of suburban developers, who first planted residential tracts without any town centers, then separate malls, and finally separate industrial parks. This rigidly zoned separation of housing, commerce, and

Kentlands, Maryland, showing residential area with trees and grass creating a buffer space between houses and sidewalk. New Urbanist community designed by Andres Duany and Elizabeth Plater-Zyberk. Photograph by Sandy Sorlien, © 2011 Sandy Sorlien from www.transect-collection.org.

industry, as Duany and Plater-Zyberk wrote, is what needs to be overcome and what the New Urbanism was designed to bring back together.[33] Initiating a new beginning, the New Urbanism—also known as "Traditional Neighborhood Design," "sustainable development," "neotraditional planning," and "livable communities"—articulated a set of guidelines in the early nineties at a meeting of planners and city officials. The Ahwahnee Principles, as they became known, have been widely promulgated through the growing network of New Urbanists.

The Ahwahnee Principles address multiple factors in the design of communities: the integration of work, school, and housing; a town size that permits walking; pedestrian paths and bike paths; diversity of housing types, allowing for different income levels; open space for squares and parks; location within a larger transit network; a well-defined edge (agricultural or wildlife), protected from development; a balanced ecology, providing for efficient use of water and conservation of resources. As Judith Corbett, a regional planner and developer, writes, "Towns of the type built earlier in this century—those compact, walkable communities where you could walk to the store and kids could walk to school, where there was a variety of housing types from housing over stores to single-family units with front porches facing tree-lined, narrow streets—these towns provided a life style that now seems far preferable to today's neighborhoods."[34] Plater-Zyberk connects past to present and future even more assertively when she responds in an interview to the charge that the New Urbanism is fixated sentimentally on the past:

> You know, sentimental and nostalgic, since you attach it to critics, might appear to be pejorative words. But in fact we don't think they are. Especially in this time of technological change, constant change, people change jobs very easily. The idea that your place of residence might have some kind of stability and some kind of connection with a larger picture, whether it's a larger community than just your household, or your daily life; a longer history that you might be contributing to a community that has some history and looks forward to having some future as well, I think makes a tremendous amount of sense.[35]

In short, the New Urbanism, contrary to the revolutionary rhetoric of the era of Le Corbusier, for example, or of Frank Lloyd Wright, would see the house and community as anchoring points, tying the individual to a sense of tradition that is needed in times of uncertainty—all of which can be seen as an echo of the rhetoric of Main Street and the small town that we saw dominating the Great Depression of the thirties.

Looking more closely at New Urbanism, one sees behind the principles a careful consideration of our total dependence on the automobile since at least the 1950s. Every developer must ask, What do we do with the car? For the New Urbanist, the answer is to park it in a back alley, behind the house, thus allowing the house to stand comfortably on the street and close to the sidewalk without the obtrusive presence of the car and garage. This might remind one of the Radburn solution (parking and garages behind the houses, which front on open common spaces); yet unlike Radburn, which separated vehicular traffic from pedestrian movement, the New Urbanist community affirms the multifunctional street as a familiar and still relevant fact of life, an essential aspect of an urbanism that celebrates mixed purposes.[36] Eyes on the street—Jane Jacobs's famous dictum—is also the goal of the New Urbanism, and indeed the vision of community that Jacobs famously invokes in her description of Greenwich Village (*Death and Life of Great American Cities*) is in some ways a model for the idealized urbanism that the New Urbanists strive for. And if Jacobs

Kentlands, Maryland, showing shops and residences around a grassy commons area with a central public sculpture. New Urbanist community designed by Andres Duany and Elizabeth Plater-Zyberk. Photograph by Sandy Sorlien, © 2011 Sandy Sorlien from www.transect-collection.org.

has been accused of transporting an ideal of small-town America to her ideal of city life, the New Urbanists have in some ways done the reverse, taking Jacobs's idea of urbanism and adapting it to their own vision of an urban suburbia.[37]

The physical space of the New Urbanist community of course varies considerably from one development to another, but certain characteristics are shared, as one might expect from a movement that has rigorously defined its tenets, through sets of principles, congresses, lists, and promulgations. Thus, the "Traditional Neighborhood Development Checklist," an appendix to *Suburban Nation*, by Duany, Plater-Zyberk, and Jeff Speck, encompasses about 150 particulars for planners and architects. The guidelines include ensuring that new communities preserve as much surrounding nature as possible; that neighborhoods be about a quarter of a mile from edge to center and that elementary schools be within walking distance; that neighborhood centers have retail space and mixed-use buildings (i.e., apartments above stores); that open space function as plazas and parks; that blocks be short and street width strictly graduated, from broader collector roads to narrow residential streets and narrower back lanes and alleys; that cars be parked in garages in back alleys, but that parking be allowed on streets; that there be a diversity of housing types, from apartments to two- and three-family houses, to row houses, to cottages, to larger houses on their own lots; and that subsidized hous-

Kentlands, Maryland, showing the mixed-use town center, with shops and residences, in a variegated row-house design. New Urbanist community designed by Andres Duany and Elizabeth Plater-Zyberk. Photograph by Sandy Sorlien, © 2011 Sandy Sorlien from www.transect-collection.org.

ing be stylistically indistinguishable from market-rate units. Where there are porches, they should be close to the street, fostering the intimacy of community. The New Urbanism is, in short, an effort to re-create the small town, to create it *ab ovo*, wherever the land is ripe for development, not at a crossroads, but often in the middle of nowhere.

Consistent with the checklist above, the two most obvious markers of the New Urbanism are its traditional neighborhood design and the traditional architectural styles that are insisted on by the community's building codes. Thus, traditional styles (e.g., colonial, Georgian, Victorian, craftsman, or other vernacular styles rooted in long-established regional architecture) are used and constructed from local materials, creating the familiar feel of the small town. Duany and Plater-Zyberk are forthright in their defense of these traditional styles, arguing that "authentic traditional" is what most people want (as opposed to, say, modern) and that this is far superior to the "traditional" housing of the suburbs.[38] (Robert A. M. Stern had sounded this turn of thought in 1981 in *The Anglo-American Suburb*: "Now many of the traditional values of our society are attractive again. Artists in all fields are rediscovering bourgeois virtues denied to the avant-garde as recently as ten years ago.")[39] The New Urbanists counter their architectural brethren who associate traditional style with conservative ideology by affirming that the underlying town planning ideas at the heart of the New Urbanism are what matter most. Modernist style, they add, would also go well in their communities if the audience were sufficiently advanced to accept it, as would advanced ideas of planning and regional development. In short, they are being pragmatists, and indeed some of the designs done after *Suburban Nation* have incorporated modernist idioms. But it would be foolish to assume that the traditional architectural style of the New Urbanist community does not carry with it, for residents, a weight of cultural meaning and association—all of which are part of the marketing of the New Urbanism around family values and a nostalgia for the comfort, safety, and presumed sanity of the mythical small town.

The impact of the New Urbanism has been profound on new community development throughout the United States, with particular visibility in Florida, California, and the Mid-Atlantic. In fact, what began as an insurgent movement has quickly become mainstreamed, a strategy of choice for developers and town planners, redefining what "community" means in America. Yet contemplating the range of New Urbanist communities, one realizes that utopian space does not always a utopian community make. There may, for example, be a town center in the community, but—given the relatively limited scale of New Urbanist developments—the community may have an insufficient population to support its commercial establishments. The most successful new communities manage to attract outsiders, either as tourists (as in the Disney-created Celebration, outside Orlando) or as nearby residents, as when a community's town center doubles as a shopping and entertainment magnet for surrounding suburban communities (as in Kentlands, Maryland). And while the theory of the New Urbanism speaks of integrating workplace and residence, few if any New Urbanist communities have integrated businesses or companies or manufacturing beyond the local service level. Despite their attractiveness as living spaces—and one cannot deny their appeal and the sustaining power of their real estate values—these new communities have more often functioned as smarter suburban developments, with a few more amenities, rather than as nurturing laboratories for a future society.

But it is as a promised model of American society that the New Urban-

Victorian pattern book for Celebration, outside of Orlando, Florida, designed to guide architects in creating appropriate styles. From Michael Lassell, Celebration: The Story of a Town *(2004).*

ism bears further consideration. What of the social dimensions of the New Urbanist Main Street?

Along with their evil twin, the gated community, New Urbanist towns have constituted the dominant paradigm for the late twentieth century and early twenty-first. But where the gated community has unabashedly turned its back on the world outside, fashioning its own heavenly perfection in isolation from the gritty and grasping realities of the "real" world, the New Urbanism has aimed higher. It has attempted to provide not only the material basis for the good life but also a model for the good society, incorporating a social mix that reflects an ideal of diversity. "The choice is ours," declare Duany, Plater-Zyberk, and Speck, "either a society of homogeneous pieces, isolated from one another in often fortified enclaves, or a society of diverse and memorable neighborhoods, organized into mutually supportive towns, cities, and regions."[40]

In speaking of "a society of diverse and memorable neighborhoods," Duany, Plater-Zyberk, and Speck point us in the right direction, though their phrasing suggests that diversity may be found not in the single neighborhood but rather in the multiplicity of neighborhoods. And there is little in the landmark *Suburban Nation* that would suggest how diversity—which we can translate into economic, ethnic, and racial differences—can be achieved within the individual neighborhood.[41] Nevertheless, Duany, Plater-Zyberk, and Speck do articulate two important points that bear on achieving a mix of income levels. The first is that "affordable housing should not look different from market-rate housing"; it should not be visibly stigmatized. The second is that affordable housing must be dispersed, rather than concentrated in large developments, at the rate of about one in ten within a given neighborhood.[42] Some New Urbanist communities, at least, have achieved this desired mix, interspersing housing types within close range, thus making it possible for people to stay in a community, moving up to a larger house or downsizing, as circumstances change. The New Urbanism does allow continued residence rather than exile and uprooting. And—most important—at least some communities have made subsidized affordable housing visibly indistinct, blending with the surrounding housing. (Perhaps the best example is Duany and Plater-Zyberk's Kentlands, Maryland.) More generally, however, where New Urbanist designers have created housing at different income levels, consumer demand and the costlier amenities of the community have kept prices high relative to surrounding housing in the area, thus maintaining in effect a society that is relatively homogeneous in socioeconomic and racial terms and barely accessible by the middle class. The New Urbanism has yet to solve this problem.

At the heart of the New Urbanist community—what establishes its appeal and what sustains it—are rules, rules governing what can be built and how existing buildings can be changed, how properties must look, how landscaping must look, how people must behave. All societies have rules, and neighborhood public parks may include a long list of prohibitions (no fires, no biking, no dogs off leash, no loud music, etc.), which are typically ignored by the public and rarely enforced by the police. In the New Urbanist community, rules are enforced, readily and eagerly, and this is one of its appeals to residents, who are seeking an enclave of order in the disorder and chaos of contemporary society. Some might even use the rules zealously to their advantage, reporting on their neighbors' violations where people in the "outside world" might simply live and let live.

In the ideal New Urbanist community, there is no litter, the grass is cut regularly, houses are harmoniously complementary (e.g., no adjacent houses can be painted the same color unless that color is white),

Promotional card for Artisan Park, a subdevelopment within Celebration, outside of Orlando, Florida, 2009.

no trailers or boats are permitted in driveways, and so forth. Of course not everyone loves rules, and some have bridled at their sense of a claustrophobic atmosphere. The Walt Disney Company would not permit "for sale" signs on houses in Celebration, one of many self-serving rules that drove authors Douglas Frantz and Catherine Collins to write that the celebrated town's management seemed at times "totalitarian and even a little desperate."[43]

Kentlands, perhaps the most sophisticated Duany and Plater-Zyberk project, has somewhat self-consciously tried to moderate the boutique perfectionism of planned communities by designing, slyly and paradoxically, for imperfection: "Kentlands has idiosyncrasy and imperfections—intentionally. Authentic variety is achieved by allowing odd, leftover lots to remain, forcing the design of a building for just that lot. We insisted that the imprecision of design sketches be reflected in the built work. It took years for the engineers to get used to not straightening every street or making every corner ninety degrees. Those idiosyncrasies add to the charm of the place."[44] This may seem somewhat precious—in the way that "distressed" furniture, new but made to look old, can seem precious—but authenticity is sufficiently elusive, and elastic, in the twenty-first century to accommodate the precise imprecision of state-of-the-art New Urbanism.

Celebration, near Orlando, not far from Disneyworld, is the New Urbanist community that has received the most scrutiny in the media, not least because it was an early model—opening in 1996—and, more important, because it was produced by the Disney Company as a fulfillment of Walt's original vision of creating an ideal model community.[45] (See Plate 9.) Celebration has received high marks for design, but its original intention to provide housing at a range of income levels became quickly modified when demand drove up the prices, making it a more uniformly middle- to upper-middle-class (and wealthy) community. Dwelling sizes are segregated, according to type and class, with the upper end of homes (now selling for several million dollars) in areas allowing spacious private yards and grounds, and apartments (at the other end) grouped in other areas. Some dozen or more years after Celebration opened, apartments had all been transitioned to condominium ownership, thus further limiting the social mix. According to the 2000 census, approximately 94 percent of Celebration's inhabitants were white, with less than 2 percent African American and the remainder Hispanic or Asian. Given these figures, it is not surprising that one resident wrote smugly on a community website, with a sense of chauvinism unmixed with social conscience: "Our homes cost a lot more but any honest person would have to admit that part of the charm of buying here is living a life style that mimics what most American families could only hope to enjoy. No ethnic or racial problems in sight here."[46]

As Frantz and Collins, along with Andrew Ross, have documented, despite the degree of homogeneity in the community, life in Celebration in its heady early years was not always harmonious, with complaints against management directed chiefly at the delays and quality of the building and, within the community itself, regarding the much touted progressive school, which did not always deliver what parents expected. Still, at least one student from the earliest years reported on her experience in high school and in the community generally in uniformly positive terms. "How do you feel this community has helped shape the person you are today?" she was asked. "I can honestly say I know what a sense of place and sense of community means. It is because of Celebration I 'get it.' I hope that I'll find that again someday with my children. I want to thank my parents for standing in line with 5,000 people entering into a lottery for the original 350 homes. I know that by my seeing Celebration develop over the course of the past 13 years I'll have a map in my mind on how to help create a better community where I land."[47] One might respond by asking whether

Celebration, outside of Orlando, Florida, town view from across the lake. Photograph by Sandy Sorlien. © 2011 Sandy Sorlien from www.transect-collection.org.

Celebration "gets it." It is hard to know how graduates of so homogeneous and ordered a community can be prepared for the disorder and diversity of the "real" world.

But then, why should we ask New Urbanist communities to provide a model for solving society's social problems? Is it not enough for them simply to provide a better formula for land use in developing the suburbs? And yet, if New Urbanist communities become the model for future development in this country—and their influence is certainly extending—we have not only all the good that is a part of this paradigm but also the potential for something all too familiar and all too pernicious in its possible consequences. Robert D. Putnam, in his comprehensive study of community and its discontents in the late twentieth century, *Bowling Alone*, speaks of the two quite different kinds of social capital: bonding and bridging. Bonding increases the solidity and contact of members within a relatively homogeneous group; bridging increases the contact across members of different groups.[48] Both bridging and bonding "can have powerfully positive social effects," Putnam writes. "But bonding social capital, by creating strong in-group loyalty, may also create strong out-group antagonism."[49]

A perfect example of that latter point can be found on the front page of the *Celebration Independent* for May 2009. Responding to the call to form a local Anti-Tax Tea Party, about fifty residents of Celebration and neighboring Four Corners gathered in Celebration's Founder's Park to protest federal taxes. One protestor is quoted: "We own a small business and are acting responsibly to get through the recession, but we are being punished by having to bail out those who are not responsible enough to dig out themselves." These protests, representing the new populism, were diffusely directed against President Barack Obama's bailouts of financial giants but also against the "stimulus" spending, which is perceived as Obama's move toward "socialism," including what is imagined as national health care. There were no expressed objections to the news, which appeared on page 8 of the same issue, that a local congressman had arranged for $750,000 in federal funding to help fund the construction of a library for Celebration. In short, the protest in Celebration, admittedly a minor affair, represents not just a bonding within the homogeneous community but also a failure to imagine a bridging with needs outside the community.

Does the utopian community need to connect with the world outside? Or is utopia defined by its insulation and refusal to build a bridge to the world outside? In the fifties, Putnam observes, small-town America built social capital through the bonding within its communities; but in the sixties and after, it has been argued, Americans became more tolerant of one another while losing their previous close connections, an evolution that parallels the move from small towns to metropolitan areas, for it is the "size of place . . . that determines civic engagement."[50] The New Urbanism, as Putnam implies, may reverse this trend, in building spaces that have town centers and that foster community within a limited population. What he does not mention is the degree to which these communities may foster bonding at the expense of the larger bridging that is an equal goal of our larger society. One might also ask, as Emily Talen does in assessing New Urbanist communities, what *kind* of "bonding"—"casual neighboring" or "deep social bonding"—is present in New Urbanist towns, whose sense of community, she argues, is based on "resident homogeneity, not the more socially desirable goal of heterogeneity."[51]

In 1998, as the New Urbanism was gaining ground, literally, and the idea of the small town was surfacing yet again in the American spatial imagination, two films appeared that commented on our fascination with this icon of community, *Pleasantville* and *The Truman Show*. *Pleasantville* featured a main character, David, who is obsessed with the fifties television image of the small town and who, by a twist of engineering, is able to go back inside his television set, entering the lives of the TV townsfolk, while retaining his own later consciousness. David adores the small town, but he gradually realizes that the fifties black-and-white TV town lacks color both literally and figuratively. It is (as befits fifties television land) a disembodied place, without sex and unable to absorb the vitality that color represents in the arts. The hero gradually begins to change this monochromatic world to a more full-bodied and colorful one, but the town wants stasis and develops a prejudice against those who morph into color TV characters: they are, in the conceit of the film, "colored," and become correspondingly ostracized ("No Coloreds" signs appear), with ensuing violence. Eventually the town becomes all "colored," but in the film's sly satire, David still feels oppressed in the end by Pleasantville's limitations and chooses to leave the quondam paradise and return to his contemporary America.

The more spectacular *The Truman Show* was filmed in one of the first New Urbanist communities, Seaside, Florida (built in 1984–91), a pioneering work by Duany and Plater-Zyberk. (See Plate 8.) *The Truman Show* cuts both ways, showing us, on the one hand, the perfection of life in the planned community, where everything is always upbeat, sunny, and a matter of seemingly unending daily routine, marked by the minor events in the life of the sitcom's hero, David Truman; but on the other hand, the bubble that Truman lives in is literally just that—a giant bubble housing a giant movie set that has been designed to accommodate Truman's years of growing up, from his birth to the present. This most complete of reality TV shows (as it has been conceived) is, moreover, being watched by millions worldwide and directed by the producer genius—the *deus absconditus*—behind it. Like the hero of *Pleasantville*, Truman, when he gets an inkling of the scripted nature of his reality, contrives to leave it, by sailing to the ends of the "Earth." In doing so, he is cheered by his global audience, who see him as a kind of Everyman, striking out bravely for a new world beyond the confines of his closed utopian existence—even if that means the show as they know it will end. *The Truman Show* (as a TV show) had offered its viewers the purest form of the homogeneous community, reduced to the joys of the quotidian, a utopia that could exist on the television screen, if not in the real lives of the show's viewers. In cheering for David to break out of that perfection, viewers were cheering, finally—and somewhat improbably and romantically, for a popular audience—for reality, disorder, and the unknown future. *The Truman Show* (the film) reveals the mise-en-scène behind the main character's life, and in the process makes us wonder, as Jorge Luis Borges did, if our lives are not a dream within a dream, and if perfection in life is not the wrong goal after all, leaving us straddling our social need for order and our contrary need, as Richard Sennett has argued, for disorder.[52]

The traditional small town, in its mythical image, has concealed beneath the charming and homey facades of Main Street the force of exclusion that stands behind the happy community. Yet it has served again and again, throughout the twentieth century, as a model of community for the planned community, which has variously strived—and usually failed—to achieve the diverse population that our ideal notion of community in a multiracial, multicultural society requires. Behind the streets and squares of the planned community—which assumes that the good society can be achieved through the creation of the good place—lies an effort to create the bonds of community, but without paying sufficient attention to the complex balance of socioeconomic and psychological forces required to achieve that state. Can we plan the good place? Assuming we can, we have not in the process paid sufficient attention to the paradoxical nature of community, its tension between inclusion and exclusion, its effort to create bonds while excluding, de facto, racial or other minorities. With few exceptions, the history of community planning in America has been a history of good intentions gone astray, of wishing to have utopia but not having the right ingredients.[53]

But if the city—as opposed to the small town—is by its very nature a place of diversity and disorder, and also a place of the highest cultural aspirations, what happens if we bring the small town, in the form of the New Urbanism, into the city? I try to answer that question in the next chapter.

Drive through some parts of North or West Philadelphia today, less than a mile from the high-rise office buildings and luxury condominiums in the core of Center City, and you will see single-family homes and twins, constructed of brick with white-painted front doors and trim, many with front lawns and backyards, a white picket fence here and there, sidewalks, porches, and even possibly a cul-de-sac. Over the past fifteen years or so, the urban blight that had marked these areas—run-down townhouses, abandoned buildings with boarded doors and windows, broken glass and defaced walls, rubble-filled lots, the remains of derelict public housing— has been significantly mitigated, and vacant lots have been transformed into a new vision of the city.[1] Yet oddly, this vision of renewal does not come from a tradition of urbanism. Rather, it comes from the small town, with overtones of suburbia, mediated by the New Urbanism, and brought within walking distance of the heart of the metropolis. As the authors of a recent study of metropolitan Philadelphia observe, "Some city neighborhoods now resemble suburban places more than they resemble nearby sections of Philadelphia."[2]

How did all of this come about? What are the assumptions behind this new development? And where will it take the city of the twenty-first century?

The factual questions are easy to answer: These new developments are part of the complex process of urban reconstruction that has been underwritten by the federal government, with additional state and local funding, as part of the Housing and Community Development Act of 1992—or HOPE VI (Housing Opportunities for People Everywhere). The program was enthusiastically promoted by Henry Cisneros, President Bill Clinton's secretary of housing and urban development, who initiated a period of transformation in American housing that is still under way. Joining public dollars and private investment, this transformation has also been effected by private developers motivated by the federal Low-Income Housing Tax Credit Program, a dollar-for-dollar reduction (i.e., dollars invested are deducted from tax to be paid) used usually by corporations that are developing multifamily houses. Since its inception in 1986, the program has generated approximately 90 percent of affordable housing nationwide.[3]

One can see the results of this remarkable evolution nationally in much of the urban development of the last twenty years—from St. Louis to Chicago to Washington to Atlanta—where the monstrous post–World War II high-rises that had been associated with public housing and crime for decades have been demolished and replaced by lower-density housing built vaguely along the lines of New Urbanist principles. I am going to call these city versions of the New Urbanism "New City Communities" to distinguish them from their suburban cousins. To understand just how striking a change New City Communities represent, let us recall that the city has been, for 200 years, the antithesis of the small town. Only with the New Urbanism of the late twentieth century has the model of the small town come back into the mainstream of urbanism, though it is worth noting that until the mid-nineties, at least, the New Urbanist planners, in providing a better model for regional and suburban development, had turned their backs on the cities and urban renewal.[4] In the twenty-first century, we need to reassess the assumed opposition, if not contradiction, between the city and the small town in American culture.

At the same time, a closer look reveals that in fact the boundaries between city, suburbs, and small towns were challenged early in the twentieth century, when urban planners first began to think of the city as a collection of small towns and neighborhoods. Looking back on the development of New York City outside of Manhattan, Robert Stern observed in *The Anglo American Suburb* (1982), "Much of New York is a city of attached and semi-attached one-, two-, and three-family houses, interspersed with apartment blocks usually no more than six storeys high. For this reason, it can be argued that New York and most other American cities are, like London, collections of small towns—let us call them suburbs—united not by a uniform grid or by a super-highway system, but by a system of roads which generally preceded urbanisation and by underground and elevated rail systems that even now can make the suburbanisation of our cities feasible."[5] Arguing for a reversal of the post–World War II thinking that had led planners to abandon the city to seek virgin land in the suburbs to solve our urban problems, Stern advocated rebuilding within the usable city. And we can go even farther in eroding the line between city and small town, for in some ways the small town has been a recognized part of urban life since the early twentieth century. Small-town values were identified by Clarence Perry as the foundation of the neighborhood unit that he promoted as an essential feature of urban design and renewal through the thirties.

What happened to this way of thinking? Post–World War II urban renewal took, in fact, a quite different direction—emulating the high-rise developments surrounded by park land that were conceived by Le Corbusier in the 1930s as the future of urbanism. Thus, massive housing projects were built to shelter the urban poor, while a wealthier (and whiter) population fled to the suburbs, leaving the cities to fend for themselves. Meanwhile, the high-rise projects became nests of crime and vandalism, with unsupervised hallways and elevators especially dangerous. Inadequate maintenance began to erode the physical plants, while inadequate policing allowed gangs and drug lords to take over the public spaces. It took nearly thirty years of misguided building before the general consensus arrived that the high-rise project as a housing model for the poor was a disaster.

Even before the inevitable destruction of Pruitt-Igoe (built, 1954; demolished, 1972), the housing project in St. Louis that became a byword for this failed vision of the urban future and whose removal heralded the similar fate awaiting other such projects nationwide over the next decades, Jane Jacobs offered her scathing critique of modernist master plans. Under the shibboleth of urban renewal and "progress," she argued, high-rise housing had swept away low-rise neighborhoods that had been functioning quite well, neighborhoods like Boston's North End or Manhattan's Greenwich Village. With their lively sidewalks and short blocks, their mix of dense residential housing and a commercial economy, these neighborhoods had preserved the character of community. In effect (and without acknowledging the connection), Jacobs was celebrating urban life in the form of the small town, and she has been criticized in doing so for being rooted in nostalgia and slighting the cultural dynamism of city life.[6] From another angle, she was simply describing a process not uncommon in American cities, where the most successful neighborhoods have been "urban villages."[7] In fact, Jacobs's vision of urbanism provides a lens that is still useful in viewing the evolving city of the twenty-first century.

As geographer John Jakle has argued, there has been, since the beginning of the twentieth century, a dialectic between the small town and the city, and the migration into the cities of former inhabitants of small towns

Pruitt-Igoe housing project, St. Louis, Missouri. U.S. Geological Survey photograph, between 1963 and 1972.

Demolition of Pruitt-Igoe housing project, St. Louis, Missouri. U.S. Department of Housing and Urban Development photographs, April 1972. Wikipedia.

transformed the city accordingly: "Americans came to configure cities in ways highly reminiscent of their small-town roots—American cities becoming substantially small town–like if not in physical form then in social constitution and function, especially as measured at the neighborhood level."[8] In fact, Jakle argues, with an eye especially on the immigrant communities, "early-twentieth-century cities were really clusters of small towns—symbolic locales defined at the neighborhood level," and the city dweller's identity depended not on downtown public spaces but on the immediate locale and the home.

In championing the virtues of the city neighborhood, Jacobs also dismissed the whole suburban ideal of the planned garden city as itself a mirage, lacking in the vitality and civility and diversity that the city could offer. Yet Jacobs's urbanism, a covert celebration of small-town community in an urban context, was in turn a catalyst for the New Urbanist planners, who developed the suburbs so as to bring key elements of Jacobs's idealized urban neighborhood to the ex-urban community—walkable streets, houses built close to one another, a sufficiently dense population to sustain a Main Street shopping center, with the sense of community that flows from that space.

Jacobs's views were, in the 1960s, a forceful rebuke to a way of thinking that had become ingrained in the minds of civic planners, who for twenty years had built high-rises to solve all sorts of urban problems. Jakle looks at this history through a gendered lens: where men in the early twentieth century "dominated the boardrooms of big business and the halls of big government," urging big civic projects and skyscrapers to symbolize "progress," women were seen as the "essence of locality as keepers of family household," and therefore also as the stable force behind the "neighborhood," an opposition that parallels the relationship between the city and the small town.[9]

Without essentializing these characteristics as "masculine" or "feminine" it is nevertheless plausible to observe a dramatic shift in architectural and planning sensibility over the last forty years that parallels the seismic changes in cultural attitudes toward gender. Robert Venturi and Denise Scott Brown signaled the same deep change in thinking in the 1970s when—learning from Jacobs as well as from Las Vegas—they celebrated the "ordinary," the vernacular, as opposed to the "heroic" architectural models of modernism. Still, it may be no coincidence that the move from heroic to ordinary, from city to neighborhood, from high-rise to low-rise, has taken place simultaneously with what we might call (following

Ann Douglas's characterization of a nineteenth-century transformation she calls the "feminization of American culture") a second "feminization" of American society in the last decades of the twentieth century, visible across so many cultural fields, a renewal of gendered consciousness that has also coincided with a heightened awareness about environmental issues and sciences. The now widespread practice of creating "urban villages," of building New City Communities in the midst of the metropolis, is accordingly as much the expression of a generalized cultural ethos as it is a strategy for urban renewal.

In thinking about the origins of this change, the impact of the New Urbanism cannot be overstated. One of the most cogent analyses of the failures of urban planning in the last twenty years is made by Andres Duany, Elizabeth Plater-Zyberk, and Jeff Speck in *Suburban Nation* (which I discussed in chapter 7). Duany, Plater-Zyberk, and Speck argue that city government must proactively enact the kinds of zoning that will allow for the easier development of lots within the city, both for middle-class housing and for commercial development. In doing so, Duany, Plater-Zyberk, and Speck also argue against the fear of gentrification that has dominated urban housing assumptions in recent decades on two grounds: first, urban revitalization is impossible without gentrification, given that revitalization expands the tax base by bringing a vital residential population; and second, there is now adequate affordable housing available for displaced residents. Although many would argue, more than ten years after *Suburban Nation*, that their second assumption is invalid, a number of cities now have adequate space and funding to construct both affordable and middle-class housing.

One such city, dramatically altered since the mid-nineties, has been Philadelphia, and I want to use it as a case study, focusing on the signal transformation it has undergone, which illustrates the extraordinary richness of the New Urbanist paradigm, and also its limitations.[10] In more than a dozen instances, scattered throughout the city, the Philadelphia Housing Authority (PHA) has taken low-income communities that were rife with crime and dereliction, many of them high-rise, and transformed them into homes that are often indistinguishable from market-rate housing—solidly built, attractive, with contemporary utilities (central air conditioning and heating, internet, etc.).[11] These new affordable housing developments, consisting of low-rise, low-density buildings, have taken many forms, but they have generally expanded the number of rooms per unit, allowing for more spacious habitations for larger families. Most striking, the new de-

Adaptation of New Urbanism to North Philadelphia public housing, built by the Philadelphia Housing Authority. Single homes and duplexes surround a fenced-in common area, with a view of Center City Philadelphia in the background. Photograph by author, 2010.

velopments have increased the grassy areas around the units and possess an entirely different look from the public housing of the past.[12] With large backyards behind each house that join with others to create common open playing spaces, the development has adapted at least a part of the Radburn plan, but with this radical difference: the homes are encircled by a perimeter wrought-iron fence, keeping out the unwanted public and preserving the safety of the inner commons apart from the North Philadelphia streets.

Surveyed as a whole, the *stylistic* solutions to affordable housing in Philadelphia range from homes that would be comfortable in suburbia, at one extreme, to homes that fit into the urban fabric, at the other. The "suburban" housing was generally constructed at the beginning of the HOPE VI renewal effort, in an area of North Philadelphia that had become largely derelict in the nineties. Built to achieve a lower density than the city's traditional row housing, these units responded to Philadelphia housing director John Kromer's affirmation that "Philadelphia in the 1990s does not need the same high level of housing density as it did a century before, when North Philadelphia was a manufacturing center with worker housing clustered around factories."[13] With houses standing in large grassy plots, this neighborhood is perhaps the least "urban" in feel. As Michael

Johns, the chief architect at the PHA, said in 2005 about the suburban projects done in the nineties, "To get anyone to come to North Philadelphia, it better look like something done by Toll Bros [a "luxury home" builder in the Delaware Valley]. . . . It had to be dramatic if we were going to change people's notions about public housing. We were making a statement."[14] Indeed they were: with their grassy front and back yards, small porches, white doors, white window trimming, and a vaguely colonial idiom realized within a postmodern vocabulary; with occasional common green space and even an occasional cul-de-sac, these homes say "private house" loudly and clearly and even more clearly they say "suburbs."

At the other extreme are the quasi-Victorian brick row houses, which look "new" but feel like they belong in a city like Philadelphia, much of whose older stock consists of Victorian row houses. The new buildings that seem most at home blend with the existing brick streetscape, having an urban feel and sometimes being finished with details that reference the Victorian era, when much of North, South, and West Philadelphia was built. The existing Philadelphia row houses from 100 or more years ago often have more elaborate facades and ornaments, but these new ones seem like contemporary updates, even including Victorian roof cornices.

Somewhere in the middle, in terms of their fit with the urban context, are the vast majority of the New City Communities done under the aegis of the PHA, which have a deliberately New Urbanist style—vaguely neo-Victorian—featuring uniformly designed two-story red brick row houses with miniature porches, gabled windows, tiny grassy frontyards, front steps, and an occasional bay window. The quality and substance vary somewhat, but generally these are townhouse communities that are handsome and efficient in design, providing substantial and livable affordable housing (both rented and owned); they satisfy a need for privacy and respect that, again, was ignored in the mass housing developments of the post–World War II era. Not surprisingly, Philadelphia's housing program has become a model internationally for government-funded projects.[15] (See Plate 10.)

And yet an odd feeling overcomes one in looking at these new neighborhoods. They are, of course, developments, and to that extent have a degree of homogeneity within each community, each of which might occupy a lot from approximately four to sixteen square blocks in size. Such large urban developments create a uniformity of appearance that goes against the grain of a city where lots were more frequently developed in smaller units, and usually in a more piecemeal way. (New Urbanist communities

Adaptation of New Urbanism to North Philadelphia public housing, built by the Philadelphia Housing Authority. Victorian row houses inspired the design. Photograph by author, 2010.

—as I noted in the case of Kentlands—deliberately vary the styles of adjacent houses so as to simulate a more "authentic" streetscape that has evolved over time.)

Acknowledging this sign of authenticity, the sophisticated and award-winning design of the Martin Luther King row houses—the PHA's premier development to date—includes an irregular profile, in terms of elevation, as if the block had been developed in stages. Just south of Center City, the new King houses are the best example of a development that was conceived not just to provide affordable housing but to regenerate a neighborhood that had been blighted for years by the Martin Luther King high-rises. When the high-rises were imploded in 1999, the PHA received grants to redevelop the site, along with the surrounding area. In moving from high-rise to low-rise housing, the density was dramatically reduced to a total of some 250 units, including 109 homes that would be owned by residents (with subsidized mortgages). The mix of rental and owner-occupied units worked here, spurring private development in the area.

Martin Luther King row houses, South Philadelphia, built by the Philadelphia Housing Authority, 2011. The MLK houses attempt a more sophisticated urban design, with varied building heights and an occasional corner store. Photograph by Jan Pasek. Courtesy of Philadelphia Housing Authority.

But what chiefly accounts for the success of the King houses, apart from the selectivity of tenants, is the styling: rather than having a uniform appearance, the houses' facades (most Victorian in styling) vary by street and even within a given street, providing the appearance of the kind of gradual, organic development that "real" neighborhoods have. Fitting seamlessly into Philadelphia's street grid, they appear like a renewal of the urban fabric rather than an intrusion into it.

The King development may represent a future trend for public housing inspired by the New Urbanism, but with these few exceptions, the essential heterogeneity of the streetscape that is characteristic of the city is not part of the New City Community developments. As a consequence, these mini-neighborhoods have a "feel" to them that is completely different from the otherwise dominant urban texture of grassless sidewalk.

In a way, these urban versions of suburban houses beg the whole question of urban renewal: What is it? What should it look like? What does it mean to import the suburbs into the inner city? Does suburban density (or the lack thereof) meet the needs of urban development? Do the grassy yards contradict the meaning of "city," where a presumed density of population creates not only the need for row houses, but the critical mass required for cultural enterprise? Does the space of the suburban model—especially in the more extreme early developments, where a house stands alone surrounded by grass—speak to the community ethos of urban life? Or does it mimic the private suburban house that embodies the American Dream, representing a long-awaited reversal of stigmatized affordable housing in this country and the fulfillment of widely shared aspirations?

In short, stepping back to survey the differences between the urban and suburban versions of New Urbanism, one paradox immediately presents itself: where the suburban New Urbanism seeks to bring high-density design to the suburbs (with all of its attending advantages), New Urbanism in the city seeks just the opposite: to bring lower density to the city, even lower density, at times, than in New Urbanist suburban communities. The explanation for this apparent paradox is that it makes sense to bring people together in the unpopulated suburbs in order to achieve the density required to make a sustainable town center and a walkable community. But in the city, the move has been not to create such self-sustaining communities but rather to create housing that looks attractive (i.e., suburban, or vaguely New Urbanist), while leaving everything else that makes a self-sustaining community out of the equation. There is no "Main Street" for these communities, no retail corridor nearby, and there are few playgrounds and community centers.

New City Communities have become the prevailing mode of urban reconstruction for a variety of reasons. They are, for one, the opposite of the high-rise towers that had menaced the city, and they seem therefore like a fresh start in a new and better direction. And they are. Moreover, they feel safe, both to insiders and outsiders, by virtue of their simulation of the image of safety that is conjured by the mythical small town evoked by the front porches and yards. And in general the low-density affordable housing in the New City Communities represents a creative response to the troubled history of public housing in the decades following World War II.

Behind the adaption of New Urbanist principles to the inner city lies a cogent analysis provided by Oscar Newman, whose theory of "defensible space" both explained why high-rise public housing had been a fiasco and provided models for successful and safe residential patterns, based on architectural and design principles.[16] Newman, who had taught at Washington University in St Louis, was there at the construction of Pruitt-Igoe, opened in 1954, and he was there less than twenty years later at its dramatic implosion, observing firsthand over the course of these years the patterns and problems of high-rise public housing. For Newman, it is not the high-rise per se that creates an environment for crime—obviously there are luxury buildings that function quite well in this mode—but rather the nearly total absence of a monitoring presence in the public buildings: no doorman, no elevator man, no porter, no security, minimal maintenance. Newman's solution for lower-income housing was to engineer space in a way that maximizes the *private* space of the individual renter or homeowner and minimizes *public* space. In fact, the problem with the high-rise projects was precisely too much public space, communal space, for which no one could feel responsible. The result was crime and vandalism, space taken over by gangs, derelicts, prostitutes, and so on.

Newman proposed a battery of solutions, depending on the particular circumstances presenting themselves for remedy. What Newman did, where necessary, was divide the public space into segments that allowed for more individual "ownership" of previously open space, individual decorating options, along with the upgrading of public amenities and street furniture (lights, play equipment, etc.). Of course, new construction would allow for proper design to begin with, and in that case Newman, who on numerous occasions was invested with legal planning authority, insisted on creating mini-developments, wherever possible, with smaller numbers of family units that would be interspersed throughout middle-income neighborhoods, and that inevitably entailed negotiating with the middle-income NIMBYs. Each unit would be designed to fit the neighborhood aesthetically, and each unit would allow tenants control over their front and back yards. In this way, the family, whether they rented or owned, would be invested in their residence, would be "trained" for homeownership, and would "police" the public spaces in their immediate vicinity. The results, where Newman was able to create these "defensible spaces," were a dramatic decrease in crime and vandalism and an increase in surrounding property values.[17]

Oddly, Newman is rarely mentioned in the contemporary discourse of affordable housing, but his legacy remains, after his death in 2004, as a founding principle of urban renewal.[18] Newman's theories, which were endorsed by Cisneros when he was secretary of housing in the 1990s and were published by the Department of Housing and Urban Development, provided the foundation and theoretical rationale for the move from the

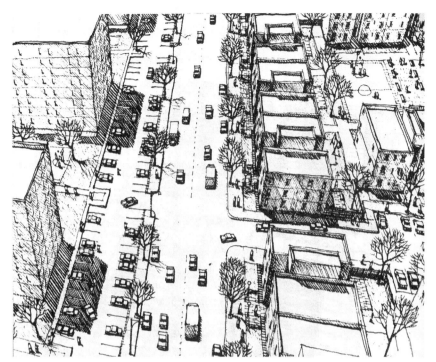

Illustration from Oscar Newman's Design Guidelines for Creating Defensible Space *(National Institute for Law Enforcement and Criminal Justice and U.S. Department of Housing and Urban Development, 1976), showing how the buildings on the right beneficially bring residents in contact with the street, with as few families as possible sharing the entries. On the left, the buildings are turned away from the street, removing residents from a sense of identification with the property and the street.*

pernicious high-rise developments to the smaller low-rise. Newman was adapting the *appearance* of the New Urbanist developments for his affordable housing units—townhouse construction, sidewalks, stoops—and he was building on the implicit values of community that would result when families were invested in their private space and in the relatively minimal common space they shared with other residents.

But the major premise of Newman's theory was a psychological inversion of the New Urbanism. While the latter sold the values of community, Newman promoted the values of the individual and of private control, of autonomy. While New Urbanist residents were willingly giving up control to the authority of the community in order to achieve aesthetic order in the larger environment, Newman counseled that residents in affordable housing should be first of all invested in "owning" the space outside their

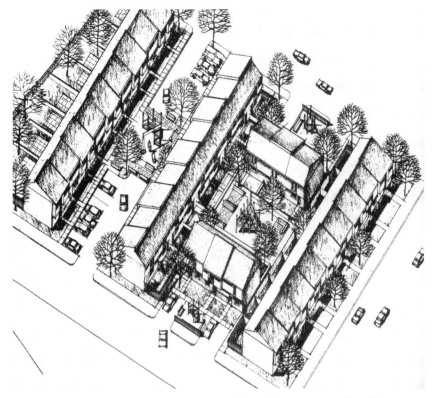

Illustration from Oscar Newman's Design Guidelines for Creating Defensible Space *(National Institute for Law Enforcement and Criminal Justice and U.S. Department of Housing and Urban Development, 1976), showing row-house cluster that emphasizes private and semiprivate areas within the housing unit, with shared play spaces for children in the center, surrounded by low-rise houses.*

apartment doors; in effect he was privatizing public housing. Residents needed to buy into the concept of ownership and responsibility in order to function as citizens in a community. At bottom he was fusing the appeal of individual homeownership that the suburbs had traditionally offered with the concept of community that the New Urbanism represented, along with the greater economies and efficiencies of New Urbanist buildings.[19]

Yet from another perspective, the location of affordable housing within the city, and usually in areas of the city that are at higher risk of crime, places yet another burden on the lower-income resident. A suburban location, with reduced crime, provides a setting where the value of "community" can be added as another luxury. For the New City Community, location makes it vulnerable to the sometimes dangerous and threatening winds that blow through the city—from gangs to homeless people to reckless teens to drug dealers and prostitutes. These are not necessarily the environmental conditions of Center City upscale neighborhoods, but they may be more likely in the marginal areas that have been subject to urban renewal. Because of the lack of reliable public safety in these areas, then, residents are compelled to "defend" their homes, their spaces, against the unknown.

We might say, in response to this description, that nothing is more "American" than defending one's property against the unknown intruder. A whole industry of gun manufacturing and sales is based on this right, as are an industry of Hollywood films and a political movement that takes no prisoners in defending the right to bear arms as the paramount freedom and privilege of an American citizen. True, when Oscar Newman talks about the need to create defensible spaces, he is not thinking of creating armed warfare within the city. He is thinking more along the lines of the vigilant citizen (as opposed to the vigilante), the "town watch" type, who is alert and defensive and does not want trouble in the neighborhood. The gun-rights advocate with his arsenal in his private house, waiting for the unruly kids on his lawn (think Clint Eastwood in *Gran Torino*), often conceals a xenophobia that is closed down to anything in the public space. Newman's ideal citizen is wary but not xenophobic, protective of private space but happily joining in the commons and the community. Still, Newman's residents clearly have a far tougher job than the residents of a utopian New Urbanist community located far from the city: it is the inner-city resident who must deal with the city's vandals and drug lords.

We do not yet know how well these communities will work in the long run, but they may, despite these reservations, be the city's best bet for renewing itself at the margins. Of course, in the best of all worlds, as Newman knew, affordable housing for low-income residents would be far better integrated into the texture of middle-class urban neighborhoods; in fact, by their appearance it would be hard to tell them apart. In some instances—to continue with the example of Philadelphia—that has indeed been the case: there are mixed-income communities constructed by the PHA (e.g., Ridge Falls and Martin Luther King) where a percentage of the housing is set aside at subsidized rates, and others are sold or rented at market rate. And today's practice, according to Carl Greene (director of PHA at the time), confirms the principle of invisibility: "The housing authority insists on designs that are virtually indistinguishable from the surrounding homes, except that they are generally smaller."[20]

The transformations of the urban center in Philadelphia and other cities have dramatically reversed the trend of urban decay and are beginning to restore an urban fabric that had badly frayed in the years since World War II. They have provided homes—with modern appliances, air conditioning, and sufficient space—to millions of people who would otherwise be excluded from this social good. They have added to the population of cities that have been losing ground steadily, and the new residents they have brought in will, one can hope, provide the critical mass to support (and spur the growth of) a commercial economy—supermarkets, cleaners, drugstores, the basics—that had all but disappeared from parts of the inner city. Most impressive, they have raised real estate values in the neighborhoods where the New City Communities have been built. (In one Philadelphia neighborhood, for example, values rose at three times the citywide average.)[21]

Yet despite their obvious appeal and the social benefits of these New City Communities, we may look at them from the perspective of the city as a whole and ask whether they have realized their own potential. Taking this broader perspective, how might one judge the results thus far of this extraordinary experiment in urban reconstruction? One might observe first that of course this lower-density housing cannot accommodate the numbers of people living previously in the old high-rises, and what happened to the displaced residents is something little pondered by urban renewal agencies.[22] In the late nineties, the Clinton administration removed the requirement that homes that were demolished needed to be replaced on a one-to-one basis.[23] Consequently, according to a recent study, for every 11,000 units demolished, 4,000 are built nationally. Only 11 percent of former residents succeed in moving back to the newly constructed housing (those with higher incomes), while 30 percent wind up with Section 8 vouchers and 50 percent transfer to other projects.[24] For the New City Communities to succeed, even as "affordable housing," it is essential that residents have the economic power to remain residents in good standing, maintaining their properties, and obviously this limits the number of potential applicants. As John Kromer, formerly Philadelphia's housing director, starkly put it, "In the late 1980s and early 1990s, the neediest and the homeless were the priority. Now it's decent families."[25] Those selected, something of an elite group, enjoy the benefits of their new homes and new communities. For the rest, the struggle continues. And in the deeply troubled economy of the twenty-first century, that is no small struggle.

The New City Community is a strategy for renewing the city through affordable housing; it is not a strategy for solving the vaster problem of poverty and housing. And it leaves open the question of whether the city is being rebuilt by repopulating it with more economically advantaged residents (still qualifying as low-income) and removing the poorest of the poor.[26] Section 8 housing—where the landlord is willing to accept government vouchers—is not a particularly happy solution, with many neighborhoods resisting the subsidized population; moreover, the limits to Section 8 housing support imposed by the city of Philadelphia (seven years, except for the disabled and elderly) assume that moving to home-ownership is a possibility in an economic marketplace where jobs have been scarce. (It is difficult to see how you solve the problem of struggling neighborhoods without addressing the issue of unemployment.)

The intention in creating affordable housing has been to avoid the stigma and isolation of such housing by designing developments that look like market housing, and this effort in more recent years has been success-ful. There has also been an effort to incorporate market-based housing as well, allowing for middle-class occupants, thus creating "mixed" commu-nities. (Most developers seem willing to accept a proportion of 10 percent of total housing as a viable set-aside figure for affordable housing occu-pants.) And this strategy, too, has met with some success. Still, to a large degree, the New City Communities in Philadelphia are largely African American, and in that sense they are the mirror image of the white New Urbanist townhouse communities outside the city. They lack the mixed-use (residential and commercial) planning that generates dynamic urban environments: few shops and restaurants adjoin these developments, and there are few corner stores of the sort visible throughout the older row-house neighborhoods of Philadelphia. Given the privatizing of space, in backyards and frontyards, there are often few places for children to play, and few public play areas.[27] These developments exist largely as islands in the urban ocean, lacking the networked connectivity that likewise gener-ates street energy within the urban scene. They impose a vision of subur-ban typology on the city. They are missing a town center, a Main Street.

In other respects, too, the New City Communities stand apart from the rest of the city. To use the example of Philadelphia again, one can observe a difference between the architectural idiom of public housing and the idiom of private housing that is evolving, though both are underwritten by New Urbanist principles. The new *private* developments look differ-ent from their public counterparts. The private developers have adapted New Urbanist principles, but within an urban modernist idiom (rather than the more traditional neocolonial porch-and-front-yard idiom of the PHA): lacking in porches, with solid front doors and facades, often with second- or third-floor balconies, they appear impregnable, offering the middle class a different approach to "defensible space."[28] Yet another Philadelphia example is Westrum Development Corporation's Brewerytown, a large middle-class development with a New Urbanist feel in a corner of North Philadelphia above gentrified Girard Avenue, set in its own precinct apart from the urban grid. Brewerytown, built on a large block of land partially made available by the city of Philadelphia under its Neighborhood Transformation Initiative, was hailed by Mayor John F. Street as a model of urban redevelopment for the city—though in fact it remains, in terms of scale, at least, a unique example.[29] As an instance of what critics see as gentrification, Brewerytown has been contested by some of the displaced African American population. Yet another Westrum Development, Hilltop at Falls Ridge, in the East Falls area of Philadelphia and on the site of a former notoriously derelict high-rise public housing development, is more traditionally New Urbanist in design (i.e., neocolonial) and again occupies a space separate from the urban grid, with winding roads through the community.

WHERE RESIDENTS of affordable housing's New City Communities have purchased the suburban feel of their housing at the expense of having to "defend" their space, middle-class residents seem to be allowed the luxury of living in more secure fortresses. Look at the designs from one of Philadelphia's major firms, which works across the spectrum, from affordable housing to upscale suburban developments and historic properties.[30] The stylistic vocabulary is flexible but firmly distinguishable: at one end of the firm's practice, stylistically, is the public housing idiom, homey townhouses, traditionally "Victorian" in design, grassy yards, somewhat suburban in feel. At the other extreme are the "hip" urban designs, the "chic" housing (to use the language of their promotional literature), appealing to urban professionals who want something more neomodern, vaguely postmodern, clean lines, striking fenestration, new materials (glass, steel, plastic), as opposed to brick and porches and front steps. These private developments, like the public housing, are conceived along New Urbanist lines (scale, use of space, orientation toward street, etc.), but the idiom and the ethos of the designs say "urban," not "suburban." One might imagine a deliberate effort to distinguish the new middle-class housing from what has now become the defining idiom of public housing. Where the

Brewerytown, a market-rate private development in a previously marginal area of Philadelphia, not far from Center City. Photograph by author, 2010.

public housing embodies traditional values and the idea of family, the upscale chic urban housing is making a lifestyle statement about freedom, modernity, technology, and urbanism.

Leaving these caveats aside, what the example of Philadelphia demonstrates is that the New Urbanist principles (derived from Jane Jacobs) that govern the development of Main Street and the new towns can be just as valuable in thinking about the development of the central districts of American cities. By many measures, Philadelphia has become, in the twenty-first century, a model of urban redevelopment, a success story. And although the net effect of the New City Communities has been to decrease the population of these areas, to de-densify them, they have nevertheless managed to attract the mix of income levels (including middle-class residents) that would supply a growing tax base for sustaining the city. Private developers in Philadelphia, as in other cities, are beginning to build on parcels in the city that are closer to the retail centers.[31] This is a huge accomplishment. In this way, the wheel comes full circle, from Jacobs's idealized small town as model for the urban neighborhood to the urban neighborhood as model for suburban development to suburban New Urbanism as model for the new Center City neighborhood.

But the dramatic changes in the way people are living in the city in the twenty-first century are only half the story of the influence of Main Street, as mediated by the New Urbanism. Commercial design, along with a new concept of the "town center"—a mix of entertainment and retail and residential housing—is the other half, and it is to an examination of this new mix, yet another manifestation of the Main Street ideal, that I turn in the conclusion.

Conclusion
Consuming Main Street

One might see a kind of poetic justice in this circle of history: the cities that decimated the small towns during the first half of the twentieth century were themselves brought to the brink of disaster by a burgeoning suburbanization movement, including the outlandish growth of shopping centers and malls outside the city. Then, with the decline of suburban malls in the late twentieth and early twenty-first centuries, the small towns began to establish their own functional identity by re-creating (or inventing) themselves as incarnations of nostalgia, even while the suburbs have tried to redefine themselves as small towns, with Main Street "town centers" or, at best, a commercial and residential center around a commuting rail station—so-called transit villages.[1] Meanwhile, the suburban malls—those not yet turned to brownfields—have tried to disguise themselves as versions of Main Street![2] Well into the twenty-first century, small towns, decoupled commercially from their surrounding populations by the ease of e-commerce, meet yet new challenges as they are bankrupted by prevailing economic conditions and forced to shrink their fire and police departments.[3] Yet even as the real small town continues to struggle for its material survival in the twenty-first century, Main Street has become one of the leading paradigms for the construction and reconstruction of public space, including, remarkably, urban space.

It has been argued that we have evolved toward a new eclecticism in American urbanism, one that attempts to combine several strands in American practice; yet behind each of them one can see the power of the Main Street idea. Emily Talen identifies four components that are, or should be, part of a new flexible urbanism: the incrementalism associated with Jane Jacobs (small improvements wherever possible); the grander visions of the City Beautiful movement associated with Daniel Burnham and his heirs, which include vistas and monuments and boulevards; the regional planning tradition of Lewis Mumford and his associates; and the garden city tradition that mutates into the New Urbanism.[4] Main Street is nothing if not incremental in its rate of change; and, of course, it is an essential piece of the regional planning traditions represented by Mumford and the New Urbanism. Main Street may seem least allied to the grand visions of the City Beautiful, but even here we might argue that the town center, at its best, has been the site of an active street life, festivals, and parades.

In the earlier model—beginning in the 1960s with Victor Gruen's Midtown Plaza in Rochester, New York—cities were in competition with the suburbs. The challenge was to get *homo automobilus* into the city and out of his or her car; and the means to do this was to make the city as friendly to private transportation as possible—meaning expressways from the suburbs to the cities and, once the car had arrived, ample parking lots in which to leave it. Out of the car, the shopper would then be enveloped by an indoor mall, usually of vertical construction, given the denser land use in the city center. Spacious shopping galleries, dramatic entrances, escalators, indoor entertainment spaces, restaurants, indoor food courts, an ice-skating rink now and then—these were the magnets used to draw the suburbanite into the city, and they could be coupled with hotels and transportation centers as well.[5]

These indoor urban malls, many still thriving, are immune to weather changes (once the car has arrived in the parking lot), but they are also, for that reason, a static environment, a sealed atmosphere, a walled universe, with only seasonal decorations to remind us of the changing world outside and zombie music to propel us through the corridors—punctuated by an occasional fountain or artificial tree—at an even pace. Ultimately the malls, whether urban or suburban, have come to seem, to many, dead spaces, sterile environments, even (to borrow Henry Miller's 1945 phrase) air-conditioned nightmares.

The New Urbanist downtown is another scene entirely. (See Plate 11.) With streets arranged in the familiar grid and an occasional pedestrian walkway, the new center city area draws people in by virtue of restaurants, outdoor cafés, shops, and arts festivals; with playful sculptures, fountains, seating areas, and small performance spaces here and there, the urban precinct is an entertainment center as well. At best, residential areas are mixed with commercial areas in a zone that provides the values of the walkable neighborhood.[6] Ghirardelli Square, in San Francisco, which opened in 1964, was a precursor to this type of development, and the idea was carried forward by James Rouse in Boston's Faneuil Hall, opening in

1976.[7] Rouse's example, which exploited the marketing potential of historic buildings and places, in turn inspired a new way of thinking about the attractive possibilities of cities in the 1980s. Especially successful was Rouse's Baltimore waterfront development, Harborplace, which mixed commercial and residential properties, hotels, museums, restaurants, all in a festive and dramatic setting. Where Main Street had offered, at best, a movie theater and drugstore soda fountain, the new urban entertainment centers offer game parlors, theaters, theme restaurants, concerts, and holiday celebrations; where Main Street stores catered to the everyday needs of the town—cleaners, tailors, hardware, bakery, grocery, pharmacy, gas station, café—the new urban marketplaces feature boutique stores, electronics stores, home furnishings, gift shops, high-end shoes, camping equipment, card shops, and themed restaurants. Main Street might have had a Woolworth or Kresge; the new marketplaces have a variety of national chains, from toy stores to branded clothing to department stores.

Though anathema to some critics for its factitiousness (like Manhattan's South Street Seaport, another Rouse production, it was not so much a historical preservation as an ersatz creation), Rouse's Baltimore Harborplace brought people back to the city for the excitement it afforded— the crowds, the activity, the spirit of celebration, the outdoor scene, the cafés. The new town centers in downtown areas might not have the special resources of a seaport, but they aimed to create a magnet by fashioning walkable streets, diverse housing types, street benches and lampposts, trees, outdoor dining areas, public sculpture, and human-scale architecture.[8] And at their best they have attracted diverse populations (a mix of age, race, ethnicity, and income), who come for the human drama, the sense of community, the spontaneity of street life.[9] Rather than shutting out the world through enclosed spaces, as the malls have done, the new Main Street downtowns aim to incorporate "reality," or at least a festival version of it, modeled on Disneyland's utopian Main Street.

Moreover—and this may be the most important ingredient of their success—all of this takes place within an environment that is free from crime and disorder, an environment that is "safe." What was appealing in the malls, especially as people were fleeing from the troubled cities, was their safety. You could stroll the corridors knowing that security guards were close at hand and that the mall was protected by a long list of prohibitions, publicly visible, that insured a decorous and civil environment. The small town—at least in myth—always had a sense of safety and community; and it is what the city, competing with the mall, has had to provide.

Westfield Horton Plaza, San Diego, California, the new urban solution: town center,
outdoor mall, and Main Street combined into one, 2008. Photograph by Coolcaesar.
Wikicommons.

The New Urbanist marketplaces do provide an assurance (if not a guar-
antee) of safety, by virtue of their own downtown private police forces.
Private security zones—as in many parts of Los Angeles, San Diego, New
York, and the downtown area of Fort Worth, where it is supported by
the philanthropy of the Bass brothers—have provided that assurance of
safety, ensured by a private security force that offers the visible and ef-
ficacious presence needed to keep order, working hand in glove with the
public police departments. These safe urban zones are called Business Improvement Districts—or BIDs—and they have deterred crime and revived
business in their areas, making it possible for the downtown streets to
come alive at night.[10] In place since the 1980s in many cases, they have
also reversed declining real estate values, improved the cleanliness of
downtown areas, and drawn the public to the areas they govern.

Yet their status as quasi-governmental entities is ambiguous and po-
tentially problematic. BIDs can be constructed in a variety of forms, as
subunits of municipal government or as charitable institutions, but they
function with some of the authority of governmental units. One BID in

Center City Philadelphia, for example, runs a court for petty crime where offenders are given community service punishments instead of jail time.[11] Yet the accountability of BIDs is somewhat unclear, since they are governed by boards that are not elected by voters but rather appointed by City Hall; moreover, their funding is the result of mandatory assessments on businesses and institutions in the area. Having the power to make improvements to sidewalks, paving, plantings, sewers, water lines, and so on, and using their own funds, BIDs have the power to do strategic planning with positive results, but they inevitably affect public space in ways that are not fully responsive to residents' needs, and that residents have no power to check. And while crime may be reduced in one area under patrol, it can also migrate to other areas in the city where safety patrols are less in evidence. Evaluating the function of these urban safety zones is thus complicated, when viewed from the perspective of the city as a whole.[12]

No one can object to the creation of safe downtown areas that draw local residents and tourists to the streets and enliven the civic space, creating the kind of vital, safe urban spaces that Jane Jacobs would celebrate and that embody the virtues of the small town in its idealized form—a space of community, civic engagement, recreation, and entertainment. But we cannot fail to observe that insofar as they are made possible by BIDs, they are quasi-public spaces, the result of a kind of privatizing of public space. (New York City's POPS—Privately Owned Public Spaces— offer the most salient example of this paradox.)[13] And we cannot fail to associate the trend in its largest sense with a movement that has become increasingly visible in the twenty-first century on a national scale as well: the privatizing of government functions, the outsourcing of security, of the military, of prisons, of disaster relief, of whatever can be outsourced.[14]

Importing the suburban model of New Urbanism into the city has in many cases helped reverse the declining fortunes of cities in the late twentieth century; it has become the new paradigm of urban development for the twenty-first century, a simulacrum of the Jacobs neighborhood ideal, an allusion to the messy commercial vitality that Robert Venturi had urged us to learn from in the lessons of Las Vegas. And to the extent that it succeeds, it may well help to humanize the city, restore the broken fabric of neighborhood life, and act as a magnet to revitalize the dynamic civilizations of American cities. But the process is not without its complexities and its trade-offs.

IN CHAPTER 2, I discussed the fate of real small towns as they have struggled to survive into the twenty-first century, and I am ending now with Main Street as the new paradigm of the new century. The instant "town"—with shopping, entertainment, restaurants, and housing, in one walkable community—can now be implanted in the middle of nowhere or in the middle of a decaying inner city: it is the portable solution of our era to community development. Obviously there is continuity between these two versions of Main Street—the real town and the ersatz town as created entertainment center; and yet from another angle there is contradiction. The real small town is a place of conflict and difference, of exclusion and social distinction; the idealized small town is a place of harmony, a symbol of democracy, of community, but likewise a place of social homogeneity. We have strived to create more perfect places out of the reality of Main Street, and sometimes we have come close to success. But the perfection of Main Street—or its seeming perfection—can be found at hand now chiefly in the imagined town centers of the suburban shopping malls and the newly invented downtown entertainment centers, patrolled by security guards. It can be found, in other words, in places that strive to emulate the perfection of Disneyland and its Main Street. To the degree that these are corporate environments, or privately supported ones, they represent the usurpation of the public ideal of Main Street. What began as a symbol of the commons, of the good life, of democracy, in contrast to the corporations that own America, has become in the twenty-first century an ersatz environment, an unreal thing, a corporate creation, the shadow of the Platonic ideal.

And yet for the consumer it is powerfully attractive—as an ideal, as an artificial environment, as a simulacrum of democracy and community. If we have failed to realize this ideal in the real small towns that are struggling to survive and are places of diversity and conflict (as the real world is), we have to some degree succeeded in creating it as an imagined environment. The myth of Main Street—nurtured by our popular culture and by the many representations of small towns that have drawn millions of tourists from the early twentieth century to the present—continues to sustain our core values and now, in the twenty-first century, is remaking our cities. We may not have the real thing, but we can have the consumer version of it, the one we can enjoy precisely as consumers. And that is where we live today in America, in so many ways: deeply attached to our imagined ideal of community, as represented by Main Street, and glad enough if we are privileged to enjoy the facsimile of community in an environment comfortingly guarded for us by the watchful patrolling of private security forces. Our nostalgia for what we have lost, the mythic Main Street of our dreams, is at least partly assuaged by these iconic facsimile environments—New Urbanist neighborhoods, urban and suburban "town center" shopping areas—that can even at times surpass the real thing. In the ersatz environment of the urban Main Street, we can once again enjoy the illusion of a safe community in a harmonious society.

IT IS THE ARGUMENT of this book that Main Street and America are conjoined historically and in the imagination: Walt Disney was both reflecting American popular culture and creating it when he constructed his theme parks with an entrance through Main Street. But, as I affirmed at the outset, Main Street is both a place and an idea, and we need to keep the two distinct if we are not to confuse reality with dream. The small town that so many grew up in is also the small town that assiduously kept out the stranger. It is also the town from which so many have tried to escape. The mentality of the small town that Sinclair Lewis excoriated remains today in many ways the mentality of half of America: Grundyism, with its relentless effort to legislate morality, is still one of the strongest forces in American politics. But Main Street simultaneously remains for the twenty-first century a dream to pursue; the nostalgic turning back to the small town that began in the 1930s with the photographers of the Farm Security Administration, with *Our Town* and *It's a Wonderful Life*, is still a powerful force in American culture, causing us to look wherever we can find it for that idealized Main Street, packaged with ribbons of nostalgia, street lamps, and corner drugstores.

Small towns have died a thousand deaths in reality, yet they have also lived, some at least, by refashioning themselves as an image of the dream; meanwhile, the idea of Main Street has inspired dreams of community and small-town life that have been embodied in countless suburban developments, inner cities, and urban town centers. The meaning of Main Street in American culture is thus a story of contradictions—of the power of a symbol to contain some of our highest ideals in a democratic culture at the same time that it reveals, beneath the surface, a history of social exclusion and the crushing power of convention. Main Street clearly has value as a commodity, indeed a fetish, in our consumer society; its value to our political culture may be even greater if we can see it not as the oppressive and homogeneous society it so often was in reality but as an ideal of comity in our increasingly factionalized national culture.

Thus do we recover from the past what we want to imagine in the future. (Shades of F. Scott Fitzgerald here: "So we beat on, boats against the current, borne back ceaselessly into the past.") The persistence of Main Street into the twenty-first century, indeed its increasing power as a symbol in the political and commercial marketplace, speaks to the authority of the myth to sustain our ideals and nurture a sense of community in a society that is otherwise a scene of fragmentation and social disintegration.

Notes

INTRODUCTION

1. In 2009, Republican former vice presidential nominee Sarah Palin tried to reclaim Main Street for the Right in a speech in Hong Kong to more than 1,000 investors and bankers: "I'm going to call it like I see it, and I will share with you candidly a view right from Main Street—Main Street, U.S.A." Associated Press, "Palin Takes 'Main Street' to Hong Kong," *New York Times*, Sept. 24, 2009, http://query.nytimes.com/gst/fullpage.html?res=9C04E4D91430F937A1575AC0A96F9C8B63&scp=1&sq=&st=nyt, accessed June 28, 2010.

2. Robert Pinsky, *Thousands of Broadways: Dreams and Nightmares of the American Small Town* (Chicago: University of Chicago Press, 2009), 15.

3. F. O. Matthiessen, *The American Renaissance: Art and Expression in the Age of Emerson and Whitman* (New York: Oxford University Press, 1941), xx.

4. Thomas Bender, *Community and Social Change in America* (New Brunswick, N.J.: Rutgers University Press, 1978), 6, 7.

5. As a student of New Urbanism observes: "Many studies substantiate the idea that physical factors can act as a mechanism to promote resident interaction." Emily Talen, "The Problem with Community in Planning," *Journal of Planning Literature* 15, no. 2 (Nov. 2000): 177. I will deal with this issue more extensively in later chapters.

6. Linda Lyons, "Teens Drawn to Bright Lights, Big Cities," May 25, 2004, www.gallup.com/poll, accessed June 29, 2010.

7. See Rob Kroes, "The Small Town: Between Modernity and Post-modernity," in *The Small Town in America: A Multidisciplinary Revisit*, edited by Hans Bertens and Theo D'haen (Amsterdam: VU University Press, 1995), 7.

8. Robert Bellah et al., *Habits of the Heart: Individualism and Commitment in American Life* (New York: Perennial, 1986), 251.

9. Lasch also observed: "Traditions embody conflict as well as consensus; in many ways this is their most important aspect." Christopher Lasch, "The Communitarian Critique of Liberalism," in *Community in America: The Challenge of Habits of the Heart*, edited by Charles H. Reynolds (Berkeley: University of California Press, 1988), 178.

10. See Ning Wang, "The Feasibility and Significance of Applying the Main Street Approach to Preservation-Based Economic Development in Contemporary China," master's thesis, University of Pennsylvania, 2009.

11. Published first in *The Snow Image and Other Twice-Told Tales* (1852), it was reprinted as a separate book in 1901, with an introduction by Hawthorne's son, Julian Hawthorne. Nathaniel Hawthorne, *Main-Street* (Canton, Pa.: Kirkgate, 1901).

12. Ibid., 46.

13. From the epigraph: "Main Street is the climax of civilization. That this Ford car

might stand in front of the Bon Ton Store, Hannibal invaded Rome and Erasmus wrote in Oxford cloisters. What Ole Jenson the grocer says to Ezra Stowbody the banker is the new law for London, Prague, and the unprofitable isles of the sea; whatsoever Ezra does not know and sanction, that thing is heresy, worthless for knowing and wicked to consider." Sinclair Lewis, *Main Street* (New York: Harcourt Brace, 1920).

14. From 1880 to 1940, many local opera houses in New England towns had painted curtains depicting the town Main Street, successors to Hawthorne's panorama. See Katie Zezima, "The Curtain Rises on Old Vermont," *New York Times*, June 25, 2006.

15. On "*nonplaces*," also see George Ritzer, *The Globalization of Nothing*, 2nd ed. (Thousand Oaks, Calif.: Pine Forge, 2007).

CHAPTER 1

1. The Mapping Main Street project affirms that there are "over 10,466 streets named Main in the United States." A glance at the images on the website, a collective documentary project, reveals the enormous diversity and range of "Main Street." The project's founders have structured the website as a collaboration with viewers, who are invited to add their pictures and stories, some of which are broadcast on National Public Radio. Yet the Mapping Main Street project is actually a more limited survey of small-town America than it might appear, since it restricts itself to Main Streets that literally use the name "Main Street." There are a myriad of streets that are de facto Main Streets but have other names. See http://www.mappingmainstreet.org/, accessed July 10, 2011. Also see, for a cultural geographer's perspective on the range of types, Richard V. Francaviglia, "Space and Main Street," in *Main Street Revisited: Time, Space, and Image Building in Small-Town America* (Iowa City: University of Iowa Press, 1996), 65–129.

2. Susan Fenimore Cooper, "Village Improvement Societies," *Putnam's Magazine*, n.s., 4, no. 21 (Sept. 1869): 359–66, http://external.oneonta.edu/cooper/susan/village.html, accessed July 11, 2011.

3. Randolph S. Bourne, "The Social Order in an American Town," *Atlantic Monthly* 111 (1913): 227–36.

4. Thorstein Veblen, "The Country Town," in *Absentee Ownership and Business Enterprise in Recent Times* (1923); rpt. in *The Portable Veblen*, edited by Max Lerner (New York: Viking, 1948), 407.

5. John W. Reps, *Bird's Eye Views: Historic Lithographs of North American Cities* (Princeton, N.J.: Princeton Architectural Press, 1998), 12. My discussion of the maps draws on this very useful book.

6. Towns were also pictorially represented, from the 1870s through the early 1900s especially, in "souvenir books," which consisted of images of a particular town sold locally to tourists. These topographical books, usually no more than six by nine inches, featured images of houses, institutions, cemeteries, parks, and principal streets, sometimes with minimal textual descriptions and sometimes without. One major producer was the Wittemann Brothers, who traveled widely, taking pictures that were reproduced as lithographs, later (with the new photomechanical process) as Albertypes, and then, in the early twentieth century, as photogravures. As pictorial summations of a given town or city, they sought to boost the place's reputation and solidify its social and economic status. More than 400 such books were produced by the Wittemanns and are described in David Brodherson, "Souvenir Books in Stone: Lithographic Miniatures for the Masses," *Imprint* 12, no. 2 (Autumn 1987): 21–28. I am grateful to Barbara Natanson, Head of Prints and

Photographs at the Library of Congress, for calling to my attention the library's collection of these items.

7. Walt Whitman, *Democratic Vistas* (1871), in *Leaves of Grass and Selected Prose*, edited by John Kouwenhoven (New York: Modern Library, 1950), 494.

8. As Michael Kammen points out, the tension between tradition and progress is a leitmotif that is worked out in many different ways, from the nineteenth century to the present. Kammen, *Mystic Chords of Memory: The Transformation of Tradition in American Culture* (New York: Vintage, 1993), 14.

9. Edwards Roberts, "Two Montana Cities," *Harper's New Monthly Magazine*, Sept. 1888, 587.

10. Edith Wharton, *Summer* (1917; New York: Berkley, 1981), 121.

11. Dona Brown, *Inventing New England: Regional Tourism in the Nineteenth Century* (Washington, D.C.: Smithsonian Institution Press, 1995), 139.

12. Ibid., 133. This period would soon be followed in the early twentieth century by Wallace Nutting's popularization of the colonial revival style in home furnishings.

13. Max Page, *The Creative Destruction of Manhattan, 1900–1940* (Chicago: University of Chicago Press, 1999), 252.

14. Nostalgia can also elevate self-esteem and alleviate feelings of "existential threat," according to Constantine Sedikides et al., "Nostalgia: Past, Present, and Future," *Current Directions in Psychological Science* 17 (2008): 304–7.

15. See Susan Stewart, *On Longing: Narratives of the Miniature, the Gigantic, the Souvenir, the Collection* (Durham, N.C.: Duke University Press, 1993), 58–60.

16. Gieringer went to New York City frequently, focusing his attention on the miniatures at the American Museum of Natural History and the Metropolitan Museum of Art.

17. Maurice Halbwachs, *On Collective Memory*, edited by Lewis Coser (Chicago: University of Chicago Press, 1992), 38. Also see Barry Schwartz, "The Social Context of Commemoration: A Study in Collective Memory," *Social Forces* 61, no. 2 (1982): 374.

18. James D. McCabe, *The Illustrated History of the Centennial Exhibition* (1876; Philadelphia: National Publishing Company, 1975), 239–40; cited in Jay Anderson, *Time Machines: The World of Living History* (Nashville, Tenn.: American Association for State and Local History, 1984), 25.

19. See Stephen Conn, *Museums and American Intellectual Life, 1876–1926* (Chicago: University of Chicago Press, 2000), 160.

20. "Danger to our country is to be apprehended not so much from the influence of new things as from our forgetting the values of old things"; Ford, quoted in John L. Wright et al., "Report of the Curriculum Committee, 1981," unpublished report of the Edison Institute, Ford Archives, Henry Ford Museum; cited in Kammen, *Mystic Chords*, 355–56. On Ford's Greenfield Village, see Conn, *Museums*, 152–60; and Anderson, *Time Machines*.

21. Edith Wharton, *Age of Innocence* (1920; New York: Modern Library, 1943), 205.

22. Mike Wallace, "Visiting the Past: History Museums in the United States," *Mickey Mouse History and Other Essays on American Memory* (Philadelphia: Temple University Press, 1996), 15.

23. See Roland Marchand, *Creating the Corporate Soul: The Rise of Public Relations and Corporate Imagery in American Big Business* (Berkeley: University of California Press, 1998), 312–13.

24. Ibid., 336.

25. Ibid., 346–47.

26. See ibid., illustrations, 352, 350.

27. Baldwin makes this statement in the documentary film *Paradise Lost: The Child Murders at Robin Hood Hills* (1996), directed by Joe Berlinger and Bruce Sinofsky.

28. "The Testimony of Walter E. Disney before the House Committee on Un-American Activities," in *Walt Disney: Conversations*, edited by Kathy Merlock Jackson (Jackson: University Press of Mississippi, 2006), 40.

29. Miranda Joseph, *Against the Romance of Community* (Minneapolis: University of Minnesota Press, 2002), 6.

30. For a fuller discussion of Disneyland, see "Understanding Disneyland: American Mass Culture and the European Gaze," in Miles Orvell, *After the Machine: Visual Arts and the Erasing of Cultural Boundaries* (Jackson: University Press of Mississippi, 1995), 147–59.

31. Even in an article about the visible slippage of Disney's theme parks, written in 2005, the author concludes with a paean to the magic of Main Street: "Seeing the cobblestone streets and the rows of old-timey shops, I can't help but buy into the fantasy that is Walt Disney's Main Street, designed after the one in his boyhood home of Marceline, Mo. Some might call it synthetic, but that's missing the point: It never pretends to be real." Charles Passy, "Some Ask If the Disney Magic Is Slipping," *New York Times*, July 31, 2005.

32. See discussion in Richard V. Francaviglia, *Main Street Revisited: Time, Space, and Image Building in Small-Town America* (Iowa City: University of Iowa Press, 1996), 145–67. Also see Karal Ann Marling, "Imagineering the Disney Theme Parks," in *Designing Disney's Theme Parks: The Architecture of Reassurance*, edited by Karal Ann Marling (Paris: Flammarion, 1997), 86–90.

33. Robert A. Iger, quoted in David Barboza and Brooks Barnes, "Disney Plans Lavish Park in Shanghai," *New York Times*, Apr. 7, 2011, http://www.nytimes.com/2011/04/08/business/media/08disney.html?_r=1, accessed July 7, 2011.

34. Glenway Wescott, *Good-Bye, Wisconsin* (New York: Harper & Brothers, 1928), 6.

35. See Francaviglia, *Main Street Revisited*, 147. Goff's early sketches can be seen in *Walt Disney Imagineering: A Behind the Dreams Look at Making the Magic Real*, by The Imagineers (New York: Hyperion, 1996), 12–13.

36. "Second Inaugural Address of William McKinley," Avalon Project: Documents in Law, History and Diplomacy, Yale University, http://avalon.law.yale.edu/19th_century/mckin2.asp, accessed Sept. 11, 2010.

37. The magazine then had a circulation of 2 million. Jan Cohn, *Creating America: George Horace Lorimer and the "Saturday Evening Post"* (Pittsburgh: University of Pittsburgh Press, 1989), 9–10; quoted in Anne Knutson, "The Saturday Evening Post," in *Norman Rockwell: Pictures for the American People*, edited by Maureen Hart Hennessey and Anne Knutson (New York: Harry Abrams, 1999), 144.

38. One such group actually appears on a *Saturday Evening Post* cover for April Fool's Day, 1948.

39. See Neil Harris, "The View from the City," in Hennessey and Knutson, *Norman Rockwell*, 131–42.

40. Eric Sevareid, "Home Again," *Colliers*, May 11, 1956, 38–68; quoted in John R. Stilgoe, "Treasured Wastes: Spaces and Memory," *Places* 4 (1987): 71.

41. Rockwell's range as an artist was much greater than the *Post* covers, as one can see from the very different modes he could employ in advertisements, in historical paintings, in book illustrations, and on the covers of the *Literary Digest*, where caricature is absent. For examples, see Christopher Finch, *Norman Rockwell's America* (New York: Harry Abrams, 1985), figs. 158, 159, 169, etc.

42. For examples, see Susan E. Meyer, *Norman Rockwell's People* (New York: Harry Abrams, 1981).

43. Photographer Jim Richardson's images of Cuba, Kansas, taken over a thirty-year period, evince the continuing power of Rockwell's vision: http://ngm.nationalgeographic.com/ngm/0405/feature2/index.html, accessed June 9, 2010.

CHAPTER 2

1. Henry J. Fletcher, "The Doom of the Small Town," *The Forum* (Mar. 1895): 214–23, quotation on 214.

2. Bob Greene, "Empty House on the Prairie," *New York Times*, Mar. 2, 2005.

3. John Fiske, "The Story of a New England Town," *Atlantic Monthly* 86, no. 518 (Dec. 1900): 731, 734.

4. John J. Raskob, chairman of Finance Committee of General Motors, quoted in Newton Fuessle, "Pulling Main Street Out of the Mud," *Outlook*, Aug. 16, 1922, 640.

5. For a broader discussion of Milburn, an underappreciated figure in American literature, see Lawrence Rodgers, "Oklahoma on His Mind: The Folklore Legacy of George Milburn," *Folklore Historian* 21 (2004): 3–15. My thanks to Professor Rodgers for calling this to my attention.

6. "There'll Be Jobs for Veterans Up and Down Main Street," *Saturday Evening Post*, Oct. 28, 1944.

7. Margaret L. Wise, "Report to the Editors: He Wants a Beachhead on Main Street," *Saturday Evening Post*, Oct. 2, 1945.

8. Godfrey Miebhar, "Pro: Does the Chain Store System Threaten the Nation's Welfare?," *Congressional Digest* 9, nos. 8–9 (Aug.–Sept. 1930): 214.

9. R. W. Lyons, "Con: Does the Chain Store System Threaten the Nation's Welfare?," *Congressional Digest* 9, nos. 8–9 (Aug.–Sept. 1930): 214–15.

10. See Steven Lagerfeld, "What Main Street Can Learn from the Mall," *Atlantic Monthly*, Nov. 1995, 118.

11. Richard Moe and Carter Wilkie, *Changing Places: Rebuilding Community in the Age of Sprawl* (New York: Holt, 1997), 144. Also see Michael Southworth, "Reinventing Main Street: From Mall to Townscape Mall," *Journal of Urban Design* 10 (June 2005): 152.

12. Mall of America brochure, 10; quoted in Mark Gottdiener, *The Theming of America: Dreams, Visions, and Commercial Space* (Boulder, Colo.: Westview, 1997), 86.

13. Catherine Bauer and Clarence Stein, "Store Buildings and Neighborhood Shopping Centers," *Architectural Record* 75 (Feb. 1934): 185; quoted in M. Jeffrey Hardwick, *Mall Maker: Victor Gruen, Architect of an American Dream* (Philadelphia: University of Pennsylvania Press, 2004), 110; also see ibid., 77–78. I am indebted to Hardwick's book for my discussion of Gruen.

14. For a thorough discussion of the legal history of free speech within private malls, see Mark C. Alexander, "Attention, Shoppers: The First Amendment in the Modern Shopping Mall," *Arizona Law Review* 41, no. 1 (1999): 1–47. The U.S. Supreme court ruled against free speech in malls, and most state supreme courts that have adjudicated the issue, as Alexander observes, "have held that individuals do not have a right to engage in expressive activity in shopping malls," on the grounds that their state constitutions "do not confer broader speech rights than those guaranteed by the First Amendment to the United States Constitution" (31). Alexander argues strongly the need for free speech in malls, on

the grounds that malls have become integral and unavoidable public (or quasi-public) spaces and that democracy depends on such free exchange of ideas.

15. Jacobs, "Downtown Is for People," in *The Exploding Metropolis*, by Editors of *Fortune* (Garden City, N.Y.: Doubleday, 1958), 157–84; quoted in Hardwick, *Mall Maker*, 180.

16. Morris Lapidus, "Store Design: A Merchandising Problem," *Architectural Record* 89 (Feb. 1941): 113; quoted in Hardwick, *Mall Maker*, 55.

17. See Charles Fishman, *The Wal-Mart Effect* (New York: Penguin, 2006). Advocates of big box stores argue that they can save desperate small towns from extinction by virtue of the taxes such businesses pay, the jobs they provide (such as they are), and the cheap goods. This might fall, sadly, under the category of eating crumbs to avoid starvation. See James Daubs, "Deserted Village: Could Wal-Mart Save My Midwestern Hometown?," *Politics Daily*, Jan. 9, 2010, http://www.politicsdaily.com/2010/01/19/deserted-village -could-wal-mart-save-my-midwestern-hometown/, accessed June 9, 2010. Also see Elena G. Irwin and Jill Clark, "Wall Street vs. Main Street: What Are the Benefits and Costs of Wal-Mart to Local Communities?," *Choices*, 2nd quarter 2006, 117–21.

18. Southworth, "Reinventing Main Street," 152.

19. The Streets at Southpoint and Main Street, in Durham, North Carolina, is one such mall, with both indoor shopping and an outdoor simulated town center, with fountain, walking streets, etc. It is, according to *USA Today*, one of the "10 Great Places to Spend It All in One Place," where "each storefront is styled with a small-town feel"; http://www.usatoday.com/travel/destinations/10great/2004-11-25-shopping_x.htm, accessed June 11, 2010.

20. Alison Isenberg, *Downtown America: A History of the Place and the People Who Made It* (Chicago: University of Chicago Press, 2004), 91–94. German geographer Walter Christeller developed his "central place theory" in the early 1930s to explain the distribution of smaller and larger urban centers within a given demographic zone.

21. Ibid., 93.

22. See ibid., 68–69, for an example.

23. Gabrielle Esperdy, *Modernizing Main Street: Architecture and Consumer Culture in the New Deal* (Chicago: University of Chicago Press, 2008), 9.

24. In the 1854 Act of Incorporation, the city of Philadelphia took over governance of what had been the entire county of Philadelphia.

25. Plater-Zyberk made this remark in "The New Urbanism," lecture at Chestnut Hill Academy, 1992 (sponsored by the Chestnut Hill Historical Society).

26. David R. Contosta, *Suburb in the City: Chestnut Hill, Philadelphia, 1850–1990* (Columbus: Ohio State University Press, 1992); Elijah Anderson, *Code of the Street: Decency, Violence, and the Moral Life of the Inner City* (New York: Norton, 1999); Witold Rybczynski, *Last Harvest: How a Cornfield Became New Daleville* (New York: Scribners, 2007). *Last Harvest* focuses not on Chestnut Hill but on the construction of a New Urbanist development outside of Philadelphia.

27. Rybczynski, *Last Harvest*, 3–5.

28. Anderson, *Code of the Street*, 15–16.

29. Ibid., 16.

30. Ibid., 17.

31. I am indebted to the assistant archivist of the Chestnut Hill Historical Society, Alexander B. Bartlett, for indispensable help with materials in the society's collection. I am also indebted to Contosta's chapters on Wells in *Suburb in the City*, esp. 216–33.

32. The Chestnut Hill shops promoted their new parking plan in a large advertisement

taken in a local paper, the *Herald*, Mar. 13, 1952: "The concepts of diagonal parking and planting are recent innovations being utilized throughout the nation in community shopping areas. Examples close by are the blueprints of Fairless Hills and Levittown's 'park and shop perimeters,' and Ardmore parking plazas."

33. Wells uses the term "horizontal department store" in an interview conducted in 1989. *Interviews with Lloyd P. Wells*, Environmental Research Group: Jon Lang, Walter Moleski, Sept. 18, 20, and 21, 1989, Chestnut Hill Historical Society. Also see Contosta, *Suburb in the City*, 221. Wells also called it a "horizontal shopping center"; Paula M. Riley, "A Lightning Rod for Controversy for 50 Years, Lloyd Wells: His Impact Still Felt Daily on Hill," *Chestnut Hill Local*, Feb. 1, 2007, http://www.chestnuthilllocal.com/issues/2007.02.01/locallife2.html, accessed June 18, 2010.

34. Lloyd Wells, conversation with the author, Aug. 14, 2011.

35. Wells also credited a like-minded colleague, Joe Sims, who had worked on historic preservation in Philadelphia during the 1930s, with the inspiration. Wells recalls Sims saying, "We've got to get some sort of architectural integrity in the buildings. It's got to look like a village. It's got to look like a colonial village. It's got to be attractive to people. We've got to get the ladies to come here because they want to come here." For Wells this meant taking down "the visual vulgarity, the visual noise, meaning neon signs." *Interviews with Lloyd P. Wells*, 10. Wells uses the term "romantic fantasy" in an e-mail to the author, July 30, 2011.

36. See Contosta, *Suburb in the City*, 225. Contosta also suggested, in conversation with the author, the relevance of Williamsburg to Philadelphia's restoration project. On the strong influence of Williamsburg on the restoration of Independence National Historical Park, see also Constance M. Greiff, *Independence: The Creation of a National Park* (Philadelphia: University of Pennsylvania Press, 1987), 258–61. On this point also see Charlene Mires, *Independence Hall in American Memory* (Philadelphia: University of Pennsylvania Press, 2002), 218.

37. Isenberg, *Downtown America*, 256.

38. One example of Victorian transformation was the Chestnut Hill Hotel, originally a turreted structure, which was radically and somewhat awkwardly "restored" to an imagined colonial appearance.

39. Conversation with author, Aug. 14, 2011.

40. Thomas H. Keels and Elizabeth Farmer Jarvis, *Images of America: Chestnut Hill* (Philadelphia: Chestnut Hill Historical Society; Charleston, S.C.: Arcadia, 2002), 123.

41. Chestnut Hill has also suffered from a vigorous anticommerce movement led by people living close to Germantown Avenue who do not want to see their parking spaces lost to transient customers. Their NIMBY resistance to restaurants and other development that might increase traffic has been frequent and vociferous, and they have discouraged outside developers from coming into the town. Another problem has been one of the major local landlords, who has left properties vacant for many years while waiting for the "perfect" tenant (e.g., an antique store), and whose feuds with the town have adversely marked it. See *Chestnut Hill Local*, Oct. 19, 2006. Also see Kristin Pazulski, "Bowman Properties Faults CHCA for Teenagers Inc. Displacement," *Chestnut Hill Local*, Sept. 28, 2006, http://www.chestnuthilllocal.com/issues/2006.09.28/opinion.html; "From Our Readers," *Chestnut Hill Local*, Nov. 16, 2006, http://www.chestnuthilllocal.com/issues/2006.11.16/letters.html, accessed June 18, 2010. For a more recent story on Chestnut Hill, see Andrew Maykuth, "Downturn Reigns in Upscale Enclave," *Philadelphia Inquirer*, June 15, 2009.

42. "The Main Street Four-Point Approach," *Main Street National Trust for Historic*

Preservation, http://www.preservationnation.org/main-street/about-main-street/ the-approach/, accessed June 15, 2010. The necessity for full community engagement in the Main Street renewal process is stressed in Louis Lopilato II, *Main Street: Some Lessons in Revitalization* (Lanham, Md.: University Press of America, 2003).

43. On the struggle of Superior, Nebraska, for survival, see Timothy Egan, "Amid Dying Towns of Rural Plains, One Makes a Stand," *New York Times*, Dec. 1, 2003. On the effort of a Kansas town, driven by a longtime Kansan, that is remaking itself successfully as an arts center, see Stephen Kinzer, "Sowing Art on the Kansas Prairie," *New York Times*, Jan. 22, 2004. On the revival of old movie houses on Main Street as social anchors, see Patricia Leigh Brown, "Old Movie Houses Find Audiences in the Plains," *New York Times*, July 5, 2010. Other survival strategies are noted in "America the Creative: Can Statues of Killer Bees and Storytelling Festivals Stop the Country's Smallest Towns from Withering Away?," *The Economist*, Dec. 23, 2006.

44. For a detailed discussion of the economics of rehabilitation in one such town, see Jessie Swigger, "Reconstructing Main Street: Memories, Place, and the San Marcos Main Street Program," *Journal of the American Studies Association of Texas* 34 (Oct. 2003): 35–57. A reality TV show, *Town Haul*, begun in 2005, featured the renovation of small towns, or at least some Main Street buildings; see Karrie Jacobs, "Makeovers Make a Move to Main Street," *New York Times*, Jan. 16, 2005. In at least one case, Main Street has been resurrected through the efforts of a single businessman, who bought up the buildings along a dying Main Street in Mount Morris, near Rochester, New York, and has restored and rented them, attracting new life to what was once a picturesque small town. See Charles V. Bagli, "Resurrecting a Village by Buying Up Main Street," *New York Times*, Nov. 12, 2010.

45. The maximum allowable grant under this program is $1 million. "Main Street Grants Notice of Funding Availability," July 11, 2011, http://portal.hud.gov/hudportal/ HUD?src=/program_offices/public_indian_housing/programs/ph/hope6/grants/ mainstreet, accessed July 11, 2011.

46. Nick Reding's *Methland: The Death and Life of an American Small Town* (New York: Bloomsbury USA, 2010) concerns another challenge to towns, especially in farming regions—methamphetamine addiction. Focusing on Oelwein, Iowa (pop. 6,000), Reding sees the local meth labs as a product of high unemployment and available ingredients. He argues that Oelwein's problems are representative of a regional drug problem, though he notes that after 2008, as the town's economy improved, meth production began to decline.

CHAPTER 3

1. Lewis would not appear for ten years in the pages of the *Saturday Evening Post*, except to be denounced on the editorial page. See Richard Lingeman, *Sinclair Lewis: Rebel from Main Street* (New York: Random House, 2002), 144, 152.

2. See William L. Andrews, "Goldsmith and Freneau in 'The American Village,'" *Early American Literature* 5 (1970): 15.

3. Carl Van Doren, "The Revolt from the Village," *The Nation* 12 (Oct. 1921): 407–12; rpt. in Carl Van Doren, *Contemporary American Novelists, 1900–1920* (New York: Macmillan, 1931).

4. A valuable treatment of the full range of this attack on Middle America can be found in Anthony Hilfer, *The Revolt from the Village, 1915–1930: The Literary Attack on American Small-Town Provincialism* (Chapel Hill: University of North Carolina Press, 1969), 84–157.

5. The prevalence of the theme is suggested by Van Wyck Brooks's remark in a 1941 essay: "A few years ago, as a publisher's reader, I ran through a novel every day by some

young man or woman who had grown up in the West or South. They could not seem to forgive the town they were born in—just to escape from those towns and tell the world how ugly, false and brutal they were seemed almost to be the motive of those writers in living." Brooks, "On Literature Today"; quoted in D. N. Jeans, "Fiction and the Small Town in the United States: A Contribution to the Study of Urbanisation," *Australian Geographical Studies* 22 (Oct. 1984): 269.

6. See Mark Schorer, *Sinclair Lewis: An American Life* (New York: Dell, 1961), 176–77.

7. Randolph Bourne, "The Social Order in an American Town," *Atlantic Monthly* 111 (1913): 227–36.

8. The continuation of the revolt from the village in the post–World War II era is visible in Bob Dylan's remark in an interview about his separation from his small-town background and his old friends: "They still seem to be in the same old way. They still have a feeling that's tied up, where it's tied up in the town, in their parents, in the newspapers that they read which go out to maybe five thousand people. . . . I'm not putting them down. It's just my road and theirs, it's different. . . . They're not thinking about the same things I'm thinking about." "Radio Interview with Studs Terkel, WFMT (Chicago), May 1963," in *Bob Dylan: The Essential Interviews*, edited by Jonathan Cott (New York: Wenner, 2006), 9.

9. Sinclair Lewis, *Main Street* (New York: Harcourt Brace, 1920), 246. Subsequent references to *Main Street* will be given in the text.

10. Van Doren, *Contemporary American Novelists*, 162. Cf. William Allen White's claim, in 1906, of the cultural parity of the small town and the big city; White, *In Our Town* (New York: McClure, Phillips, 1906), 7–8.

11. See Schorer, *Sinclair Lewis*, 290–91.

12. H. L. Mencken, "Puritanism as a Literary Force," in *A Book of Prefaces* (New York: Knopf, 1917), 280.

13. Ibid., 227–28.

14. Van Wyck Brooks, *America's Coming-of-Age: Three Essays on America* (New York: Dutton, 1970 [1934]), 17.

15. Ibid., 16.

16. Ibid., 35.

17. Ibid., 20.

18. Meredith Nicholson, *The Valley of Democracy* (New York: Scribner's, 1918), 25.

19. Ibid., 26.

20. Ibid., 283–84.

21. "'Let Main Street Alone!' Says Meredith Nicholson," *Current Opinion* 70 (June 1921): 799.

22. Ibid., 800.

23. Ibid.

24. The passage continues: "Other towns she came to know by anecdote: a prairie village where the wind blew all day long, and the mud was two feet thick in spring, and in summer the flying sand scarred new-painted houses and dust covered the few flowers set out in pots. New England mill-towns with the hands living in rows of cottages like blocks of lava. A rich farming-center in New Jersey, off the railroad, furiously pious, ruled by old men, unbelievably ignorant old men, sitting about the grocery talking of James G. Blaine. A Southern town, full of the magnolias and white columns which Carol had accepted as proof of romance, but hating the negroes, obsequious to the Old Families. A Western mining-settlement like a tumor. A booming semi-city with parks and clever architects, visited by famous pianists and unctuous lecturers, but irritable from a struggle between union

labor and the manufacturers' association, so that in even the gayest of the new houses there was a ceaseless and intimidating heresy-hunt" (429).

25. Henry H. Vail, *A History of the McGuffey Readers* (Cleveland: Burrows Brothers, 1911), 2, Project Gutenberg eBook, released Apr. 7, 2005.

26. Ford first saw the ruins of the McGuffey birthplace, a log cabin in western Pennsylvania, in 1932, and by 1934 the cabin had been redesigned and rebuilt in Ford's capsule of American history, along with the McGuffey School, built from logs in the Holmes family barn. The McGuffey buildings may have been slightly ersatz, but Ford's devotion to the Readers was genuine, and his McGuffey collection, begun in 1910, eventually encompassed 145 editions of the books.

27. Lewis Atherton, *Main Street on the Middle Border* (Bloomington: Indiana University Press, 1954), 65–72.

28. The lyceum system lasted for thirty-five years, until the Civil War, and was more focused on educational lectures, designed for artisans, farmers, etc. See Carl Bode, *The American Lyceum: Town Meeting of the Mind* (New York: Oxford University Press, 1956).

29. Andrew C. Rieser, *The Chautauqua Moment: Protestants, Progressives, and the Culture of Modern Liberalism* (New York: Columbia University Press, 2003), 103, 85, 88.

30. Ibid., 125, 286.

31. A more acerbic treatment of this relativism can be found in Arthur L. Lippmann's 1926 poem, "Main Street, New York," which contrasts the country hayseed, awed by Wall Street, with city dwellers who, thronging against a window display of safety razors, are themselves no less "boorish" than the "rube": they are "hayseeds from Manhattan." Lippmann, "Main Street, New York," *Life Magazine*, June 17, 1926.

32. See Joseph S. Wood's important revisionary study *The New England Village* (Baltimore: Johns Hopkins University Press, 1997).

33. Societies sprang up in the 1870s and 1880s in New England and the Mid-Atlantic, inspired in part by Susan Fenimore Cooper's "Village Improvement Societies," which extolled the American village as superior to the European but also pointed out room for improvement—in water, streets, trees, sidewalks, benches, parks, etc. *Putnam's Magazine*, n.s., 4, no. 21 (Sept. 1869): 359–66.

34. See Thomas J. Campanella, *Republic of Shade: New England and the American Elm* (New Haven, Conn.: Yale University Press, 2003).

35. As E. W. Burgess put it, Grundyism is the "subjection of the individual to continuous observation and control by the community." Burgess, editor's preface to Albert Blumenthal, *A Sociological Study of a Small Town* (Chicago: University of Chicago Press, 1932), xii.

36. As Jaime Harker describes Lewis's critique of Carol, "For Lewis, the reform cure is as debilitating as the sickness of American mediocrity and hypocrisy." See Harker, "Progressive Middlebrow: Dorothy Canfield, Women's Magazines, and Popular Feminism in the Twenties," in *Middlebrow Moderns: Popular American Women Writers of the 1920s*, edited by Lisa Botshon and Meredith Goldsmith (Boston: Northeastern University Press, 2003), 121.

37. William James, "What Is the Significance of Life?," in James, *Talks to Teachers on Psychology, and to Students on Some of Life's Ideals* (London: Geo. H. Ellis, 1910), 269. See the discussion of James's essay in Alan Trachtenberg, *The Incorporation of America: Culture and Society in the Gilded Age* (New York: Hill & Wang, 1982) 140–45, on which I draw for this discussion.

38. James, "What Is the Significance of Life?," 271.

39. Ibid., 273.

40. Ibid., 275. James adds in a footnote that he wrote this essay before the Cuban and Philippine wars, mere episodes, he argues, in a process that is "everywhere tending toward the Chautauqua ideals" (274).

41. Lewis's skepticism about heroism is evident in regard to the war in Europe as well, including the supposed heroism of soldiers and the national uplift of spirit it was to bring about. As Miles Bjornstam says to Carol, "Well, have you become a patriot? Eh? Sure, they'll bring democracy—the democracy of death. Yes, sure, in every war since the Garden of Eden the workmen have gone out to fight each other for perfectly good reasons—handed to them by their bosses" (276). Earlier, Carol had said to Guy Pollock, realizing that he fell short of her dream of masculine mystery and romance, "I'm not heroic. I'm scared by all the fighting that's going on in the world. I want nobility and adventure, but perhaps I want still more to curl on the hearth with some one I love" (202).

42. Theodore Dreiser, "Typhoon," in *Chains* (New York: Boni & Liveright, 1927), 183.

43. Thorstein Veblen, *Absentee Ownership and Business Enterprise in Recent Times: The Case of America* (New York: B. W. Huebsch, 1923), 152. The effects of this are far-reaching and corrosive on the moral character, as Veblen observes, congruently with Lewis: "One must avoid offense, cultivate good-will. . . . One must eschew opinions, or information, which are not acceptable to the common run of those whose good-will has or may conceivably come to have any commercial value" (159).

44. Sinclair Lewis, "Main Street's Been Paved," *The Nation*, Sept. 10, 1924, 255.

45. Ibid., 256.

46. Ibid., 259.

47. Ibid.

48. Ibid., 259, 260.

49. Henry Anatole Grunwald, "Main Street in 1947," *Life Magazine*, June 23, 1947, 101.

50. Ibid., 104.

51. Ibid., 114.

52. Ibid.

53. Sinclair Lewis, "The Long Arm of the Small Town"; quoted in Schorer, *Sinclair Lewis*, 7.

CHAPTER 4

1. Sinclair Lewis, *Babbitt* (New York: Harcourt Brace, 1922), 119.

2. Ibid., 32.

3. See Gabrielle Esperdy, introduction to *Modernizing Main Street: Architecture and Consumer Culture in the New Deal* (Chicago: University of Chicago Press, 2008); and Alison Isenberg, *Downtown America: A History of the Place and the People Who Made It* (Chicago: University of Chicago Press, 2004), chap. 2.

4. See Frank R. Kent, "Big Business Conquers Main Street," *The Independent*, June 27, 1925, 715.

5. Editorial, *Saturday Evening Post*, July 18, 1931.

6. R. L. Duffus, "The Small Town," in *America Now: An Inquiry into Civilization in the United States*, edited by Harold E. Stearns (New York: Scribner's, 1938), 389.

7. Ibid., 392.

8. Ibid., 394.

9. In his famous 1903 essay "The Metropolis and Mental Life," Simmel contrasted the "tempo and multiplicity of economic, occupational, and social life" in the city as against

the "slower, more habitual, more smoothly flowing rhythm of the sensory-mental phase of small town and rural existence." The result, for Simmel, was a metropolitan personality that was protective and rational, with a mentality that is "least sensitive and which is furthest removed from the depths of personality." Georg Simmel, *Simmel on Culture: Selected Writings*, edited by David Patrick Frisby and Mike Featherstone (Thousand Oaks, Calif.: Sage, 1998), 175.

10. Robert Pinsky, *Thousands of Broadways: Dreams and Nightmares of the American Small Town* (Chicago: University of Chicago Press, 2009), 13.

11. Archibald MacLeish, *Land of the Free* (New York: Harcourt Brace, 1938), 51. Lange's other images of Sallisaw confirm the townsfolk's general sense of idleness and worry.

12. Roy Stryker, "The Farm Security Photographer Covers the American Small Town," Roy Stryker Papers, University of Louisville Photographic Archives, 1.

13. For a discussion of Lynd and Stryker, see James Curtis, *Mind's Eye, Mind's Truth* (Philadelphia: Temple University Press, 1989), 101–3.

14. Stryker, "The Farm Security Photographer," 1.

15. Roy Stryker and Nancy Wood, *In This Proud Land: America 1935–1943 as Seen in the FSA Photographs* (New York: Galahad, 1973), 15. The emotional significance of the railroad track was articulated as early as 1885, in an essay by M. H. Leonard, "Southwestern Kansas Seen with Eastern Eyes," *Atlantic Monthly*, July 1885: "Yet even the track is a welcome sight to the prairie dweller, for it connects him with his early home and Eastern friends, and the great world of civilization on whose edge he dwells." Willa Cather incorporates the railroad as an essential ingredient in the small-town culture of Moonstone, Colorado, in *Song of the Lark* (1915).

16. Walker Evans, "Main Street Looking North from Courthouse Square," *Fortune Magazine*, May 1948.

17. See Jeff Rosenheim, *Walker Evans and the Picture Postcard* (New York: Metropolitan Museum of Art and Steidl and Partners, 2009).

18. For a fuller discussion of the Pie Town project, see Curtis, *Mind's Eye*, 111–22.

19. James Curtis notes that Lee failed to place a longer version of the Pie Town article—some 6,000 words—in *Collier's* or *Reader's Digest* (ibid., 122). Possibly the backwater quality of the town was thought to lack a connection with the mainstream readership of these magazines.

20. Rosskam edited the photographs as well as the text, reducing it, according to Michael Lesy, from 60,000 to 20,000 words. Lesy, *Long Time Coming: A Photographic Portrait of America, 1935–1943* (New York: Norton, 2002), 321.

21. Sherwood Anderson, *Home Town* (New York: Alliance, 1940). See, for examples, Arthur Rothstein's Montana town (49) and his Iowa streetscape in fall (62); Ben Shahn's Middlesboro, Kentucky (12), and his Ohio town—possibly Lancaster—with strollers under a movie marquee (42); Russell Lee's San Augustine, Texas (10), as well his Marshall, Texas, courthouse on a Saturday afternoon (99). Subsequent references to *Home Town* will be given in the text.

22. "A Small Town's Saturday Night: *Life* Visits Franklin, Ind.," *Life*, Dec. 1940.

23. Thornton Wilder, *Our Town*, foreword by Donald Margulies, afterword by Tappan Wilder (New York: Perennial Classics, 1998), 107. Subsequent references to *Our Town* will be given in the text.

24. See *Pullman Car Hiawatha* and *The Happy Journey to Trenton and Camden* (both 1931).

25. Though Wilder's association of photography with literal realism was a common one,

in fact, the "documentary realism" of the FSA photographers under Stryker was aiming at a typical representation of reality, where the particular represented the general.

26. Wilder's relative complacency had already been fiercely and famously attacked by radical critic Mike Gold in "Wilder: Prophet of the Genteel Christ," *New Republic* 64 (Oct. 22, 1930): 266–67.

27. Frank R. Kent, "Filth on Main Street," *The Independent*, June 20, 1925, 686. Nellie B. Miller, literature chair of the General Federation of Women's Clubs, chimed in a few months later to confirm the dire problem and add that "the respectable residence section just off Main Street is so placidly unaware of it." Miller, "Fighting Filth on Main Street," *The Independent*, Oct. 10, 1925, 411.

28. Frank C. Hanighen, "The Gangs of Main Street," *North American Review*, Apr. 1932, 345.

29. Irving Bacheller, "Main Street up-to-Date," *The Forum*, Mar. 1934, 185.

30. Yet another example of the recovery of the small town in post–World War II culture is Paul Strand's 1962 *Tir a' Mhurain*, a photographic study of the Outer Hebrides. Strand connected his work with the American small town of the early twentieth century: "Growing up in America, one of my earliest memories of a book that had moved me deeply was the *Spoon River Anthology* by Edgar Lee Masters. Like Masters, I had got the idea that it would be interesting to make a portrait of a village in photography not taking images off the graves, as Masters did, but photographing a village as it is now with the people who live in it"; "Excerpts from Correspondence, Interviews, and Other Documents," in *Paul Strand: Sixty Years of Photographs*, edited by Michael Hoffman (London: Gordon Fraser 1976), 165; quoted in Martin Padgett, *Photographers of the Western Isles* (Edinburgh: John Donald, 2010), 192. Given the exigencies of the McCarthy period, Strand fulfilled the project in venues outside the United States.

CHAPTER 5

1. "Homes for Rent in Park Forest," advertisement in *Chicago Tribune*; rpt. in Gregory C. Randall, *America's Original GI Town: Park Forest, Illinois* (Baltimore: Johns Hopkins University Press, 2000), 111. William H. Whyte writes shrewdly about the development of community in Park Forest in his 1956 best seller and classic, *The Organization Man* (1956; Philadelphia: University of Pennsylvania Press, 2002), 283.

2. John A. Jakle, "America's Small Town/Big City Dialectic," *Journal of Cultural Geography* 18 (Spring–Summer 1999): 3.

3. William Allen White, *In Our Town* (New York: McClure, Philips, 1906), 217, 124; Sinclair Lewis, *Main Street* (New York: Harcourt Brace, 1920), 202.

4. Norman Mailer, *Armies of the Night: History as a Novel, the Novel as History* (New York: New American Library, 1968), 173.

5. Sherrilyn A. Ifill, *On the Courthouse Lawn: Confronting the Legacy of Lynching in the Twenty-First Century* (Boston: Beacon, 2007), 16. I am grateful to Sharon O'Brien for calling my attention to this book.

6. Ibid., 17.

7. James W. Loewen, *Sundown Towns: A Hidden Dimension of American Racism* (New York: New Press, 2005).

8. Richard Wright, "The Ethics of Living Jim Crow," in *Uncle Tom's Children* (1940; New York: Harper and Row, Perennial Library, 1965), 10.

9. Loewen, *Sundown Towns*, 79–80. By 1970, population growth in the United States

was largely suburban, with more people living in suburbs than in cities. The range of figures is broad because Loewen "could not and did not locate every sundown town in America." He confirmed approximately 1,000; based on random sampling and inferential statistics, the others are probable but unconfirmed.

10. Ibid., 60.

11. See Jean Pfaelzer, *Driven Out: The Forgotten War against Chinese Americans* (Berkeley: University of California Press, 2008), which concentrates on the late nineteenth century, when Chinese residents were driven out of scores of towns in California. On gays and lesbians, see Loewen, *Sundown Towns*, 329–31.

12. Willie Wallace, "Eyewitness to Jim Crow," *The History of Jim Crow*, http://www.jimcrowhistory.org/resources/narratives/Willie_Wallace.htm, accessed Aug. 23, 2011.

13. Loewen, *Sundown Towns*, 101, 103.

14. Ibid., 129. In 1926, the Supreme Court ruled that restrictive covenants were acceptable (*Corrigan v. Buckley*). See ibid., 257.

15. Ibid., 129–30.

16. There is also the story, beginning shortly after the Civil War, of the creation of all-black towns, in response to the segregationist practices of most white towns. See photographs and narrative in Wendel A. White, *Small Towns, Black Lives: African American Communities in Southern New Jersey* (Oceanville, N.J.: Noyes Museum of Art, 2003). Most famously, the Harlem Renaissance writer Zora Neale Hurston grew up in all-black Eatonville, Florida, which profoundly shaped her views of racial relations. Unlike her contemporary Richard Wright, for example, she escaped a Jim Crow childhood and tended to minimize racial conflict in the United States.

17. Loewen, *Sundown Towns*, 131. A 1989 study of the 1980 census reveals the nearly total absence of blacks from small towns, except in the South. See Glenn V. Fuguitt, David L. Brown, and Calvin L. Beale, *Rural and Small Town America*, Census Monograph Series (New York: Russell Sage Foundation, 1989), 430.

18. Edward J. Blakely and Mary Gail Snyder, *Fortress America: Gated Communities in the United States* (Washington, D.C.: Brookings Institution Press, 1997), 148–49.

19. Ibid., 3.

20. John R. Stilgoe, *Borderland: Origins of the American Suburb, 1820–1939* (New Haven, Conn.: Yale University Press, 1988), 55.

21. Frank M. Bryan, *Real Democracy: The New England Town Meeting and How It Works* (Chicago: University of Chicago Press, 2004), 280.

22. Ibid., 286, 297. Bryan does not claim that town meetings teach tolerance; rather, he argues that they ingrain forbearance in the face of difference (288).

23. Sherwood Anderson, *Home Town* (New York: Alliance, 1940), 95.

24. Granville Hicks, *Small Town* (New York: Macmillan, 1946), 13.

25. Ibid., 16, 273.

26. Ibid., 274.

27. Robert S. Lynd and Helen Merrell Lynd, *Middletown: A Study in Modern American Culture* (New York: Harcourt Brace, 1929); Lynd and Lynd, *Middletown in Transition: A Study in Cultural Conflicts* (New York: Harcourt Brace Jovanovich, 1937).

28. Muncie was likewise considered "typical" by readers of *Middletown*, precisely because of the relative (and uncommon) absence of foreign or African American populations in the city. It was this focus on the "normal" that made the Lynds' study so striking in the growing sociological literature. See Sarah E. Igo, *The Averaged American: Surveys, Citizens, and the Making of a Mass Public* (Cambridge: Harvard University Press, 2008), 84.

29. Lynd and Lynd, *Middletown in Transition*, 405–8.

30. Ibid., 417.

31. Ibid., 481–84.

32. Ibid., 444–45.

33. Ibid., 457; Lewis Corey, *The Crisis of the Middle Class* (New York: Covici-Friede, 1935).

34. Dwight Hoover, introduction to *Middletown Jews: The Tenuous Survival of an American Jewish Community*, edited by Dan Rottenberg (Bloomington: Indiana University Press, 1997), xxxi.

35. Ewa Morawska, *Insecure Prosperity: Small-Town Jews in Industrial America, 1890–1940* (Princeton, N.J.: Princeton University Press, 1996), 190.

36. Luke E. Lassiter et al., *The Other Side of Middletown: Exploring Muncie's African American Community* (Walnut Creek, Calif.: AltaMira, 2004).

37. Lynd and Lynd, *Middletown in Transition*, 464. The lynching is the subject of Cynthia Carr's *Our Town: A Heartland Lynching, a Haunted Town, and the Hidden History of White America* (New York: Crown, 2006), which argues that the KKK in Indiana organized the violence.

38. Lassiter et al., *The Other Side of Middletown*, 62.

39. Ibid.

40. Lynd and Lynd, *Middletown in Transition*, 458–60.

41. "Muncie, Ind. Is the Great U.S. 'Middletown,'" *Life*, May 10, 1937.

42. Lynd and Lynd, *Middletown in Transition*, 450, 451.

43. From a *Life* advertisement from the late 1930s: "LIFE's mind-guided cameras have gone forth across the vast face of America and pictured its normal, pleasant expressions— its college life and smalltown folkways, its wheat ripening in the sun, and its research proceeding patiently in busy laboratories. Out of LIFE's resolve to make pictures responsible—as well as powerful—LIFE's editors have made a tremendous discovery: that millions of people can be as deeply interested in pictures of calm, daily life as in pictures of the accidental, the sudden, the explosive which makes the news." Quoted in Samantha Baskind, "The 'True' Story: LIFE Magazine, Horace Bristol, and John Steinbeck's *The Grapes of Wrath*," *Steinbeck Studies* 15, no. 2 (Fall 2004): 57.

44. Personal narratives dealing with the boundaries of acceptance and rejection in small-town America can be found in John Preston, ed., *Hometowns: Gay Men Write about Where They Belong* (New York: Plume, 1992); and Louise A. Blum, *You're Not from Around Here, Are You? A Lesbian in Small-Town America* (Madison: University of Wisconsin Press, 2001).

CHAPTER 6

1. See Ruckel Properties Inc., www.ruckelproperties.com, accessed May 20, 2009.

2. Tradition website, http://www.traditionfl.com/main.php, accessed May 21, 2009.

3. For an example of seventeenth-century planning, see John R. Stilgoe, "The Puritan Townscape: Ideal and Reality," *Landscape* 20 (Spring 1976): 3–7. I am indebted to Kerry Ahearn for calling my attention to this article. For utopian communities of the nineteenth century, see Dolores Hayden, *Seven American Utopians: The Architecture of Communitarian Socialism, 1790–1975* (Cambridge: MIT Press, 1976). Hayden estimates that by 1840 "at least one hundred thousand idealistic citizens" were involved in "hundreds of communistic experiments" (9). For a study of the most famous company town, Pullman, Illinois, see Carl Smith, *Urban Disorder and the Shape of Belief: The Great Chicago Fire, the Haymar-*

ket Bomb, and the Model Town of Pullman (Chicago: University of Chicago Press, 1995), 183–87. A more remote example is the Ford Company's Fordlandia, built in 1928 in the Amazon jungles of Brazil as a prefabricated town for rubber workers. See Greg Grandin, *Fordlandia: The Rise and Fall of Henry Ford's Jungle City* (New York: Metropolitan, 2009).

4. See Simon Parker, *Urban Theory and the Urban Experience: Encountering the City* (Oxon, U.K.: Routledge, 2004), 57. Also see David Schuyler, introduction to *From Garden City to Green City: The Legacy of Ebenezer Howard*, edited by Kermit C. Parsons and David Schuyler (Baltimore: Johns Hopkins University Press, 2002), 4.

5. Though greatly inspired by Bellamy, Howard qualified Bellamy's socialistic thinking in favor of privatized agriculture and industry and noted the influence of three British projects before his own: Edward Gibbon Wakefield's promotion of colonization to relieve overcrowding, Thomas Spence's system of land tenure, and James Silk Buckingham's model city. Ebenezer Howard, *Garden Cities of To-morrow*, edited by F. J. Osborn (Cambridge: MIT Press, 1965), 119.

6. Edward Bellamy, *Looking Backward, 2000–1887* (New York: Modern Library, 1942), 27.

7. In the epigraph to chapter 1 of *Garden Cities of To-morrow*, Howard quotes John Ruskin, who envisioned building houses in units that were "walled round, so that there may be no festering and wretched suburb anywhere, but clean and busy street within and the open country without, with a belt of beautiful garden and orchard round the walls, so that from any part of the city perfectly fresh air and grass, and sight of far horizon might be reachable in a few minutes' walk." Ruskin, *Sesame and Lilies* (New York: H. M. Caldwell, 1871), 239. Also see Schuyler, introduction to *From Garden City to Green City*, 5.

8. Martha Munzer and John Vogel Jr., *New Towns: Building Cities from Scratch* (New York: Knopf, 1974), 45.

9. See Stephen V. Ward, "Ebenezer Howard: His Life and Times," in Parsons and Schuyler, *From Garden City to Green City*, 224.

10. Robert Fishman, "The Metropolitan Tradition in American Planning," in *The American Planning Tradition*, edited by Robert Fishman (Washington, D.C.: Woodrow Wilson Center Press; Baltimore: Johns Hopkins University Press, 2000), 67.

11. Gwendolyn S. Wright, *Building the Dream: A Social History of Housing in America* (Cambridge: MIT Press, 1981), 174. As Wright observes, "After 1900, fears of isolation and a romantic nostalgia for the homogeneous fellowship associated with small towns infused much of the discussion about housing" (175). Incidentally, Heineman went on to create the first motel in California in 1925.

12. Based on the tally in Louis Graves, "A Model Village under Way," *Building Progress* 2 (Jan. 1912): 18–24; quoted in John R. Stilgoe, *Borderland: Origins of the American Suburb* (New Haven, Conn.: Yale University Press, 1988), 235.

13. Ibid., 227. For the influence of the rural picturesque style, see Jonathan Barnet, *The Elusive City: Five Centuries of Design, Ambition and Miscalculation* (New York: Harper & Row, 1986), 66.

14. Olmsted, in *Forest Hills Gardens* (New York: Sage Foundation, 1909), 16–18; quoted in Stilgoe, *Borderland*, 226.

15. Olmsted and Atterbury were both influenced by the major British town planners of the early twentieth century, Barry Parker and Raymond Unwin, who were in turn influenced by William Morris in taking the medieval village as the ideal. See Walter L. Creese, *The Search for Environment: The Garden City Before and After* (New Haven, Conn.: Yale University Press, 1966), 169–70.

16. Independence Day Program, July 4, 1915, RSF, series 3, box 19, folder 154, *Bulletin* 1,

no. 21 (July 1, 1916); quoted in Susan L. Klaus, *A Modern Arcadia: Frederick Law Olmsted Jr. and The Plan for Forest Hills Gardens* (Amherst: University of Massachusetts Press, 2002), 140.

17. See Stilgoe, *Borderland*, 233.

18. Raymond Unwin, *Town Planning in Practice*, preface by Andres Duany, introduction by Walter L. Creese (Princeton, N.J.: Princeton Architectural Press, 1994 [1909]), 382.

19. Clarence Arthur Perry, *Housing for the Machine Age* (New York: Russell Sage Foundation, 1939), 213.

20. Shelby M. Harrison, introduction to Clarence Arthur Perry, *The Neighborhood Unit*, in *Neighborhood and Community Planning, Regional Survey*, vol. 7 (New York: Committee on Regional Plan of New York and Its Environs, 1929), 23.

21. Perry, *Housing for the Machine Age*, 22–23.

22. For a discussion of Perry's thinking and the later entanglement of his ideas with the politics of urban renewal, see Howard Gillette Jr., "The Evolution of Neighborhood Planning: From the Progressive Era to the 1949 Housing Act," *Journal of Urban History* 9, no. 4 (Aug. 1983): 421–44.

23. Peter Geoffrey Hall, *Urban and Regional Planning*, 4th ed. (London: Routledge, 2002), 38.

24. Perry, *The Neighborhood Unit*, 25, 28.

25. Ibid., 94.

26. Ibid., 100. In his 1939 *Housing for the Machine Age*, Perry briefly celebrates diversity when he exclaims against the dullness of the rule-bound conformist society: "That which makes existence bright, exciting, and colorful is variation, not conformity; difference, rather than sameness." The next sentence makes clear that he means the individual's growth of personality and distinction, which the homogeneous neighborhood unit makes possible. Perry, *Housing for the Machine Age*, 220.

27. See Stilgoe, *Borderland*, 232, 238.

28. Millard F. Rogers Jr., *John Nolen and Mariemont: Building a New Town in Ohio* (Baltimore: Johns Hopkins University Press, 2001), 99.

29. Ibid., 201.

30. Ibid., 200.

31. Benton MacKaye, *The New Exploration* (Urbana: University of Illinois Press, 1962 [1928]), 59. Even "Main Street," which was "neither village nor city," was too big for MacKaye. "If it is yet a community it hopes soon not to be: it dreams to become, not a social structure like ancient Athens, but a social gelatin like modern New York. It is not a unit of humanity, it is an incipient 'massing of humanity'" (68).

32. See "The Townless Highway," in MacKaye, *The New Exploration*, 229–35; rpt. from *New Republic*, Mar. 12, 1930.

33. Richard T. Ely, "The City Housing Corporation and Sunnyside," *Journal of Land and Public Utility Economics* 2 (Apr. 1926): 181, 173.

34. Molly Turner, "A Thoroughly Conscious and Workable Community," www.place inhistory, accessed Feb. 9, 2004.

35. Clarence Stein, *Toward New Towns for America* (Cambridge: MIT Press, 1957), 33–34.

36. Lewis Mumford, *Green Memories* (New York: Harcourt, Brace, 1947), 30; quoted in Stein, *Toward New Towns*, 27.

37. Lewis Mumford, *Sketches from Life: The Autobiography of Lewis Mumford, the Early Years* (Boston: Beacon, 1982), 419.

38. Stein, *Toward New Towns*, 34.

39. Marcus W. Brauchli, "If You're Thinking of Living in Sunnyside," *New York Times*, July 23, 1983, http://www.nytimes.com/1983/07/03/realestate/if-you-re-thinking-of-living-in-sunnyside.html?&pagewanted=all, accessed July 2, 2009.

40. Stein, *Toward New Towns*, 31.

41. "No garage of any kind or nature[,] . . . no fences, hedges, outbuildings, clothes poles or lines, radio poles or lines, signs or awnings shall be erected. . . . No changes, alterations or additions of any kind shall be made to the porches or exterior of any building on said premises, including exterior painting in any different color than at present, without written consent of said Trustees." *Declaration of Easements and Restrictions*, 1926; quoted in *Sunnyside Gardens Neighborhood History*, Place in History website, http://www.placeinhistory.org/proof/projects/sunnyside_gardens/, accessed July 5, 2009. For 1949 photographs of inner courtyards with hedges, see Stein, *Toward New Towns*, 30–33. The fact that Stein printed these in his own book suggests that he accepted the hedges as an acceptable addition to the original idea.

42. "Sunnyside Passes City Council Subcommittee Vote," *News and Views from the Historic Districts Council*, posted Oct. 24, 2007, http://www.nyccouncil.info/pdf_files/newswire/102_102407_sunnyside.pdf, accessed July 6, 2011. The City Council approved landmark designation on October 29, 2007. See Courtney Gates, "City Government," *Gotham Gazette*, Oct. 30, 2007, http://www.gothamgazette.com/article/searchlight/20071030/203/2334, accessed July 9, 2011.

43. I am indebted to Jane Lyle Diepeveen, Fair Lawn borough historian, for sharing her knowledge and experiences at Radburn over many years, and for a walking tour.

44. Evan McKenzie, *Privatopia: Homeowner Associations and the Rise of Residential Private Government* (New Haven, Conn.: Yale University Press, 1994), 48.

45. Stein, *Toward New Towns*, 60.

46. Ibid., 61. In early years of the town, "the school with 95% Radburn students, the pools and the many adult activities, together with its isolation from other neighborhoods, resulted in a close-knit community where nearly everyone knew everyone else." Jane Lyle Diepeveen, e-mail to author, Jan. 17, 2011.

47. Stein, *Toward New Towns*, 61.

48. Ibid.

49. Residents do now "vote for seven of the nine Trustees of the Corp., but the Trustees nominate those who run for office." The Radburn Citizens Association elects one representative to the Radburn Association Board of Trustees. A committee of the Radburn Association Trustees reviews applications for exterior construction, thus regulating the aesthetic appearance of the community. For years the committee was fairly relaxed in its review, resulting in some slightly incongruous reconstructions, for example, picture windows or floor-to-ceiling windows in a community that the town historian describes as "mostly colonial revival or Tudor revival." Jane Lyle Diepeveen, e-mails to author, May 9 and 28, 2009.

50. Louise Orlando, quoted in Peter Applebome, "Our Towns: A Difference of Opinion, in the Real World, Upsets the Order of an Ideal Community," *New York Times*, Oct. 16, 2005.

51. See online newsletter of the association, http://www.radburncitizens.org/, accessed July 6, 2009.

52. McKenzie, *Privatopia*, 57, 58.

53. Stein, *Toward New Towns*, 73.

54. Stein was also involved in planning the impressive Harbor Hills Public Housing De-

velopment, completed in 1941, in Lomita, California. The architect was Reginald Johnson, who devoted the latter part of his career to public housing in the modern idiom.

55. Mark Luccarelli, *Lewis Mumford and the Ecological Region: The Politics of Planning* (New York: Guilford, 1995), 153–56.

56. Benton MacKay worked for the Tennessee Valley Authority; Frederick Ackerman, Clarence Stein, and Henry Wright went to the Public Works Administration; and Catherine Bauer advised the Federal Housing Authority. See Harry Francis Mallgrave, *Modern Architecture* (Cambridge: Cambridge University Press, 2005), 317.

57. Yorkship Village, now known as Fairview Village, consists of two-story row houses in a concentric street design surrounding a commercial town square and village green.

58. See Howard Gillette Jr., *Civitas by Design: Building Better Communities, from the Garden City to the New Urbanism* (Philadelphia: University of Pennsylvania Press, 2010), 136.

59. Stein, *Toward New Towns*, 122–23.

60. Ibid., 150.

61. Joseph L. Arnold, *The New Deal in the Suburbs: A History of the Greenbelt Town Program, 1935–1954* (Columbus: Ohio State University Press, 1971), 139. On the progressive legacy of Greenbelt, see Cathy D. Knepper, *Greenbelt, Maryland: A Living Legacy of the New Deal* (Baltimore: Johns Hopkins University Press, 2001).

62. Cedric Larson, "Greenbelt, Maryland: A Federally Planned Community," *National Municipal Review* 27 (Aug. 1938): 413–20; quoted in Arnold, *The New Deal*, 143.

63. Arnold, *The New Deal*, 151.

64. Mark Clapson, *Suburban Century: Social Change and Urban Growth in England and the USA* (New York: Berg, 2003), 71. An increasing number of Jews moved to Greenbelt in the thirties and forties, though they met some hostility. See ibid., 149.

65. Though government-sponsored housing would take off after World War II in Europe, U.S. federal sponsorship was first.

66. Luccarelli, *Lewis Mumford*, 25–26.

67. See Howard Gillette Jr.'s discussion of *The City* in *Civitas by Design*, 49–50.

CHAPTER 7

1. Peter Geoffrey Hall, *Cities of Tomorrow: An Intellectual History of Urban Planning and Design in the Twentieth Century*, 3rd ed. (Oxford, U.K.: Blackwell, 2002), 316–19. I am indebted to the website Levittown: Documents of an Ideal American Suburb, by Peter Bacon Hales, for essential background and materials on Levittown; http://tigger.uic.edu/~pbhales/Levittown.html, accessed Mar. 2, 2009.

2. On the New York Levittown, see Geoffrey Harold Baker and Bruno Funaro, *Shopping Centers: Design and Operation* (New York: Reinhold/Chapman and Hall, 1951), 261; and Howard Gillette Jr., *Civitas by Design: Building Better Communities, from the Garden City to the New Urbanism* (Philadelphia: University of Pennsylvania Press, 2010), 78.

3. Jon Blackwell, "1951: American Dream Houses, All in a Row," *The Trentonian*, http://www.capitalcentury.com/1951.html, accessed Mar. 1, 2009.

4. Quoted in Richard Lacayo, "Suburban Legend: William Levitt," *Time*, July 3, 1950.

5. "Memo re: President's Civil Rights Message on the Armed Forces, May 11, 1948," Subject File, Clifford Papers, Harry S. Truman Library and Museum, http://www.truman library.org, accessed Mar. 20, 2009.

6. See James W. Loewen, *Sundown Towns: A Hidden Dimension of American Racism* (New York: New Press, 2005), 127.

7. Herbert J. Gans, *The Levittowners* (New York: Vintage, 1967), 372.

8. Ibid., 379.

9. Ann Forsyth posits three typical conditions for planning innovation: structural circumstances (political and economic context), key individuals, and a reformist technical milieu that fosters new ideas. All were present with Columbia. Forsyth, *Reforming Suburbia: The Planned Communities of Irvine, Columbia, and The Woodlands* (Berkeley: University of California Press, 2005), 43.

10. James Rouse, "Great Cities for a Great Society," speech delivered at the honor awards luncheon of the Chicago Chamber of Commerce and Industry and the Chicago Chapter of the AIA, Apr. 8, 1965, 16; quoted in Nicholas Dagen Bloom, *Suburban Alchemy: 1960s New Towns and the Transformation of the American Dream* (Columbus: Ohio State University Press, 2001), 34.

11. Joshua Olsen, *Better Places, Better Lives: A Biography of James Rouse* (Washington, D.C.: Urban Land Institute, 2003), 172. Rouse's wife shared this vision, declaring in 1977 that Jesus would want people "to be in small communities, so they could be more loving, sharing warmth and friendships, and support one another"; Libby Rouse, "The Spiritual Dream behind Columbia and the Vision Still Hopefully ahead for It," paper prepared for the Kittamaqundi Community, Columbia, Maryland, 1977, Columbia Archives; quoted in Forsyth, *Reforming Suburbia*, 112.

12. Forsyth, *Reforming Suburbia*, 35–36.

13. See Joseph L. Arnold, *The New Deal in the Suburbs: A History of the Greenbelt Town Program, 1935–1954* (Columbus: Ohio State University Press, 1971), 22. The term *new community* is also used for large planned developments in the United States.

14. James Rouse, "It Can Happen Here: A Paper on Metropolitan Growth," paper prepared for the University of California, Berkeley, Sept. 23, 1963, 6; quoted in Bloom, *Suburban Alchemy*, 39.

15. James Rouse, "Talk at Conference on Family Happiness and Security, Insurance Company of North America," Columbia Archives, MCII James Rouse Papers, Folder 1A; quoted in Forsyth, *Reforming Suburbia*, 32; Rouse, "Columbia: A Presentation to the Officials and Citizens of Howard County, Maryland, November 11, 1964," Columbia Archives, loose file; quoted in Forsyth, *Reforming Suburbia*, 33. I am indebted to Forsyth for parts of this discussion of Rouse.

16. See Bloom, *Suburban Alchemy*, 39.

17. Libby Rouse, "The Spiritual Dream behind Columbia"; quoted in Forsyth, *Reforming Suburbia*, 12.

18. Rouse's 1964 presentation to local officials stressed the utopian promise of the village center: "Each village square will be beautifully planted and maintained. Benches for relaxing in sunlight or shade, flower-bordered pathways, all will be inviting and attractive places for people"; Community Research and Development Inc., "Columbia: A New Town for Howard County—A Presentation to the Officers and Citizens of Howard County," Baltimore, Nov. 11, 1964, 22.

19. Bloom, *Suburban Alchemy*, 168.

20. See Olsen, *Better Places*, 160, which quotes Rouse from notes of those attending a planning meeting.

21. Ibid., 196–97, 198.

22. Ibid., 200.

23. See Forsyth, *Reforming Suburbia*, 114–19.

24. Ibid., 120–21.

25. Ibid., 121.

26. Bloom, *Suburban Alchemy*, 168–69.

27. Ibid., 176.

28. Emily Talen sees the conflict between garden city design (i.e., multiple units) and the single-family house as the central conflict in American urbanism. See Talen, *New Urbanism and American Planning: The Conflict of Cultures* (New York: Routledge, 2005), 13.

29. Herbert Gans, *The Urban Villagers: Group and Class in the Life of Italian-Americans* (New York: Free Press, 1962); Gans, *The Levittowners*.

30. See James Borchert, *Alley Life in Washington: Family, Community, Religion, and Folklife in the City, 1850–1970* (Urbana: University of Illinois Press, 1980).

31. See Emily Talen's review of the literature on environmental sociology and architectural determinism, which demonstrates that design "plays a role in fostering or inhibiting resident interaction" and can serve as a catalyst for creating community; Talen, "Sense of Community and Neighborhood Form: An Assessment of the Social Doctrine of New Urbanism," *Urban Studies* 36, no. 8 (1999): 1365–75. On the freedom of designers to affect social norms, see the discussion in Margaret Crawford, *Building the Workingman's Paradise: The Design of American Company Towns* (London: Verso, 1995), 8. Eric Monkonnen, by contrast, has termed the reading of economic and social practices from an observation of the physical structure of a community as the "architectural fallacy." Monkonnen, *America Becomes Urban* (Berkeley: University of California Press, 1988): 224. Cf. Oscar Newman's more nuanced view, expressed fifteen years earlier, though obviously not a prophylactic: "We are concerned that some might read into our work the implication that architectural design can have a direct causal effect on social interactions. Architecture operates more in the area of 'influence' than control. It can create a setting conducive to realizing the potential of mutual concern. It does not and cannot manipulate people toward these feelings, but rather allows mutually benefiting attitudes to surface." Newman, *Defensible Space: Crime Prevention through Urban Design* (New York: Collier, 1973), 207.

32. Andres Duany and Elizabeth Plater-Zyberk, "The Second Coming of the American Small Town," *Wilson Quarterly* (Winter 1992): 21.

33. Ibid., 23.

34. Judith Corbett, "The Ahwahnee Principles: Toward More Livable Communities," http://www.lgc.org/freepub/community_design/articles/ahwahnee_article/index.html, accessed May 21, 2009. The Ahwahnee Lodge, in Yosemite Valley, was designed as a luxury hotel in 1925 by Gilbert Stanley Underwood, and though it seems an unlikely place for the creation of a manifesto on urbanism, it is a spectacular example of a rustic design, albeit on a grand scale, that respects and acknowledges the valley's ecology.

35. "A New Urbanism Conversation," aired on *PBS NewsHour*, July 19, 2000, http://www.pbs.org/newshour/newurbanism/plater-zyberk.html, accessed May 21, 2009.

36. Duany called the demand that "moving cars be segregated from pedestrians" a "simple minded slogan"; Andres Duany, preface to Raymond Unwin, *Town Planning in Practice: An Introduction to the Art of Designing Cities and Suburbs* (Princeton, N.J.: Princeton Architectural Press, 1994), 4. Ironically, Unwin's town plans influenced Stein (who designed Radburn, which separated foot and vehicular traffic) as much as they did Duany.

37. On Jacobs's anticipation of New Urbanism, see William Fulton, "The Garden Suburb and the New Urbanism," in *From Garden City to Green City: The Legacy of Ebenezer Howard*, edited by Kermit C. Parsons and David Schuyler (Baltimore: Johns Hopkins University Press, 2002), 164.

38. Andres Duany, Elizabeth Plater-Zyberk, and Jeff Speck, *Suburban Nation: The Rise of Sprawl and the Decline of the American Dream* (New York: North Point, 2000), 209–10.

39. Robert A. M. Stern, *The Anglo American Suburb: Architectural Design* (London: Academy, 1996 [1982]), 4.

40. Duany, Plater-Zyberk, and Speck, *Suburban Nation*, xiv.

41. The New Urbanists have come under attack for a number of sins, both real and imagined, which might be summarized as creating homogeneous communities that fail to address issues of social equity, attempting (contrarily) to engineer social diversity, privatizing public space, and creating public space that promotes a postmodern consumer culture. David Brain offers a critique of attacks on New Urbanism, concluding with an affirmation of New Urbanism's effort to create a movement that "seeks to build relationships across associational networks and policy arenas" from the local to the regional; Brain, "From Good Neighborhoods to Sustainable Cities: Social Science and the Social Agenda of the New Urbanism," *International Regional Science Review* 28, no. 2 (Apr. 2005): 231–34. Emily Talen, arguing that design can foster social diversity, also speaks positively of New Urbanism's challenge to builders to answer the question "How does place provide 'cross-cutting identities' that enable, sustain, or manage diversity?"; Talen, "Design That Enables Diversity: The Complications of a Planning Ideal," *Journal of Planning Literature* 20 (2006): 242.

42. Duany, Plater-Zyberk, and Speck, *Suburban Nation*, 52, 53.

43. Douglas Frantz and Catherine Collins, *Celebration, U.S.A.: Living in Disney's Brave New Town* (New York: Henry Holt, 1999), 333.

44. Jason Miller, "Walking in Kentlands," *Traditional Neighborhood Design*, www.TNDhomes.com, accessed May 15, 2009.

45. In addition to Frantz and Collins, *Celebration, U.S.A.*, see Andrew Ross's shrewd ethnography, *The Celebration Chronicles: Life, Liberty, and the Pursuit of Property Value in Disney's New Town* (New York: Ballantine, 1999).

46. Quoted in Jayson Blair, "Failed Disney Vision: Integrated City," *New York Times*, Sept. 23, 2001.

47. Quoted in Elizabeth Purcell, "Then and Now—A Celebration Graduation; Ashlee Hawk—Class of 2009," *Celebration Independent*, Apr. 15, 2009, 3.

48. Loewen argues strongly for the positive effects of such contact across race in assessing what is lost in towns that are all white or all black; Loewen, *Sundown Towns*, 337, 353.

49. Robert D. Putnam, *Bowling Alone: The Collapse and Revival of American Community* (New York: Simon and Schuster, 2000), 23.

50. Ibid., 352, 207. Putnam refers to the work of Michael Schudson and Alan Wolfe, who ask, "Might not the gain in liberty be worth the cost in community?"; quoted in Putnam, *Bowling Alone*, 352. See Schudson, *The Good Citizen* (New York: Martin Kessler, 1998); and Wolfe, *One Nation after All* (New York: Viking, 1998).

51. Emily Talen, "Sense of Community and Neighborhood Form: An Assessment of the Social Doctrine of New Urbanism," *Urban Studies* 36, no. 8 (1999): 1375, 1369.

52. See Richard Sennett, *The Uses of Disorder: Personal Identity and City Life* (1970; New York: Norton, 1992). Cf. Michael Sorkin, "Acting Urban," *Metropolis*, Aug.–Sept. 1998, http://www.metropolismag.com/html/content_0898/aug98wha.htm, accessed July 17, 2009.

53. For an incisive summary of the critique of New Urbanism—that it is "overly determinist as well as too deeply embedded in capitalist ideology"—see Gillette, *Civitas by Design*, 130–33. Gillette notes Michael Sorkin's sharp criticism of the New Urbanist plans

for post-Katrina New Orleans, which Sorkin likens, in their "unitary fantasy of perfection," to the "dreamy utopian socialist ideology" of the modernist Congrès International d'Architecture Moderne. Michael Sorkin, "Will New Plans for the Gulf Drown It Again, This Time in Nostalgia?," *Architectural Record* (Feb. 1, 2006); quoted in Gillette, *Civitas by Design*, 130–31.

CHAPTER 8

1. The revival of cities that was well under way by the mid-1990s, despite the dire predictions of the 1980s, was partly the result of the growth of the community development corporation (CDC) movement, fueled by banks reinvesting in the inner city. The process is described by Paul Grogan and Tony Proscio in their landmark book, *Comeback Cities: A Blueprint for Urban Neighborhood Revival* (New York: Basic Books, 2001).

2. Carolyn Adams et al., *Restructuring the Philadelphia Region: Metropolitan Divisions and Inequality* (Philadelphia: Temple University Press, 2008), 5. A detailed account of the Neighborhood Transformation Initiative in Philadelphia, dating from 2001, can be found in John Kromer, *Fixing Broken Cities: The Implementation of Urban Development Strategies* (New York: Routledge, 2009).

3. In Philadelphia, the coordinating agency has been chiefly the Philadelphia Housing Authority, which manages 81,000 residents, though it is complemented by several other organizations that variously work to develop partnerships with communities, developers, and governmental agencies, including the Neighborhood Transformation Initiative, the Office of Housing and Community, the Redevelopment Authority, and the Philadelphia Housing Development Corporation.

4. See, e.g., Magali Sarfatti Larson, *Behind the Postmodern Façade: Architectural Change in Late Twentieth Century America* (Berkeley: University of California Press, 1995), 126. John Kromer, director of housing and community development in Philadelphia during the nineties, acknowledges the relevance of New Urbanist planning and design principles to urban development, but he says that "with every mile [from exurb to inner city] the new urbanism gets weaker and weaker as a guide to practice"; Kromer, *Neighborhood Recovery: Reinvestment Policy for the New Hometown* (New Brunswick, N.J.: Rutgers, 1999), 228.

5. Robert A. M. Stern, *The Anglo American Suburb: Architectural Design* (London: Academy, 1996 [1982]), 12.

6. See Max Page: "Unfortunately, it is to this nostalgia—in part spawned by Jane Jacobs—that developers have responded in the past two decades. They have simplified and bundled together various invented traditions of the bustling small town, building whole, instantaneous developments which mimic in stilted ways the principles of community development laid out by Jane Jacobs"; Page, "Maxwell Street and the Crucible of Culture," *Three Cities*, http://artsweb.bham.ac.uk/citysites/, accessed Jan. 8, 2010.

7. See Herbert J. Gans, *Urban Villagers: Group and Class in the Life of Italian-Americans*, updated and expanded ed. (New York: Free Press, 1982).

8. "A big city/small town dialectic proved remarkably resilient in shaping what American cities became"; John A. Jakle, "America's Small Town/Big City Dialectic," *Journal of Cultural Geography* 18, no. 2 (Spring/Summer 1999): 1, *Academic Search Premier*, EBSCO, Web, accessed July 21, 2010.

9. Ibid., 1.

10. One of the few studies of the New Urbanism in older industrial cities is Sabina Deitrick and Cliff Ellis, "New Urbanism in the Inner City: A Case Study of Pittsburgh," *Journal*

of the American Planning Association 70, no. 4 (Autumn 2004): 426–42. Deitrick and Ellis examine three types of projects—large-scale (refill), smaller-scale (infill), and patching (scattered-site infill)—that have resulted from planning by CDCs in Pittsburgh, noting that New Urbanist designs, especially at Crawford Square, have borrowed elements from traditional Pittsburgh neighborhoods (433).

11. Interestingly, Philadelphia has managed to keep a few high-rise developments, outfitting them with modern equipment and amenities as well as electronic security systems that have allowed for their success.

12. The city has also retrofitted some of the older flat-roofed low-rise housing, installing modern amenities in addition to peaked roofs, the latter designed to make them look more like traditional "homes" while also providing a less friendly platform for burglars.

13. Philadelphia Housing Authority, *Home in North Philadelphia*; quoted in Kromer, *Fixing Broken Cities*, 84. Kromer was seeking to develop North Philadelphia to protect current residents, stabilize the neighborhood, and protect the area as "an affordable housing resource at a time when housing costs in adjacent Center City neighborhoods continued to rise"; Kromer, *Fixing Broken Cities*, 83–84. I am grateful to Don Hinkle-Brown, president of the Reinvestment Fund, for sharing his insights on Philadelphia housing with me.

14. Quoted in Larry Eichel, "Rising from Ruins: Why Public Housing, Once the Scourge of the City, Now Is a Vital Part of Its Life and Its Future," *Philadelphia Inquirer*, Dec. 4, 2005.

15. Much of the credit for Philadelphia's public housing revolution must go to Carl Greene, executive director of the PHA from 1998 to 2010. Greene's autocratic style was never very popular, and when it was learned that sexual harassment suits against him were settled extravagantly with PHA funds, he was suspended by the PHA board in August 2010 and fired in September 2010 under a heavy cloud of misconduct charges and investigations into PHA spending on legal fees.

16. An easily accessible summary of Newman's views is available online. See Oscar Newman, *Creating Defensible Space*, U.S. Department of Housing and Urban Development, Office of Policy Development and Research, Apr. 1996, http://www.huduser.org/publications/pdf/def.pdf, accessed July 1, 2010.

17. Philadelphia Housing Authority, "New Studies Show Philadelphia Housing Authority Construction Boosts Neighborhood Property Values by 142%," http://pha.phila.gov/press/archive_studies.aspx, accessed July 5, 2010.

18. Howard Gillette Jr. is one of the few recent historians to take note of Newman, in his *Civitas by Design: Building Better Communities, from the Garden City to the New Urbanism* (Philadelphia: University of Pennsylvania Press, 2010), 140–41. The Economy League of Greater Philadelphia mentions "defensible space" (but not Newman) in "Planning for a Safer Philadelphia," http://economyleague.org/node/43, accessed June 20, 2010.

19. The Philadelphia Housing Authority boasts of one public housing renovation project, "Crime at Wilson Park dropped dramatically after the first two phases of major renovations took place. Wilson Park proves that when families have pride in their homes, neighborhoods become safer"; Philadelphia Housing Authority, *The New Look*, pamphlet, http://www.pha.phila.gov/index.html, accessed June 25, 2010.

20. Quoted in Inga Saffron, "Low-Rise, High Hopes," *Philadelphia Inquirer*, Apr. 15, 2005.

21. In the blocks surrounding the Martin Luther King development, sale prices of homes rose 161 percent from 1999 to 2004. Eichel, "Rising from Ruins."

22. John Kromer discusses the impact of forced relocation on previous residents of

high-rise housing in *Fixing Broken Cities*, 99–100. While some seem to have improved their circumstances and others seem set adrift, there is still a need for systematic study of this question.

23. The Quality Housing and Work Responsibility Act of 1998, which funded the demolition of high-rise housing under HOPE VI, permitted cities to escape the requirement of one-for-one unit replacement.

24. Sean Purdy, "False Promises: The Redevelopment of Public Housing in North America," speech delivered at Society of Fellows, Temple University, Apr. 13, 2005.

25. Quoted in Eichel, "Rising from Ruins."

26. See Adams et al., *Restructuring the Philadelphia Region*, 108.

27. My thanks to Simon Bronner for pointing this out, in discussion following a lecture at the Mid-Atlantic American Studies Association Meeting, Philadelphia, Mar. 19, 2010.

28. See, for example, *Spring Arts Point*, a development by Sam Sherman designed by artist and architect David Slovic and located within walking distance of Center City. Developer Bart Blatstein's The Piazza, a similarly modernist New Urbanist development built around a large open space inspired by Italian examples, is the core of a developing gentrified neighborhood that is more self-sufficient, the Northern Liberties area of Philadelphia, a bit farther from Center City.

29. The success and limitations of Mayor Street's Neighborhood Transformation Initiative (NTI) have been examined in detail in Steve McGovern, "Philadelphia's Neighborhood Transformation Initiative: A Case Study of Mayoral Leadership, Bold Planning and Conflict," *Housing Policy Debate* 17, no. 3 (2006). Writing in 2006, McGovern noted that subsequent for-profit development in Philadelphia, leveraged by public funds under the NTI, has been on a much smaller scale. With the election of new mayor Michael Nutter in 2008, Philadelphia's neighborhood transformation program came to a halt; instead the city government sought to assess the program's impact and unravel its finances, an effort that went on, inconclusively, for several years.

30. See, for example, the work of Blackney Hayes Architects and Pennrose, two major firms.

31. One problem for Philadelphia is the high number of properties that have been allowed to stagnate (with huge tax arrears), without going to sheriff's sale, for years, sometimes decades. This may result from pressure on the City Council by local residents who fear gentrification.

CONCLUSION

1. Station Square in suburban Ambler (outside of Philadelphia) boasts for its residents, "The best of both worlds. . . . City living in the burbs! . . . Tree-lined streets, stress-free commutes, and wooded walking trails cozy up to coffee shops, first-rate theatre, and world-class dining. Are these the quiet suburbs or the vibrant city streets? The serenity of a small town meets the best of city living at Station Square at Ambler, new townhomes in Montgomery County"; http://www.stationsquareatambler.com/, accessed June 21, 2010. Also see Brian Wolshon and James Wahl, "Novi's Main Street: Neotraditional Neighborhood Planning and Design," *Journal of Urban Planning and Development* 125, no. 1 (Mar. 1999): 2–16.

2. Mall sales have declined by 50 percent from 1995 to 2003, nearly 15 percent of malls are vacant, and another 15 to 20 percent are failing. See Michael Southworth, "Reinventing Main Street: From Mall to Townscape Mall," *Journal of Urban Design* 10 (June 2005): 152.

3. See Adam Belz, "Rural Boom Skips Main Street," *USA Today Weekly International Edition*, June 10–12, 2011; also see Roger Lowenstein, "Broke Town, U.S.A.," *New York Times Magazine*, Mar. 6, 2011, 26–29.

4. Emily Talen, *New Urbanism and American Planning: The Conflict of Cultures* (New York: Routledge, 2005), 10.

5. The indoor mall is conceived as an alternate urban space and stays open at least into the early evening; in contrast, cities like Minneapolis, Houston, and Toronto developed, as early as the 1960s, privatized indoor spaces consisting of tunnels, skyways, and concourses. Privately owned and operated, they cater to the middle-class downtown daytime office population, but they have also created "layers of pedestrian space" that fracture the social heterogeneity of the central city areas. See Jack Byers, "The Privatization of Downtown Public Space: The Emerging Grade-Separated City in North America," *Journal of Planning Education and Research* (1998): 203, 189–205.

6. For a discussion of St. Louis by the then deputy mayor for development, see Barbara Geisman, "A Renaissance in Neighborhood and 'Main Street' Business Districts," *Economic Development Journal* (Spring 2004): 65–72.

7. See Alison Isenberg, *Downtown America: A History of the Place and the People Who Made It* (Chicago: University of Chicago Press, 2004), 292.

8. See Reid Ewing et al., "Turning Highways into Main Streets: Two Innovations in Planning Methodology," *Journal of the American Planning Association* 71 (Summer 2005): 269–82. Also see Greg Dickinson, "Memories for Sale: Nostalgia and the Construction of Identity in Old Pasadena," *Quarterly Journal of Speech* 83 (Feb. 1997): 1–27.

9. See Joel Kotkin, *The New Geography: How the Digital Revolution Is Reshaping the American Landscape* (New York: Random House, 2000).

10. See John MacDonald et al., *The Neighborhood Effects on Crime and Youth Violence: The Role of Business Improvement Districts in Los Angeles* (Santa Monica, Calif.: Rand, 2009). On BIDs, also see Sharon Zukin's description of Manhattan's Union Square as a "marketplace for meeting, trading, and gaining intelligence about social life. Yet this high degree of face-to-face sociability hides a paradox, for the public space of Union Square is controlled by a private group of the biggest property owners in the neighborhood"; Zukin, *Naked City: The Death and Life of Authentic Urban Places* (New York: Oxford University Press, 2009), 127.

11. Their legal authority derives from their mandate to "provide district security services." See Goktug Morcol and Patricia A. Patrick, "Business Improvement Districts in Pennsylvania: Implications for Democratic Metropolitan Governance," in *Business Improvement Districts: Research, Theories, and Controversies*, edited by Goktug Morcol et al. (Boca Raton, Fla.: CRC Press/Taylor & Francis, 2008), 307.

12. See ibid., 315–18.

13. See Jerold S. Kayden, *Privately Owned Public Space: The New York City Experience* (New York: Wiley, 2000). A rich case study of one such space in Manhattan can be found in Ariana Orvell, "The Paradox of Privately Owned Spaces: How Design, Context, and Privatization Limit the Placemaking Process at Park Avenue Plaza," senior thesis, Columbia University, 2011.

14. See Margaret Kohn, *Brave New Neighborhoods: The Privatization of Public Space* (New York: Routledge, 2004), 5. For a variety of approaches to the erosion of public space, see Setha Low and Neil Smith, eds., *The Politics of Public Space* (New York: Routledge, 2005).

Index

NOTE: Page numbers in italics refer to illustrations.

Evangelical Christianity, 80
Evans, Walker, 104, 105, 107–9, *107*, *108*, 111
Exclusion. *See* Social division

Fair Housing Act, 136
Fair Lawn, N.J., 174
Fairview Village, N.J., 261 (n. 57)
Falmouth, Mass., 90
Faneuil Hall, Boston, 236–37
Faneuil Market, Boston, 192
Farmer's Museum, 35
Farms. *See* Agriculture
Farm Security Administration (FSA), 104–
    13, *105*, *107–9*, *111*, *112*, *115*, 128, *135*, *137*,
    177–79, 241, 254–55 (n. 25)
Federal Arts Projects, 101–2
Federal Housing Authority (FHA), 101, 136,
    261 (n. 56)
Federal Theater Project (FTP), 118
Federal Writers Project, 118
Feminization of American culture, 220
Ferber, Edna, 96
FHA. *See* Federal Housing Authority
Films: *American Graffiti*, 128–29; as change
    agents, 114; on community, 212–14; and
    fear of mass unrest in 1930s, 127; *Fury*,
    127, 132; on garden cities, 179–82, *183*;
    Gran Torino, 229; and gun ownership,
    229; *It's a Wonderful Life*, 121–27, 241;
    Last Picture Show, 128; on mass society
    and problem of the individual, 160; *Meet
    John Doe*, 121–22; *Meet Me in St. Louis*,
    66, 127–28; *Miracle of Morgan's Creek*,
    127; *Mr. Blandings Builds His Dream
    House*, 185; *Out of the Past*, 1; *Paradise
    Lost: The Child Murders at Robin Hood
    Hill*, 246 (n. 27); *Pleasantville*, 212–13;
    Shadow of a Doubt, 1; small towns in
    1940s films, 1; social division in, 132–33;
    The Stranger, 1; suburbs in, 185; *The
    Truman Show*, 212, 213–14; *The Village*,
    132–33; violence in, 132; *Why We Fight*
    documentary series, 127
First Amendment, 131, 247–48 (n. 14)
Fishman, Robert, 154
Fiske, John, 48–49
Fitzgerald, F. Scott, 242
Florida, 64–65, 66, 149–50, 206, 209–14
Fontainebleau, 32
Ford, Henry, 24, 28–32, 84, 245 (n. 20), 252
    (n. 26)
Ford, John, 127, 184
Ford Company, 179, 258 (n. 3)
Ford (Henry) Museum, 28
Fordlandia, 258 (n. 3)
Forest Hills, N.Y., 90, 161–62
Forest Hills Gardens, N.Y.: aesthetic
    consistency of, 156, 157, 161; architecture
    of, 155; author's youth near, x, xi;
    bird's-eye view of, *156*; funding for, 155;

middle-class residents of, 155, 160; and
    neighborhood planning, 159–61, 176;
    Perry as resident of, 159–60; photograph
    of, *159*; planners of, 155; principles in
    design of, 156–59, 161; roads in, 155–56;
    town center in, 156, 158–59, *158*, *159*; in
    twenty-first century, 161; utopian vision
    and garden city ideal of, 155–61, 182–83
Forsyth, Ann, 262 (nn. 9, 15)
Fort Collins, Colo., 41
Fortune, 107–8
Fort Worth, Tex., 54, *55*, 238
Four Freedoms, The (Rockwell), 42
Fourier, Charles, 151–52
Fowler, T. M., *18*
Francaviglia, Richard V., 4, 244 (n. 1)
France, 39, 42
France, Anatole, 79
Franklin, Ind., 114
Frantz, Douglas, 209, 210
Freeman, Mary Wilkins, 74
Free speech, 247–48 (n. 14)
Freneau, Philip, 74
Freud, Sigmund, 78, 86
Frost, Robert, 30
FSA. *See* Farm Security Administration
FTP. *See* Federal Theater Project
Fury (film), 127, 132
F. W. Woolworth's chain stores, 51, 101

Gale, Zona, 75, 79
Gangs, 126, 217, 226, 229. *See also* Crime
Gans, Herbert J., 190–91, 198, 199, 200
Garden cities: community in, 163–70, 174;
    documentary film on, 179–82, *183*; early
    influences on, 258 (n. 5); in England, 9,
    151–59, *153*, *156*, *158*, *159*; fencing and
    hedges in, 168–69, 172, 260 (n. 49); in
    Forest Hills Gardens, N.Y., x, xi, 90, 155–
    61, *156*, *158*, *159*, 176; friction between
    surrounding towns and, 174; governance
    structure of, 174–75, 260 (n. 49); and
    Great Depression, 173, 175–76; Jacobs's
    critique of, 219; mandatory conformity
    in, 161, 166, 174, 260 (nn. 41, 49);
    Mariemont, Ohio, 162; neighborhood
    planning and development, 159–61, 173–
    74, 176; "new town" as term replacing,
    193; and New Urbanism, 236; population
    of, 152, 173, 193, 199; Radburn, N.J.,
    162, 163, 170–75, *170–73*, 182–83, 188,
    189; roads and automobiles in, 162, 172,
    177, 181, *181*, 183; single-family house
    versus garden city design, 263 (n. 28);
    Sunnyside Gardens, N.Y., 162–70, *164–
    66*, 172; superblocks in, 172, 173, 177. *See
    also* Planned communities
Garden Cities of To-morrow (Howard), 152,
    153
Garden City, England, 154

House Un-American Activities Committee, 37–38
Housing: for African Americans, 178; American Dream of owning single-family home, 184–92, 200; civil rights legislation on, 136; in Columbia, Md., 194–96, *197*, 199; complexity of housing development, 182; in early twentieth century, 202–3; in Forest Hills Gardens, N.Y., 155; in gated communities, 136–37; gentrification and urban housing, 220, 232, 267 (n. 28); in government-sponsored greenbelt towns, 175–79, *177–79*; government-sponsored housing in Europe, 261 (n. 65); and homeownership, 136, 164–67, 171, 184–93, 200, 228, 231; in Levittowns, 185–92, *186–89*; in Mariemont, Ohio, 162; in Muncie, Ind., 144–47, *145, 146*; in New City Communities, 220–25, *221, 223, 224,* 229–30; Newman's theory of "defensible housing," 225–29, *227, 228*; in New Urbanist communities, 202–5, *202, 204, 205, 207,* 208, 208–10, *209,* 210, *211*; in New York City, 216; in Philadelphia, 220–25, *221, 223, 224,* 229, 231–32, *233,* 266 (nn. 11–14); post–World War II loans to homeowners, 136; prefab houses, 185, 258 (n. 3); public housing projects for urban poor, 216, 217–19, *218,* 225–26; in Radburn, N.J., 171, *171;* restrictive covenants in, 136, 256 (n. 14); Section 8 housing, 231; segregation in, 136, 178; in Sunnyside Gardens, N.Y., 163–64, *166,* 168–69; tract housing in suburbs, 184, 185, 192, 205. *See also* Architecture; Housing, affordable
Housing, affordable: in Columbia, Md., 195–96; HOPE VI funds for, 70, 215–16, 221, 250 (n. 45), 267 (n. 23); in Levittowns, 187, 188; Low-Income Housing Tax Credit Program, 215–16; in "mixed" communities, 231; in New City Communities, 220–25, *221, 223, 224,* 229–30; and New Deal programs, 176; Newman's theory of "defensible housing," 225–29, *227, 228;* in New Urbanist communities generally, 208; in Philadelphia, 220–25, *221, 223, 224,* 229, 231–32, 266 (nn. 11–13); public housing projects for urban poor, 216, 217–19, *218,* 225–26; Section 8 housing, 231; in suburbs generally, 186
Housing and Community Development Act (1992), 215–16
Housing and Urban Development Department, U.S., 13, 226
Housing for the Machine Age (Perry), 259 (n. 26)
Houston, George, 60

Houston, Henry, 62
Houston, Tex., 268 (n. 5)
Howard, Ebenezer: Bellamy as influence on, 151–52, 258 (n. 5); Democracity at New York World's Fair influenced by, 180; garden city model of, 151–55, *153,* 158, 173, 193, 199; influence of, 151, 155, 160, 162, 180; influences on, 258 (nn. 5, 7); and Mumford, 152; New Urbanism influenced by, 151; visits to United States by, 151
Hudson Valley region, 70
Hurston, Zora Neale, 256 (n. 16)
Hutchinson, Anne, 131
Hybridity of Borderland, 6–7

Ibsen, Henrik, 119
Ideal communities. *See* New City Communities; New Urbanism; Planned communities
Ifill, Sherrilyn A., 133
Illinois, 134
Immigrants: in Boston, 22; in ethnic enclaves in cities, 113, 219; in Lewis's *Main Street,* 95, 97; in Sunnyside Gardens, N.Y., 168; xenophobia against, 32–33, 229
Individualism versus community, 160, 168–70, 184
Industrialization: and automobile industry, 30; and garden cities, 154, 158; and migration, 163; and migration to Northeast, 48; in Muncie, Ind., 142; in Philadelphia, 59; and philanthropy, 35; suburban industrial parks, 52, 180–81, 201–2
In Our Town (White), 131, 251 (n. 10)
Integration, 190–92, 194–98
Interstate Highway Act (1956), 49
Interstate highway system, 49, 52
Iowa, 254 (n. 21)
Ipswich, Mass., 22
Isenberg, Alison, 4, 58, 66
It's a Wonderful Life (film), 59, 121–27, *124–25,* 241

Jacobs, Jane: critique of garden cities by, 219; critique of urban renewal by, 54, 217; incrementalism associated with, 235; as influence on New Urbanism, 203–4, 219, 233, 265 (n. 6); nostalgia and urbanism of, 265 (n. 6); and small-town virtues, 239; on urban neighborhoods, 219, 233
Jakle, John, 217, 219, 265 (n. 8)
James, William, 93, 253 (n. 40)
Japan, 39, 42, 117
Jencks, Christopher, 198
Jewett, Sarah Orne, 74
Jews: exclusion of, from planned

235; photographs of, *54–56*; safety of, 237; sterility of, 236; supermalls, 69, 188; town center associated with, 58, 248 (n. 19)
Manhattan. *See* New York City
"Man That Corrupted Hadleyburg, The" (Twain), 75
Mapping Main Street project, 14, 244 (n. 1)
Marblehead, Mass., 22
Marceline, Mo., 41, 246 (n. 31)
Marchand, Roland, 35
Mariemont, Ohio, 162
Marshall, Tex., 254 (n. 21)
Marx, Leo, 8
Masses, The, 76
Mass media. *See* Films; Radio; Television; *and specific magazines and newspapers*
Masters, Edgar Lee, 76–79, 81, 121, 255 (n. 30)
Matthiessen, F. O., 4
McCall's magazine, 44
McCarthyism, 131, 255 (n. 30)
McCrory's chain stores, 101
McDonnell Aircraft, 35
McGovern, Steve, 267 (n. 29)
McGuffey, William Holmes, 30, 84, 252 (n. 26)
"McGuffey Code," 84
McGuffey Reader, 84
McHarg, Ian, 198
McKenzie, Evan, 175
McKinley, William, 41
McMurtry, Larry, 128
Meet John Doe (film), 121–22
Meet Me in St. Louis (film), 66, 127–28
Melville, Herman, 144
Memory: Halbwachs on, 27; Main Street as created memory, 23–36; Page on, 23. *See also* Nostalgia
Memphis, Tenn., *137*
Mencken, H. L., 76, 77, 79–80
Mercer, Henry, 28
Metalious, Grace, 75
Methland (Reding), 250 (n. 46)
"Metropolis and Mental Life, The" (Simmel), 253–54 (n. 9)
Metropolitan areas. *See* Cities; Downtown areas; New City Communities
Metropolitan Museum of Art, 245 (n. 16)
Middle class: and American culture, 93; in Chestnut Hill, Philadelphia, 61–63; and citizenship, 85; in Columbia, Md., 196, 198; Corey on, 141; in Forest Hills Gardens, N.Y., 155, 160, 164; and homeownership, 136, 164–67, 171, 184–93, 200, 228, 231; in Middletown studies by the Lynds, 139–48; and New City Communities, 231, 232–33; and Newman's approach to affordable housing, 226, 229; and New Urbanist

communities, 208, 210, 220; in Radburn, N.J., 171; Radburn, N.J., as upper-middle-class suburb, 171; in Sunnyside Gardens, N.Y., 164–66; and urban downtown areas, 268 (n. 5). *See also* Garden cities; Planned communities; Social division; Suburbs
Middlesboro, Ky., *112*, 254 (n. 21)
Middletown, Conn., 48–49
Middletown studies (Lynd and Lynd), 16, 106, 126, 139–48, *145–46*, 256 (n. 28)
Midtown Plaza (Rochester, N.Y.), 54, 56, *56*, 236
Midwest: characteristics of towns in, 13; Chautauqua movement in, 85; demise of small towns in, 47, 48; drought and Dust Bowl in 1930s in, 103, 104; farms in, 48; Jews in, 141; Native Americans in, 22; Nicholson on, 81–82; railroads in, 254 (n. 15); segregation in, 134; as setting of Masters's *Spoon River Anthology*, 121; Van Doren on, 79. *See also specific cities and towns*
Migrations: to cities, 43, 48, 49, 163, 219, 271; stages of, 163; to suburbs from cities, 52, 136, 163, 217; westward migration, 163
Milburn, George, 50
Miller, Arthur, 118, 131
Miller, Henry, 236
Miller, Nellie B., 255 (n. 27)
Minelli, Vincente, 127–28
Miniature of Main Street, 23–26, *24*, *25*, 47
Minneapolis, Minn., 52, 53, *54*, 268 (n. 5)
Minorities. *See* African Americans; Asian Americans; Hispanics; Integration; Jews; Segregation; Social division
Miracle of Morgan's Creek, The (film), 127
Mizner, Addison, 64–65, 66
Moawska, Ewa, 141
Model railroad, 23–26, *24*, *25*, 46
Modernization: in Lewis's fiction, 95–96, 100; of small towns, 58–59, 61, 66, 95–96, 100–103
Modernize Main Street campaign, 101
Molly Goldberg Show, The (TV show), x
Monkonnen, Eric, 263 (n. 31)
Montana, 254 (n. 21)
Montgomery Ward, 49–50
Morris, William, 258 (n. 15)
Moundville, Ala., 111
Mount, William Sidney, 43
Mount Morris, N.Y., 250 (n. 44)
Movie houses, 250 (n. 43)
Movies. *See* Films
Mr. Blandings Builds His Dream House (film), 185
Mr. Deeds Goes to Town (film), 121, 122
Mr. Smith Goes to Washington (film), 121, 122

small towns generally, 8, 10, 70. *See also*
New City Communities
New York City: Central Park in, 155,
172; commuter rail line to, 170;
disadvantages of, 160; Greenwich
Village in, 203, 217; housing in, 216;
Landmarks Preservation Commission
of, 169; Lewis in, 76–77; MacKaye on,
259 (n. 31); Park Avenue Plaza in, 268
(n. 13); POPS (Privately Owned Public
Spaces) in, 239, 268 (n. 13); private
police forces in, 238; South Street
Seaport in, 237; Union Square in, 268
(n. 10)
New Yorker, 43
New York Times, 168
New York World's Fair (1939), 35, 179–80
Nexo, Martin Andersen, 79
Nichols, J. C., 53
Nicholson, Meredith, 81–82
9/11 terrorist attacks, 12
Nolen, John, 162
Norris, Frank, 81
North American Review, 126
Northampton, Mass., *16*
North Dakota, 111
Northeast: migration to, 48; segregation in,
134. *See also* New England; *and specific
cities and towns*
Northern Liberties area, Philadelphia, 267
(n. 28)
Northland shopping center, Detroit, Mich.,
53
Norwood; or Village Life in New England
(Beecher), 87
Nostalgia: for community, 7; and Jacobs's
urbanism, 265 (n. 6); of Lewis for his
hometown, Sauk Centre, Minn., 99; and
New Urbanism, 149–50; purposes of,
245 (n. 14); for small towns, 7, 27, 44, 71,
102–29, 235, 241
Nutter, Michael, 267 (n. 29)
Nutting, Wallace, 28, 245 (n. 12)

Obama, Barack, 212
O'Brien, Sharon, 255 (n. 5)
Occupy Movement, 2
Oelwein (Iowa), 250 (n. 46)
Old Sturbridge, Mass. *See* Sturbridge/Old
Sturbridge, Mass.
Olmsted, Frederick Law, 151, 155, 172
Olmsted, Frederick Law, Jr., 155, 157, 258
(n. 14)
On the Courthouse Lawn (Ifill), 133
Opera houses, 244 (n. 14)
Organization Man, The (Whyte), 36, 255
(n. 1)
Orlando, Fla., 206, *207*, 210
Orvell, Ariana, 268 (n. 13)

Other Side of Middletown, The (Lassiter),
142–43
Our Town (Wilder), 114–21, *116*, *117*, 150, 241
Out of the Past (film), 1
Ozzie and Harriet (TV show), x

Page, Max, 23, 265 (n. 6)
Palin, Sarah, 243 (n. 1)
Palm Beach, Fla., 64–65, 66
Palmer, Frances Flora, 19–20, *19*, 46
*Paradise Lost: The Child Murders at Robin
Hood Hills* (film), 246 (n. 27)
Park Avenue Plaza, Manhattan, 268 (n. 13)
Parker, Barry, 157, 258 (n. 15)
Park Forest, Ill., 130, 131, 255 (n. 1)
Pastoral tradition, 74–75, 103
Pater, Walter, 82
Patman, Wright, 51
Peck, John, 110
Pennrose architectural firm, 267 (n. 30)
Pennsylvania, 70, 109
Perry, Clarence, 159–61, 176, 192, 217, 259
(nn. 22, 26)
Peyton Place (Metalious), 75
Pfaelzer, Jean, 256 (n. 11)
PHA. *See* Philadelphia, Pa.: Philadelphia
Housing Authority in
Philadelphia, Pa.: Act of Incorporation
(1854) of, 59, 248 (n. 24); African
Americans in, 231, 232; Brewerytown
in, 232, *233*; Carl Mackley Houses in,
176; city government of, 66; court
for petty crime in, 238–39; high-rise
developments in, 266 (n. 11); Hilltop at
Falls Ridge in, 232; historic preservation
in, 65, 249 (nn. 35–36); Martin
Luther King row houses in, 223–24,
224, 229, 266 (n. 21); Neighborhood
Transformation Initiative (NTI) in,
232, 265 (nn. 2–3), 267 (n. 29); New
City Communities in, 215, 220–25, *221*,
223, *224*, 229–34, *233*, 267 (n. 28); New
Urbanist developments outside of, 248
(n. 26), 267 (n. 1); Northern Liberties
area of, 267 (n. 28); Philadelphia
Housing Authority (PHA) in, 221–23,
229, 265 (n. 3), 266 (nn. 15, 19); The
Piazza in, 267 (n. 28); private versus
public housing developments in, 231–33,
267 (nn. 28–29); properties in, with
tax arrears, 267 (n. 31); retrofitting of
older low-rise housing in, 266 (n. 12);
Spring Arts Point in, 267 (n. 28); Wilson
Park public housing renovation project
in, 266 (n. 19). *See also* Chestnut Hill,
Philadelphia
Photography: FSA photographs during
Great Depression, 104–13, *105*, *107–9*,
111, *112*, *115*, 128, *135*, *137*, *177–79*, 241,

254–55 (n. 25); in *Life* magazine, 114–15, 144–48, *145–46*, 257 (n. 43); "lyric documentary" mode used by Evans, 108; of Middletown studies, 144–47, *145–46*; realism of, 119, 254–55 (n. 25). *See also specific cities and towns*
Piazza, Philadelphia, 267 (n. 28)
Pie Town, N.Mex., 109–11, *111*, 254 (n. 19)
Pinsky, Robert, 3, 4, 103
Pittsburgh, Pa., 265–66 (n. 10)
Plainville, Kans., 48
Planned communities: aesthetic integrity of, 161, 166, 168, 169–70, 174, 178, 189, 198, 260 (nn. 41, 49); company towns, 151, 157, 161; congeniality model of, 160–61; cooperation within, 157; critique of, by New Urbanists, 201–2; documentary *The City* on, 179–82, *183*; exclusion of ethnic groups from, 160–61, 175, 178; garden cities, 9, 151–74; governance structure of, 174–75, 260 (n. 49); government-sponsored greenbelt towns, 175–79, *177–79*; and Great Depression, 173, 175–76; history of, 151–62, 257–58 (n. 3); and individualism of later twentieth century, 168–70, 184; MacKaye on, 163; mandatory conformity in, 161, 166, 174, 178, 189, 198, 260 (nn. 41, 49); neighborhood planning and development, 159–61, 173–74, 176; as place and as social experience, 5; purpose of, 154; roads and automobiles in, 162, 172, 177, 181, 183; superblocks in, 172, 173, 177; utopian communities of nineteenth century, 151, 157, 257 (n. 3). *See also* Garden cities; New Urbanism; *and specific planned communities*
Plater-Zyberk, Elizabeth, 59, 201–9, 213, 220
Plays. *See* Theater
Pleasantville, 212–13
Plessy v. Ferguson, 134, 136
Plimoth Plantation, 35
Plymouth, N.H., *14*
Plympton Family House, 29
Poe, Edgar Allan, 162
Politics. *See* Democracy
POPS (Privately Owned Public Spaces), 239, 268 (n. 13)
Pornography, 126
Portsmouth, N.H., 22
Poverty: in Muncie, Ind., 143–48, *145–46*; and public housing projects, 216, 217–19, *218*, 225–26, 266 (n. 19). *See also* Housing, affordable; Working class
Prairie Home Companion, A, 45–46
Prejudice. *See* Segregation; Social division
Preservation movement. *See* Historic preservation

Private space in communities, 168–69, 172, 188
Privatization, 237–39
Prohibition, 80, 126
Proscio, Tony, 265 (n. 1)
Protestantism, 140, 171
Proust, Marcel, 96
Provincetown Players, 118
Pruitt-Igoe housing project, St. Louis, 217, *218*, 226
Public housing projects, 216, 217–19, *218*, 225–26, 266 (n. 19)
Public Works Administration, 176, 261 (n. 56)
Pullman, Ill., 151, 257 (n. 3)
Puritanism, 79, 80–81
"Puritanism as a Literary Force" (Mencken), 80
Putnam, Robert D., 4, 211, 212, 264 (n. 50)

Quality Housing and Work Responsibility Act (1998), 267 (n. 23)

Race and racism. *See* African Americans; Integration; Segregation; Social division
Radburn, N.J.: architecture of, 173; commercial center of, *173*; community in, 174, 260 (n. 46); compared with Levittowns, 188, 189; design covenants of, 174, 189, 260 (n. 49); in documentary *The City,* 181; governance structure of, 174–75, 260 (n. 49); during Great Depression, 173; influence of, on Rouse, 193; photographs of, *171–73*; planners of, 162, 163; promotional brochure for, *170*; and Radburn Idea, 170, 176, 177; and RPAA, 162; roads and automobiles in, 172, 203, 263 (n. 36); social division in, 171; superblocks in, 172, 173, 177; as upper-middle-class suburb, 171; utopian vision and garden city ideal of, 162, 170–75, 182–83
Radburn Association, 174–75
Radburn Citizens' Association, 175, 260 (n. 49)
Radburn Idea, 170, 176, 177
Radio, 114, 126
Railroads: commuter trains, 36, 44, 63, 136, 155–56, 170–71, 235; depots for, *94*, 107, *108*, 111; emotional significance of railroad tracks, 254 (n. 15); and mail-order businesses, 49–50; and migrations, 163; model railroad, 23–26, *24*, *25*, 46
Reader's Digest, 254 (n. 19)
Real Democracy (Bryan), 138
Realism, 81, 82, 91, 118–19, 254–55 (n. 25)
Reding, Nick, 250 (n. 46)
Reed, John, 76

127; migration to cities from, 43, 48, 49, 217, 219; miniature of, 23–26, 24, 25, 47; modernization of, 58–59, 61, 66, 95–96, 100–103; negative images of and satire on, 2, 10, 72, 75–79, 82, 86, 92, 93, 98, 99, 120, 128, 149, 240, 241; pastoral tradition of, 74–75, 103; percentage of population living in, 73; politics of, 138–39; positive image of and nostalgia for, 7, 27, 44, 71, 102–29, 235, 241; present-day revitalization of, 235; questions on, 11, 150; real versus idealized versions of, 240–41; rebellion against repression of, 76–77; regional differences in, 13–14, 109, 251–52 (n. 24); scholarship and intellectuals on, 3–4, 15–16, 138–41; social division in, 130–48; souvenir books of, 244–45 (n. 6); survival strategies of, 47, 48, 58–71, 250 (n. 43); teens' preference for, as place to live, 6; town meetings in, 138–39, 180, 256 (n. 22); unity and homogeneity of, 6, 130, 240; values and beliefs in, 2, 83–86, 105–7, 114, 120–21, 139–41, 217, 239; vaudeville tradition of, 74, 75; worries about changes in, during 1930s and 1940s, 126–27. See also Business; Cities; Main Street; Planned communities; Suburbs; and specific towns

Smith, Henry Nash, 8

Social capital, 211–12

Social classes. See Middle class; Poverty; Social division; Working class

Social division: and Chautauqua movement, 85, 93; in Chestnut Hill, Philadelphia, 62–63; and congeniality model of community, 160–61; in films, 132–33; and gated communities, 136–37; gendered social structure in The City, 182; in government-sponsored greenbelt towns, 177–78; and Great Depression, 139–41, 148; and Hicks on small-town democracy, 138–39; history of, in North America, 131–32; ideal of community versus, 214; William James on, 93; and Jews, 83, 85, 132, 139, 141; and Ku Klux Klan, 140; in Latin America, 136; in Levittowns, 190–92; in Lewis's Main Street, 96–97, 131–32; and lynching, 133, 142–43, 150, 257 (n. 37); and Main Street as utopia, 133; and Middletown studies of Muncie, Ind., 139–48, 145–46, 256 (n. 28); mixed-income community of Sunnyside Gardens, N.Y., 164–65; and New Urbanism, 150, 207–8, 210–11; in Radburn, N.J., 171; and religious intolerance, 131, 140; segregation of African Americans, 113, 133–36, 135, 137; small-town "purity" achieved through violence, 133; in small towns, 130–48, 214, 240; in South Africa, 136; and sundown towns, 133–34, 255–56 (n. 9), 256 (n. 17), 264 (n. 48); and town meetings, 138–39, 256 (n. 22); William Allen White on, 131; in Wilder's Our Town, 119–20. See also Culture

Social planning work group, 198

Song of the Lark (Cather), 254 (n. 15)

Sorkin, Michael, 264–65 (n. 53)

South: characteristics of towns in, 13, 251 (n. 24); segregation of African Americans in, 113, 133–36, 135, 137. See also specific cities and towns

South Africa, 136

Southdale mall (Minneapolis, Minn.), 53, 54

South Street Seaport, Manhattan, 237

Southworth, Michael, 58

Souvenir books, 244–45 (n. 6)

Speck, Jeff, 204–8, 220

Spence, Thomas, 258 (n. 5)

Spirn, Anne, 198

Spoon River Anthology (Masters), 77–78, 121, 255 (n. 30)

Sprawl, 162, 189, 192–93, 195, 200, 201

Spring Arts Point, Philadelphia, 267 (n. 28)

State of the Union, 121, 122

Station Square at Ambler, Pa., 267 (n. 1)

Stein, Clarence: employment of, by Public Works Administration, 261 (n. 56); and Harbor Hills Public Housing Development in Lomita, Calif., 260–61 (n. 54); and Radburn, N.J., 162, 163, 170–76, 263 (n. 36); as regional planner, 162; and Sunnyside Gardens, N.Y., 162–70, 260 (n. 41); Unwin as influence on, 263 (n. 36)

Steinbeck, John, 48, 118, 121

Steiner, Ralph, 179

Steinmetz, Charles, 30

Stern, Robert A. M., 205–6, 216

Stewart, James, 121, 125

Stilgoe, John, 138

Stockbridge, Mass., 90

Stonorov, Oscar, 176

Stowe, Harriet Beecher, 74

Strand, Paul, 255 (n. 30)

Stranger, The (film), 1

Street, John F., 232, 267 (n. 29)

Streets at Southpoint and Main Street, Durham, N.C., 248 (n. 19)

Stroudsburg, Pa., 15

Stryker, Roy, 104–7, 110, 112, 114

Sturbridge/Old Sturbridge, Mass., 26, 35, 39

Sturges, Preston, 127

Suburban Nation (Duany, Plater-Zyberk, and Speck), 204–8, 220

Suburbs: absence of, in Gieringer's Roadside America, 25; and American

Dream of single-family home, 184–92, 200; in Capra's *It's a Wonderful Life*, 123; Columbia, Md., as, 192–99, *194–97*, 262 (nn. 9, 11); critique of, by New Urbanists, 201–2; current redefinition of, as small towns, 235; and Democracy at New York World's Fair (1939), 180; dystopia of, 154; in films, 185; flight from inner city to, 52, 136, 163, 217; gated communities in, 136–37, 207; and ideal of homeownership versus community, 200; Levittowns as, 185–92, *186–89*; Park Forest, Ill., as, 130, 255 (n. 1); population of, 255–56 (n. 9); roads and automobiles in, 49, 162, 172, 177, 181, *181*, 183, 192, 201, 236; Rockwell's illustration of, 44; shopping centers in, 52, 53, *54*, 62, 64, 188, *188*; sprawl of, 189, 192–93, 195, 200, 201; and sundown towns, 134; teens' preference for, as place to live, 6; tract housing in, 184, 185, 192, 205; transit villages, 235; transportation to cities from, 236. *See also* Cities; New Urbanism; Small towns

Sudbury, Mass., 29

Summer (Wharton), 22

Sundown towns, 133–34, 255–56 (n. 9), 256 (n. 17), 264 (n. 48)

Sundown Towns (Loewen), 133–34, 136, 264 (n. 48)

Sunnyside Gardens, N.Y.: author's childhood in, x, xi; block plan of, 163–64, *165*, 172; community garden in, *167*; community in, 163–70; democracy in, 166; design covenants of, 166, 170, 189, 260 (n. 41); ethnic groups in, 168; during Great Depression, 167–68; individual rights versus communal values in, 168–70; landmark designation for, 169, 260 (n. 42); mixed-income community of, 164–65; Mumford as resident of, 165–66; photographs of, *166–67*; planners of, 162, 163, 168, 169; present-day Sunnyside, 168–69; private space in, 168–69; promotional brochure for, *164*; and RPAA, 162; utopian vision and garden city ideal of, 162–70, 182–83

Superior, Neb., 250 (n. 43)

Supermalls. *See* Malls

Supreme Court, U.S., 134, 136, 175, 256 (n. 14)

Sustainable development. *See* New Urbanism

Sweden, 27

Talen, Emily, 212, 235–36, 263 (nn. 28, 31), 264 (n. 41)

Tales of the Wayside Inn (Longfellow), 28

Tarkington, Booth, 75

Taxation: Anti-Tax Tea Party in Celebration, Fla., 212; and big box stores, 248 (n. 17); and chain stores, 51; and gentrification, 220; high taxes as danger to democracy, 147; Low-Income Housing Tax Credit Program, 215–16; and New City Communities, 233; Philadelphia properties with tax arrears, 267 (n. 31); and Radburn, N.J., 174; sales tax revenues for small towns, 70; tax break and founding of Sunnyside, N.Y., 163; tax breaks and housing developments generally, 182; tax breaks for living in small towns, 48; tax incentives for homeownership, 192–93; and urban revitalization, 220

Television, x, 36–37, 250 (n. 44)

Tennessee Valley Authority, 261 (n. 56)

Terre Haute, Ind., 141

Theater: experimentation in American theater, 118; Wilder's *Our Town*, 114–21, *116*, *117*, 241

Thoreau, Henry David, 87

Thousands of Broadways (Pinsky), 4

Time magazine, 98, 126

Tir a' Mhurain (Strand), 255 (n. 30)

Tomorrow: A Peaceful Path to Real Reform (Howard), 151

Tom Sawyer (Twain), 126

Toronto, Canada, 268 (n. 5)

Toward New Towns for America (Stein), 168

Town centers: in Columbia, Md., 194, *196*, 199, 262 (n. 18); and community generally, 184; in Europe, 52–53; in Forest Hills Gardens, N.Y., 155–56, 158–59, *158*, *159*; in Greenbelt, Md., 176–77, 178; lack of, in New City Communities, 231; in Levittowns, 188, *188*; and Main Street generally, 184; malls associated with, 58, 248 (n. 19); in Mariemont, Ohio, 162; new urban downtowns, 234–42, *238*; in New Urbanist communities, 158, 162, 206, 212; in Radburn, N.J., 173, *173*; in suburbs generally, 235

Town Haul (TV show), 250 (n. 44)

Town meetings, 138–39, 180, 256 (n. 22)

Town planning. *See* Cities; Garden cities; New City Communities; New Urbanism; Planned communities; Suburbs; *and specific cities*

Town Planning in Practice (Unwin), 157

"Townscape Malls," 58

Tracy, Spencer, 122

Tradition, Fla., 149–50

Traditional Neighborhood Design. *See* New Urbanism

Transit villages, 235

Transportation. *See* Automobiles; Highways

Truman, Harry, 190

Truman Show, The (film), 212, 213–14

Tugwell, Rexford, 104, 176